BRINGING
DOWN
THE
GREAT
WALL

BRINGING
DOWN
THE
GREAT
WALL

WRITINGS ON SCIENCE,
CULTURE, AND DEMOCRACY
IN CHINA

Fang Lizhi

INTRODUCTION BY ORVILLE SCHELL
EDITOR AND PRINCIPAL TRANSLATOR,
JAMES H. WILLIAMS

ALFRED A. KNOPF ⟋ NEW YORK 1991

Grateful acknowledgment is made to the following for permission to reprint previously published material:
Journal of Democracy: "Peering Over the Great Wall," translated by James H. Williams. *Journal of Democracy,* Vol. 1, No. 1 (Winter 1990), pp. 32–40. Copyright © 1990 by the National Endowment for Democracy. Reprinted by permission.
Longman Group UK Limited: "Patriotism and Global Citizenship," translated by James H. Williams from *The Broken Mirror: China after Tiananmen,* edited by George Hicks. Copyright © 1990 Longman Group UK Limited. Published in the U.S. and Canada by St. James Press, Chicago. Reprinted by permission of Longman Group UK Limited.
The New York Review of Books: "China's Despair and China's Hope," translated by Perry Link (Feb. 2, 1989); "Letters from the Other China," translated by Orville Schell (July 20, 1989); "Keeping the Faith," translated by James H. Williams and Orville Schell (Dec. 21, 1989). "The End of Forgetting History," originally titled "The Chinese Amnesia," translated by Perry Link (September 27, 1990). Copyright © 1989–90 by Nyrev, Inc. Reprinted by permission.
M. E. Sharpe, Inc.: Excerpts from eight essays from the issue "The Expanding Universe of Fang Lizhi: Astrophysics and Ideology in People's China," edited and translated by James H. Williams in *Chinese Studies in Philosophy,* Vol. 19, No. 4 (1988). Reprinted by permission of M. E. Sharpe, Inc., publisher, Armonk, New York 10504.

Library of Congress Cataloging-in-Publication Data
Fang, Lizhi [Date]
Bringing Down the Great Wall / Fang Lizhi.—1st ed.
    p.   cm.
ISBN 0-394-58493-7
1. China—Politics and government—1976–   2. Human rights—China.   I. Title.
    DS779.26.F3459   1990
    951.05—dc20   90-53064   CIP

CONTENTS

THE DEMOCRAT

THE DISSIDENT

This book contains thirty-two articles, speeches, and interviews by Fang Lizhi, from the period 1979 to 1990. These materials provide for the English-speaking public a unique window not only into the mind of China's foremost dissident but also into the unfolding of events in China generally during the Deng Xiaoping era.

The selections have been organized and annotated so as to make them accessible to the general reader as well as to the China specialist. Although Fang touches on a fascinating array of topics, his works center on a few prominent themes. The book is accordingly divided into four sections: "The Cosmologist," writings on intellectual freedom in the sciences, 1979–1989; "The Cosmopolitan," a collection of letters and essays on Fang's travels abroad, 1979–1988; "The Democrat," public statements on China's economic and political reforms, 1980–1986; and "The Dissident," interviews, essays, and other materials in the period dating from Fang's expulsion from the Chinese Communist Party in January 1987 until shortly after his release from refuge within the U.S. Embassy in Beijing in June 1990.

Fang speaks and writes clearly. However, the materials in this book were, for the most part, intended for a Chinese audience, and are often addressed to debates unfamiliar to the nonspecialist. To clarify the context into which these materials are woven, Orville Schell provides an introduction to the man and to the events that have propelled him into prominence. In addition,

there are introductory essays at the beginning of each of the four
main sections. Lyman Miller discusses the debates on science and
Marxism to which Fang's essays in "The Cosmologist" are addressed. I look at some persistent questions about modernization
and Chinese culture raised by Fang's writings in my introduction
to "The Cosmopolitan," and at Fang's advocacy of democracy
against the backdrop of Deng-era politics in my introduction to
"The Democrat." Finally, David Kelly provides a comparative
perspective on Fang as a dissident, viewing him in the light of
recent events in Eastern Europe and the Soviet Union.

Additional contextual information is contained in the bibliographical headnotes, an appendix containing important reference
materials (emanating from Fang's supporters and adversaries), and
a glossary containing key terms and notes on historical background. Chinese names and expressions are rendered in the official
pinyin romanization, except for customary English spellings such
as *Tao Te Ching*.

Of the thirty-two selections, one ("A Note on the Interface
between Science and Religion") was originally composed in
English. The remainder, and all materials in the appendix, are
translated from Chinese. (Original sources are noted in the headnotes. For the Zhejiang, Anhui, and Tongji speeches, the source
of the text is *Weiji gan xia de zeren,* Singapore: World Scientific,
1989.) Perry Link translated "China's Despair and China's Hope"
and "The End of Forgetting History." Tiziano Terzani provided
the English version of his 1987 and 1990 interviews with Fang.
David Kelly translated "Philosophy Is a Tool of Physics," Geremie
Barmé provided "Chinese Democracy: The View from the Beijing Observatory," and Orville Schell contributed "Letters from
the Other China." The remaining translations are mine, though
not without ample help from Hsüeh-ling Huynh, G. K. Sun, John
Jamieson, C. P. Chen, Kenneth Young, and C. K. Lai.

Translation from Chinese is always more art than science;

nonetheless, maximum effort has been expended to provide renderings that are both faithful to the original and recognizable as English. An effort has also been made to provide unabridged translations of written compositions by Fang, namely articles, essays, and personal letters. These are presented in their entirety except where so noted. Passages deleted from speeches and interviews are duly noted with ellipses.

The materials in this volume comprise much less than half of Fang's published nontechnical works, many of which are science popularizations (for which Fang received a national award in 1988). Some items of substantial political significance have also been omitted—notably the Beijing University speech of November 1985, and the Jiaotong University speech of November 1986—in the belief that their main points are to be found elsewhere in the book. What *has* guided the selection of texts has been the desire to allow the reader to see the chronological development of Fang's major themes of science, culture, and democracy, and with them not only the unfolding of critical debates during the last decade in China, but also Fang's own evolution. His language itself changes over this time period, and this is no artifact of translation; one has the clear impression of Fang discarding the terminology and categories of Chinese Marxism as he increasingly finds his own voice. Such an evolution of language is one aspect of what has struck me repeatedly in working with these texts: Fang is constantly seeking to see the world with fresh eyes, challenging not only others' preconceptions and mindsets, but his own.

As David Kelly notes in his introduction to "The Dissident," what is perhaps most remarkable about Fang Lizhi is that he could state simply and with humor that which others either failed to see or did not dare to speak of. My main goal in preparing this volume has been to allow that simplicity and humor—and the courage and intelligence they represent—to shine through.

A number of people have provided invaluable help in the preparation of this volume, especially Lyman Miller, Timothy Cheek, Marguerite Williams, Greg Dunnington, Perry Link, Ken Conca, Jerome Grieder, Chelsea Congdon, Hsüeh-ling Huynh, and Margaret Torn.

J.H.W.

Albany, California

November 1990

INTRODUCTION
by Orville Schell

When I returned to Beijing in the fall of 1986, after an absence of six months, it was hard not to feel disoriented by the sudden change in political climate. During the previous spring and summer, political and intellectual life had begun to thaw to an extent unprecedented since the Chinese Communist Party had come to power in 1949. Following on the heels of a bold program of economic reform and of opening up to the outside world, which China's paramount leader, Deng Xiaoping, had launched in 1978, this relaxation of Party control over economic, intellectual, and political life had filled the Chinese with a heady new sense of possibility. The increasing tolerance of individualism and freedom of expression reflected the surprising but growing conviction among China's new generation of reform-minded leaders that their country would not be successful in its efforts to modernize unless some dramatic way could be found to re-energize its people and win their willing participation in a new drive toward economic development. Political reform and democratization became their new rallying cries. But to the older, hard-line Maoists, who had spent their lives fighting for a very different kind of revolution—one that stressed centralization and Party discipline, rather than individual initiative and democracy—this latest wave of reform appeared as at best an unwelcome disruption and at worst a dangerous form of apostasy. While young reformers watched enthusiastically as official publications began to bloom with articles advocating freedom of speech and the press, the separation of governmental powers, and the protection of human rights, and as intellectuals publicly called for the democratization of almost all aspects of Chinese life, revolutionary hard-liners looked on with displeasure, waiting for an auspicious moment to counterattack.

A deep wariness of speaking too freely had been burned into many senior intellectuals by the crackdowns that had, with a horrifying regularity, terminated all previous interludes of liberalism in Chinese Communist history. While it was true that fall that the boundaries of acceptable political discourse were broader than ever, most intellectuals nonetheless prudently continued to try to stay within the elusive margins of Party tolerance. But there were a few who, seemingly without regard for these margins or their futures, dared speak out openly. The most vocal of these was a fifty-two-year-old astrophysicist of international stature named Fang Lizhi, who very quickly became renowned throughout China for his forceful calls for democracy and his forthrightness in publicly saying what he believed.

When I first met Fang, in his Beijing apartment in the fall of 1987, what impressed me about him first was his good cheer and guilelessness. He laughed easily—an infectious laugh that spiraled spontaneously into something like a whinny, carrying everything with it in a burst of unpremeditated mirthfulness. He was dressed simply, in a knit shirt, a tweed coat, and permanent-press slacks. Tortoiseshell glasses gave him a slightly owlish look. He made an initial impression of ordinariness—until, that is, he began to talk. Then I instantly sensed that I was in the presence of a man of not only keen intelligence and conviction but of intellectual boldness. The longer I was with him, the more this quality struck me. Far from being a studied posture adopted as a means of appearing to resist intimidation, Fang's fearlessness appeared deeply rooted in his personality, which in spite of its manifest self-confidence betrayed no suggestion of arrogance. Seldom have I met a man who, although at the center of an intense and dangerous national controversy—the Communist Party had laid the blame for the student demonstrations of the previous winter on his frequent speeches to student groups, in which he openly advocated Western democracy—so lacked the kind of polemical energy that often makes zealots of a lesser kind shrill and self-justifying. Although Fang obviously cared deeply about the cause of democracy in China, he was not one to thrust his views upon anyone; and although he had been politically persecuted throughout much of his life, there was no hint of rancor or resentment in his politics. What he was for was so much ascendant over what he was against that the notion of enemies seemed quite alien to his intellectual, political, and emotional vocabulary.

What made being with him strangely uncharacteristic of so many other experiences in China was his complete lack of the self-censorship that renders many other Chinese intellectuals of his generation incapable of speaking their minds. Without overriding his thoughts and feelings with the usual subtle (and frequently unconscious) genuflections to the official political line of the moment, Fang spoke so openly about what he was thinking and what he believed that one had to suppress the urge to warn him of the dangers of such candor. Although such warnings were, in fact, coming from many quarters, Fang seemed impervious to them. "Everything I have ever said is open," he told me, "I have nothing to hide. And since I have already said everything that I believe many times in public, what is the point of trying to hide things now, in private?"

. . .

Fang's life began in Beijing in 1936, when he was born into the family of a postal clerk from the city of Hangzhou. He entered

Beijing University (Beida) in 1952, as a student of theoretical and nuclear physics, and although he quickly distinguished himself as an unusually capable scientist, politics soon began to attract him. His first recorded brush with political dissent occurred one February day in 1955, during the founding meeting of the university chapter of the Communist Youth League (an organization that arranges political and recreational activities for young people and that anyone who intends to become a Party member must join). The league branch secretary from the physics department had been addressing the gathering, in the auditorium of Beida's administration building, and had just begun discussing the role of the league in stimulating idealism among China's youth when Fang Lizhi, then a nineteen-year-old student, dashed up onto the stage, indicating his desire to speak.

"Some of us students in the physics department thought the meeting was too dull, just a lot of formalistic speeches, so we decided to liven things up a bit," Fang once remembered. "When it came time for our branch secretary to speak, he let me express my opinion, since I had the loudest voice." Taking over the stage from the secretary, Fang redirected the discussion to the more general subject of the Chinese educational system. "I said that this kind of meeting was completely meaningless. I asked what kind of people it was that we were turning out when what we should have been doing was training people to think independently. Just having the Three Goods [good health, good study practices, and good work] is such a depressing concept and hardly enough to motivate anyone! After I spoke, the meeting fell into complete disorder."

"The next day the Party committee secretary, who was the top person in charge of ideological work for students at Beijing University, spoke all day. He said that although independent thinking was, of course, all well and good, students should settle down and study."

In spite of his attraction to politics, Fang did in fact settle down to study, earning straight *A*s at Beida. There he met his future wife, Li Shuxian, who was a fellow student in the physics department, which she ultimately joined as a faculty member. In 1956, at the age of twenty, Fang graduated from Beida and was assigned work at the Chinese Academy of Sciences' Institute of Modern Physics. But a year later the Anti-Rightist Movement began, and Chinese intellectuals who had spoken up during the previous Hundred Flowers Movement were ruthlessly persecuted. Because he had written a lengthy memorial on the need to reform China's educational system so that politics would not stifle scientific research, Fang was severely criticized. Unlike many other intellectuals under pressure, he refused to recant his alleged misdeeds and was expelled from the Party in 1958.

"For a long time after the Anti-Rightist Movement, I continued to believe in Communism," Fang told me at one of our first meetings. "Even after I was expelled from the Party, I continued to have faith in Chairman Mao and believed that it must have been I who was wrong."

Wrong or not, as a promising young scientist he was greatly needed by China in its early efforts to industrialize and was allowed to keep his position at the Institute of Modern Physics. He was ultimately even sent to help organize a new department of physics at the University of Science and Technology (Kexue Jishu Daxue, or Keda for short), which was just then being set up in Beijing. During the next few years, while teaching classes in quantum mechanics and electromagnetics, Fang also conducted research on solid-state and laser physics. Despite his previous political troubles, and because of his obvious talent in his field, in 1963 he was promoted to the position of lecturer.

But no sooner had Fang's life and career begun to resume a more normal course than the Cultural Revolution broke out, and like so many other Chinese intellectuals in 1966, Fang once more ran afoul of politics. This time he was "struggled against," branded a "reactionary," and incarcerated in a *niupeng,* or "cow shed"—a form of solitary confinement used by the Red Guards for intellectuals of the so-called "stinking ninth category," who were often dubbed "cow spirits." After a year's imprisonment he was released and "sent down" to the countryside in Anhui Province to work both in a mine and on a railroad. Here, because of the paucity of scientific books available to him, he was forced to change the focus of his scholarly work and to concentrate on the study of relativity and theoretical astrophysics.

"I had only one book with me—the Soviet physicist Lev Landau's *Classical Theory of Fields,*" Fang told me. "For six months I did nothing but read this book over and over again. It was this curious happenstance alone that caused me to switch fields from solid-state physics to cosmology."

But there was another equally important change brewing in his life. "It was then that I began to feel that perhaps Mao was not so good for the country," he remembered. "But because at the time most of us intellectuals still believed in Communism, we were left with a difficult question: If not Mao, whom should we follow? There was, of course, no one else, and he was the embodiment of all idealism.

"After the Cultural Revolution started, everything became much clearer. I realized that the Party had not been telling the truth, that they had in fact been deceiving people, and that I should not believe them anymore. You see, a sense of duty, responsibility, and loyalty to the country had been inculcated within me as a youth, but what I saw around me made me feel that the leaders weren't similarly concerned about the country and weren't shouldering responsibility for its people."

In 1969, when the Academy of Sciences began to move several of the undergraduate departments of Keda from Beijing to the provincial capital of Hefei, in Anhui Province, Fang, along with several dozen other academics who had been stigmatized with rightist labels, was exiled with them. In Hefei, Fang began to study and teach astrophysics, but because of the political cloud hanging over him, he was able to publish the results of his research only under a pseudonym.

His full rehabilitation did not come about until 1978, two years after the fall of the Gang of Four. At this time he regained his Party membership and received tenure at Keda, shortly thereafter becoming China's youngest full professor. The next few years were perhaps his most creative, from a scientific point of view. Fang, who was increasingly interested in the cosmology of the early universe, began to publish frequently on this subject, now under his own name. (By 1986 he had more than 130 articles to his credit.) In 1980 his popularity at Keda led to his being elected director of the fundamental physics department, with more than 90 percent of the faculty's 120 votes. However, his political outspokenness and progressive views on education continued to cause the Party to distrust him. Because of secret reports from a fellow professor impugning his political reliability, Fang, though nominated several times, was rejected for the post of vice president of the University of Science and Technology.

What was ultimately to have the profoundest political impact on Fang were his readings in politics and his travels abroad, which became possible as a result of Deng Xiaoping's open-door policy. In 1978 Fang left China for the first time, to attend a conference on relativistic astrophysics in Munich. Subsequent trips took him to the Vatican, for a cosmology conference; to Bogotá, Colombia, for another conference; to Italy, as a visiting professor at the University of Rome; to England, as a senior visiting fellow at the Institute of Astronomy at the University of Cambridge; to Japan, as a visiting professor at Kyoto University's Research Institute for Fundamental Physics; and finally to the United States, where he was in residence at the Institute for Advanced

Study, in Princeton, from March through July of 1986. These trips abroad were to influence deeply the way that Fang looked at both the Chinese socialist system and the role of intellectuals within it.

In spite of many years of political harassment and periodic near-total isolation from the world scientific community, Fang had now become one of the very few scientists from the People's Republic ever to have received such international scientific attention and acclaim. What made Fang even more unusual was his interest in education, philosophy, and politics—interests that grew out of his conviction that in any truly creative mind, science and philosophy, of which he took politics to be an extension, were indissolubly bound together. Just as scientific research was a way of bearing witness to truths about the natural world, so, Fang believed, intellectual and political inquiry were ways of bearing witness to truths about the political and social world.

. . .

In 1984 Fang Lizhi was finally promoted to the position of vice president of the University of Science and Technology, and Guan Weiyan, a colleague in physics, was appointed president. Clearly, Fang's star was now rising.

The next year the Ministry of Education issued a report, "The Reform of China's Educational Structure," calling for dramatic changes in the country's university system. It recommended that administrators be elected to top positions by committees of academics, rather than being appointed by the Party. Encouraged by the report, Fang and Guan designed and proposed a radical plan to redistribute power horizontally at Keda. Instead of keeping all authority concentrated in the hands of top-level administrators, allowing them to control research funding, the awarding of degrees, and faculty promotions, they proposed that these functions be spread out among special committees and academic departments themselves.

A second reform proposed in the plan involved establishing the right of faculty and staff members to audit all administrative meetings. Fang held that since the socialist system claimed to have made the people the masters of their own country, the people should have the right to know what their leaders were up to. This was an especially important concept for Fang, because he believed that a major defect of Chinese society was that in the absence of oversight provisions, problems and grievances piled up unsolved until they became explosive.

A third area of reform that concerned Fang and Guan was free speech. They wished to establish firmly the right of students and faculty members not only to speak out on campus but also to free themselves from other subtler but no less crippling forms of ideological repression. Fang and Guan wished to create an open academic and political environment at Keda, and since in their view diversity was something to be cultivated, not suppressed, it was their conviction that anyone should be able to put up a handbill and hold an event on campus without having to seek prior approval from some higher authority.

This was indeed a bold vision of academic freedom, such as the People's Republic of China had never known. But Fang and Guan did not stop there. To foster openness and engender a more cosmopolitan academic atmosphere, they also sought to establish as much contact as possible with the outside world. By the end of 1986 more than 900 faculty members and students from Keda had been sent abroad to visit, lecture, and study, more than 200 foreign scholars had visited Keda, and exchange programs had been set up with educational institutions in the United States, Japan, Britain, Italy, and France.

Fang's experience with this reform process made him more

convinced than ever that one of the most meaningful tasks he could undertake in China was pressing for change in the country's educational system. "I am determined to create intellectual and academic freedom—this will be my top priority," he said, with his usual directness, when asked about his future plans. In the context of a Western democracy, where traditions like intellectual and academic freedom are taken for granted, such a declaration might sound commonplace, but coming from a university vice president in China just as the country was emerging from the Cultural Revolution, his words had the effect of throwing down a gauntlet to Party hard-liners.

Moreover, while Fang was helping to fashion these educational reforms at Keda, he was by no means shutting himself off from the broader political issues and currents of the country at large. In fact, in 1985 and 1986 Fang seemed to turn up whenever and wherever there was open political discussion or ferment, a habit that caused consternation among those hard-liners in the Party hierarchy whose conception of the "mass line" had never included radical educational reform, much less spontaneous political campaigns for the democratization of Chinese life, led by roaming freethinkers like Fang.

• • •

Meanwhile, so successful were Fang and Guan's reforms at Keda that the official Party newspaper, the *People's Daily,* which was itself caught up in China's new dalliance with democratic thinking, ran a series of five articles in October and November of 1986, describing them in the most adulatory way, which was tantamount to giving them the Party's seal of approval. In fact, the writer, Lu Fang, was so impressed by what he had seen at Keda that from the very first sentence of the first article he seemed unable to control his enthusiasm. Instead of reciting a litany of facts and statistics to introduce his subject, as this genre of news feature often calls for, he dove right in and gushed, "During my trip to Keda, everywhere I breathed the air of democracy." Lu went on to praise the openness and "unconstrained atmosphere" of this university in which students and faculty members worked openly together.

Still mindful during those halcyon days of democratic dialogue that even the warmest political climate in China can suddenly frost over, the *People's Daily* published another article that fall asking rhetorically if it was not a concern that the radical experiments in educational reform at Keda might someday be branded as "wholesale Westernization," a derogatory phrase used by Party hard-liners to describe any overtly Western phenomenon. "Perhaps someone will bring up the question," the article admitted, before going on to answer itself. "In applying a system of 'separate and balanced powers' to run a college, is there not always some danger of being suspected of imitating Western capitalism? But the methods used at Keda are actually in accordance with the directions of Party Central regarding the 'practical application of democratization to every aspect of social life.' They are in accordance with the Constitution, which prescribes academic freedom. It [democracy] is not something that is being 'sneaked in the back door' here. We should have no suspicion about that."

The effect of these articles in the *People's Daily* was both to publicly transform Keda into a post-Mao model university and to elevate Guan and Fang to the status of semi-official national heroes. The glare of the spotlight, far from cowing Fang into silence as it might have some intellectuals, seemed hardly to faze him. In November, Shanghai's *World Economic Herald* ran an article that quoted Fang as declaring that China's intellectuals "lack their own independent mentality and a standard of value, always yield to power, and link their futures to an official career," and that once they become officials themselves, they change their attitude. "From being absolutely obedient to higher levels," he said, they become "absolutely conceited, and begin to suppress and attack other intellectuals."

Fang went on to call on intellectuals to remake themselves and, instead of being slavishly obedient to those above them, to "straighten out their bent backs." And then, as if he were uncertain whether the older generation would be able to reform themselves, he ended with an appeal to Chinese to "place their hopes in those younger intellectuals who are growing up during the 1980s."

It was one thing to crusade for educational reforms, even to discuss democracy, human rights, or government checks and balances in the abstract, but here was Fang Lizhi implicitly appealing to youthful intellectuals (and also his academic peers) to form a new check against Party power. This was a bold challenge indeed, for Fang seemed to be implying that the Party's failure to reform itself from within now justified pressure from without.

• • •

By putting into words what many of his colleagues thought but dared not utter in public, Fang's speeches were like detonations beneath the whole edifice of Party thought control. After thirty-five years during which almost all alternative or oppositional thoughts had been suppressed, here at last was a man who when he spoke made no effort to censor forbidden ideas or divide his thoughts between the private and the public. Because Fang and a small number of other dissidents, including Liu Binyan and Wang Ruowang, writers who in spite of almost constant Party persecution had continued to write exposés and critiques of Party malfeasance and stupidity, continued to speak out and to suggest alternative ways of looking at the Party, China, and the world, political discourse in China had acquired a new depth of field, a three-dimensionality in which Party orthodoxy at least momentarily lost its monopoly.

Early that winter, just as Fang and many other Chinese intellectuals began evincing some sense of hope that China might succeed after all in evolving politically toward greater democratization, a series of events that no one had anticipated erupted. Beginning in Hefei, at Fang's own university, on December 5, and ending in Beijing on January 1, twenty large Chinese cities were suddenly racked by demonstrations in which students demanded a speedup in political reform. Tens of thousands of protesters flooded the streets of urban China carrying placards and banners emblazoned with such slogans as "No Democratization," "No Modernization," and "Government of the People, by the People, and for the People." Dreary campuses became festooned with wall posters proclaiming such anti-Party sentiments as "I Have a Dream, a Dream of Freedom. I Have a Dream of Democracy. I Have a Dream of Life Endowed with Human Rights. May the Day Come When All These Are More Than Dreams."

Alarmed by the specter of political chaos, the Party reflexively acted not only to quell the disturbances, but to locate and root out their causes. Urged on by Maoist hard-liners, for whom the student uprising had been the embodiment of their worst fears about reform, the Party launched a swift counterattack.

. . .

On January 12 Zhou Guangzhao, a member of the Central Committee of the Chinese Communist Party and the vice president of the Chinese Academy of Sciences, summoned the Keda faculty to a special meeting. In the very center of the front row of the large meeting hall were two conspicuously empty seats. When the room fell silent, Zhou Guangzhao announced that the Party Central Committee and the State Council had decided to remove

Guan Weiyan, the president of the university, and Fang Lizhi, the vice president, from office and to reassign them, respectively, to the Institute of Physics and the Beijing Observatory, both in the capital.

After announcing this coup, Zhou Guangzhao accused Fang of having "disseminated many erroneous statements reflecting 'bourgeois liberalization' " and of having departed from the Four Cardinal Principles (i.e., adherence to the socialist road, to the people's democratic dictatorship, to the leadership of the Communist Party, and to Marxist–Leninist–Mao Zedong Thought). He continued his attack by saying that Fang's "ideas of running the school by attempting to shake off the Party leadership and departing from the socialist road had resulted in extremely nasty consequences for Keda. These erroneous ideas were fully revealed in the recent disturbance created by students of this university."

Over the next few days endless articles in the official press railed against Fang. These attacks were so relentless, repetitive, and overblown that it sometimes seemed as if the Party despaired of convincing even its own members, not to mention other intellectuals, of the righteousness of its actions, except by the sheer force and volume of its rhetoric. Any lingering uncertainties about whether the orders for Fang's ouster had come from the very top of the Party were dispelled when, a day after Fang's dismissal, Deng Xiaoping himself denounced Fang Lizhi, along with writers Liu Binyan and Wang Ruowang, by name during a meeting with Noboru Takeshita, then the Secretary General of the Japanese Liberal-Democratic Party, and soon to become Japan's Premier.

· · ·

The Fang Lizhi affair quickly became a cause célèbre in China. Within days of his dismissal, members of the foreign press and the diplomatic community in Beijing were referring to him as

"China's Sakharov." Chinese intellectuals, even those who did not completely agree with Fang's uncompromising vision of democracy for their country, applauded him for his unwavering boldness. The Party, desperate to stem this hagiographic treatment of Fang, was relentless in its media campaign against him. Even the *People's Daily,* which only two months earlier had lionized Fang and Guan for having created a model university at Keda, now blamed and ridiculed them, claiming that by "waving the banner of running universities in a democratic way" they were actually only "passing fish eyes off as pearls" and letting "vulcanized copper masquerade as gold." This was certainly not the first time that a Chinese publication had been forced to reverse itself—and surely there are few kinds of intellectual debasement worse than the forced repudiation by a writer or an editor of passionately held and publicly expressed beliefs—to keep its political position parallel to the flip-flopping Party line.

Fang's outspoken espousal of democracy and human rights had put the Party in a difficult bind. Having vigorously tried to cultivate intellectuals at various times during the previous years with ever wider calls for ever greater freedom and democracy, it now seemed bent on persecuting them again in a way that could not but remind them of the Anti-Rightist Movement, which had followed Mao's call for the Hundred Flowers Movement, in the mid-1950s. Sometimes it appeared as if the Party, unable to find the "golden mean" *(zhongyong)*—the middle way revered by classical Chinese political philosophers—hoped at least to create an optical illusion of moderation by oscillating back and forth rapidly between the extremes, alternately coddling and punishing its intellectuals. When, some months later, I asked Fang if he believed that democratization could ever take place in China under such conditions, he replied prophetically, "In China the concept of democratization has often been nothing more than a poker chip in what is really a game of power. Maybe there are

still a few idealistic leaders, but on the whole most are preoccupied with the struggle for power, and they use such concepts
as democracy as just another means of defeating their opponents.
One side will say, 'I stand for reform and you don't, so you
shouldn't be here!' The other will say, 'No! Reform is wrong,
so you shouldn't be here!' In the end it is the Chinese people who
suffer, because they get used as playthings."

The Party's treatment of Fang pointed up the contradiction
embedded within its whole modernization program and within
its past as well. It was a contradiction that did not bode well for
the future. If China was to modernize, the Party urgently needed
to rally to its cause those students, technocrats, and intellectuals
who had been alienated from it for so many years. The key
element of this mobilization process included both granting them
more freedom and opening China's doors to the outside world.
However, the predicament in which the Party soon found itself
was that along with foreign capital, technology, science, lan-
guages, and management techniques came foreign political ideas
and values that by their very nature challenged the notion of
one-party rule, and led to the kind of hard-line neo-Maoist
reaction to which Fang, like so many intellectuals before him in
Chinese Communist history, had fallen prey. What was the Party
to do? Allow such subversive heresies as democracy, freedom, and
human rights to spread unchecked, or crush the students and
intellectuals and risk losing their creative energies for the paramount task of developing and modernizing China?

Neither alternative seemed acceptable. Desperately needing to
find some compromise position, the Party did the only thing it
could: It acted inconsistently. By slapping down Fang Lizhi it
sent out a signal that while intellectuals might be granted unprecedented new freedoms, public political discourse was not to
be among them. However, by limiting its punitive actions to
what by historical Party standards were mild ones, it sought at

the same time to reassure intellectuals that China was not returning to the political dark ages of the Anti-Rightist Movement and
the Cultural Revolution. In effect, the message was this: "As long
as you are willing to leave the supremacy of the Communist
Party unchallenged, we will grant you considerable freedom. If
you challenge the supremacy of the Party and socialism as its
official canon, you will be punished." The reformers in the Party
were trying to keep a delicate balance between the imperatives
of modernization and those of control. But that January, when
it was rocked by renewed factional struggle after the tumultuous
student demonstrations of the previous month, this balance was
already beginning to teeter ominously.

. . .

Once purged from the Party, Fang Lizhi disappeared for a while
from public view, although hardly from the consciousness of
Chinese intellectuals. Still, he came in for frequent and strenuous
criticism in Party propaganda, being accused of having almost
single-handedly incited the nationwide student demonstrations of
1986. Although his activities were severely limited, he was allowed to receive friends, to continue his work, and to attend
certain public functions. Fang was even allowed to go abroad for
a scientific meeting. But he was explicitly forbidden to meet any
Western journalists. He remained in this strange sort of limbo
as the contending factions within the Party waged their slow-
motion struggle for ideological supremacy and political power.

   Fang's situation was unique for another reason as well. His
wife, Li Shuxian, had won a seat in the local People's Congress
in Haidian, the Beijing district where most of the city's universities are situated. Taking advantage of her new celebrity status, she
met with foreign reporters, telling them that she believed the
Party had been wrong to discharge her husband and that, in due
course, history would "prove that he was right." In the months

that followed, Li Shuxian also came to serve as a kind of local people's advocate, speaking out not only about the injustice of her husband's situation but also protesting on behalf of her student constituents, who were frequently harassed with unannounced searches of their dormitories and sometimes even with detention by police.

On February 28, 1987, Fang made his first post-purge public appearance, in Beijing, when he showed up at the Fourth National Congress of the Chinese Physics Society to deliver a paper titled "Progress in Modern Cosmology." His return was widely reported in the Chinese press, as was the fact that the meeting was chaired by none other than his old friend at Keda, Guan Weiyan. Clearly, this was an all too self-conscious attempt by the Party to reassure scientists that there might now be life after political purgatory.

In June, Fang was heartened when his application to go abroad was approved at the very highest level of Party leadership, and he was allowed to leave China briefly to take part in the annual meeting of the International Center for Theoretical Physics, being held in Trieste. He was refused permission, however, to go on to Great Britain for a conference commemorating the tercentenary of the publication of Isaac Newton's *Principia*. But no sooner had Fang gotten out of China than he was descended upon by hopeful reporters, and instead of holding back, he expounded to them on his political views as fearlessly as he had done the previous fall in China.

• • •

In the months that followed Fang's return, the Party made it abundantly clear that it took a very dim view of all that he had said while abroad. Unable to get another exit permit, Fang settled in at home, going each morning to the Beijing Astronomical Observatory, writing and breaking the Party's embargo by granting interviews to a procession of foreign writers who beat a track to his apartment door. He also managed to participate in several impromptu gatherings at Beijing University, where freethinking students, such as Wang Dan at Beijing University, had taken to organizing *shalong,* or "salon," discussion groups to debate new scientific, literary, philosophical, and political ideas.

In January 1989 Fang electrified Chinese intellectuals by writing a personal letter to Deng Xiaoping in which he called on him to release all political prisoners, including the celebrated Democracy Wall Movement activist, Wei Jingsheng. Wei had been in jail since 1979 for, in the words of the Party, "openly agitating for the overthrow of the government of the dictatorship of the proletariat and the socialist system in China." Fang's simple but audacious act presaged a whole series of open petitions from other members of the intelligentsia that called for more freedom of expression, and helped usher in a period of open criticism against the Party that was unprecedented in recent Chinese history.

This ground swell of dissident energy reached a crescendo of sorts when President George Bush arrived in Beijing at the end of February 1989. He left home with the mistaken impression that he could fly into China from Japan on a whistlestop tour, throw a U.S. anchor windward against the upcoming Sino-Soviet summit scheduled for May by glad-handing Deng Xiaoping and other high-ranking Chinese leaders, and then, without grappling with the thorny issue of democracy and human rights in China, leave a day and a half later. But things did not quite work out that way. Just as Fang and Li were about to arrive at the Great Wall Hotel to attend a farewell presidential barbecue, to which they had been invited, their car was stopped by Chinese security police. They were not only denied entrance to the banquet but, bizarrely, forced out into the streets to wander through Beijing on foot for several hours in the dark with a phalanx of Public Security Bureau plainclothesmen trailing after them.

Appearing at a mass press conference later that night before hundreds of members of the Western media who had been accompanying George Bush on his trip, Fang not only protested his own exclusion from the U.S. presidential dinner but eloquently raised the larger question of human rights abuses in China in a way that no Chinese had before. Appearing on television screens and on the front pages of newspapers around the world, Fang instantly became China's first celebrity dissident, as well as a great embarrassment to the Chinese government.

Ironically, when the student democracy movement finally did erupt into street protests in April of 1989, Fang and his wife were virtual bystanders. They played no part in organizing any of the demonstrations, made no grand pronouncements, and, indeed, never even went to Tiananmen Square. Instead, they remained at home in their Beijing apartment watching television, receiving friends, giving interviews to foreign journalists, and biding their time. They kept a deliberately low profile to avoid giving the Party any excuse for branding the movement as their own manipulation, a presumption that conspiracy-minded hard-line leaders had been too eager to make in 1987.

"I am sure what I have been doing and saying has had a strong influence on what the students think, and, of course, we support what they are doing," Fang told me just before martial law was declared in May. "But neither they nor I want to give the government any pretext for saying that I am the hand in the glove. The truth is that I have had no organizational role at all in these demonstrations. This movement was completely spontaneous and self-supporting."

But it was a measure of Fang's intellectual influence that he was nonetheless blamed as being at the center of a "very small group of people" responsible for bringing about this "counter-revolutionary rebellion." Ironically, like the mythological Hydra of Lerna, which grew two new heads each time one was severed, every time the party lambasted Fang, far from being diminished, his renown only seemed to increase.

Even when, fearing for his life after the June Fourth massacre, Fang reluctantly sought refuge with his wife in the American Embassy in Beijing, his renown did not cease to grow. Although trapped in a nether region between China and the outside world, he continued to do scientific research, to read, to write, and to bide his time until the uncertain moment of his release. But still hoping to besmirch his name, the Chinese government launched a massive propaganda campaign against him. They accused him of "counterrevolutionary propaganda and instigation," officially labeled him "the scum of the intelligentsia," and even issued a warrant for his arrest.

In failing to understand that ideas and symbols could not be stifled, imprisoned, or killed like human beings, the government continued to misjudge the elusive power of the ideas that had come to oppose it in China. Unable to fathom the depth of this power, which was so clearly manifesting itself elsewhere throughout the socialist bloc in 1989, the Party moved toward repression. But never in the last forty years had it been so precariously balanced on so little popular support. Never had there been such people as Fang Lizhi, who, in spite of this repressive power, still dared publicly to proclaim. "That Marxism no longer has any worth is a truth that cannot be denied. It is a thing of the past . . . and like a worn-out dress it should be discarded."

· · ·

For a year, suspended in diplomatic limbo between China and the United States, Fang and Li waited in the embassy in Beijing for some kind of negotiated settlement that would allow them and their twenty-two-year-old younger son, Fang Zhe, to go abroad. What made their case so intractable for U.S. negotiators to resolve was that not only had Fang ideologically challenged the sanctity of the Chinese Communist Party's right to rule with a monopoly of political power, but in the process his unrepentant critiques of the country's leadership had also infuriated Deng Xiaoping in a very personal way. Although, by 1989, technically Deng had largely retired from his official positions, he still remained as China's de facto paramount leader, and as such did not suffer kindly slights to the throne, much less humiliating losses of face. As is so often the case in totalitarian societies where the interests of a country are regularly compromised by the distorting effects of an aging Big Leader's personal vendettas, China's ability to yield on the matter of Fang Lizhi had become hostage to Deng's personal animosity.

I later asked Fang whether he had ever thought about just walking out of the embassy grounds and throwing himself on the mercy of world opinion to protect him. He reflected for a few moments, and then said: "Yes, we did think about this as a possibility. But if I had put myself in the hands of the Party, I don't think they would have treated me in ways recognized by the world community. They never would have given me a public trial. One can cite many examples in the past, such as the case of Hu Feng, who was sentenced without a public trial in the fifties, and countless other cases during the Cultural Revolution starting with Liu Shaoqi. All were dealt with secretly. So we were apprehensive that if we had walked out, our case too would have had no impact on the public and that the world community would have been hardly aware of us."

I could not help but think that Fang still had an all-too-Chinese view of the outside world, which over the past decade had, in fact, gathered a more hopeful collective conscience about human rights violations through groups like Amnesty International and Human Rights Watch. A good example of this new collective conscience was the Robert F. Kennedy Human Rights Award, which Fang himself won in 1989 while he was in the

U.S. Embassy, and which could have afforded him just the kind of protection, by fixing world attention on his plight, that he feared would be absent.

In fact, during a telecast of the Kennedy Award ceremony which took place in Washington on November 15, 1989, Senator Edward M. Kennedy praised Fang in absentia, saying, "What Andrei Sakharov was in Moscow, Fang Lizhi became in Beijing. . . ."

Lech Walesa, who was the keynote speaker, memorialized Fang and all the previous winners of the Kennedy Award by saying, "They did not shrug their shoulders, they did not turn away, they did not cross the street when they saw another human being harmed."

· · ·

As negotiations between the United States and China dragged on over the next seven months, Fang and Li made no further public utterance. But the Bush administration's conviction that political silence was the best way to aid negotiations for his release did appear to make Fang somewhat uneasy. In a personal letter written at the beginning of June 1990, just before a new flurry of discussions finally led to their release, Fang expressed a keen awareness of his responsibility to continue speaking out even as he felt temporarily compelled to restrain himself.

"We know we have a responsibility and obligation to say something about China's present and future, especially now at the time of the Tiananmen incident's anniversary," he wrote. But, acknowledging that the continuing negotiations still made it awkward for him to make provocative statements, he admitted that he found it "very hard to find a balance between these two opinions."

During the beginning of Fang and Li's tenure in the U.S. Embassy, the Chinese government was seemingly implacable in its demands that these "criminals" be handed over so that they could be "dealt with according to Chinese law." The only circumstance under which they appeared willing even to consider release was if Fang and Li would make public admissions of guilt.

"In the beginning the Chinese government insistently demanded that we admit our guilt and express a desire to reform," Fang recounted after his release. "Of course, we refused."

But once China had passed the anniversary of the Beijing massacre without any incidents, their hard-line negotiating position began to change as more hard-line leaders seemed to conclude that it was now in the interest of their country to resolve the bedeviling matter of Fang and Li so that relations with the outside world could begin to be normalized again. It was not long before negotiations with the United States began to center on a face-saving device for resolving the matter.

In May a perfect opportunity presented itself when Fang reported experiencing some minor heart palpitations. Although he was checked out by a Western doctor who found no serious medical problems, and although Fang himself later dismissed his chest pains as being the result of "drinking too much coffee," U.S. negotiators were not so quick to dismiss the matter. After news of how Fang was "stricken" had been leaked in Washington to the San Francisco *Examiner,* where it quickly garnered a front-page headline reading, "China Dissident Suffers Heart Attack," the year-long deadlock began to break in the Beijing negotiations.

· · ·

On June 25, 1990, Fang and Li left the U.S. Embassy and flew to England, where he was to take up residence at the Institute of Astronomy, Cambridge University. When I met with Fang there, I was struck by how he had succeeded in keeping his intellectual clarity and political balance, when the world around him had been changing with such unpredictable and often frightening rapidity.

"If circumstances allow I will go immediately back to China to make whatever contributions I can, because I can only really function there," he said matter-of-factly, as if, having barely had time to confront the present, he had already decided about the future.

Asked whether he thought his final departure from China was a victory or a failure, he replied with his usual unpolemical candor: "It is hard to say. It is a victory in the sense that the Chinese government finally had to let me out because they were under pressure. But it can also be seen as a failure because I have left my own country, my colleagues, and also many of my acquaintances and friends, and naturally my effectiveness will now be marked by this."

Then, as if he did not wish to seem too gloomy about the situation, he recounted a list of other Chinese leaders, including Kang Youwei, Liang Qichao, and Sun Yatsen, who in the past had succeeded in having considerable impact on the course of Chinese history from abroad. When asked if he did not feel a certain ambivalence at having escaped China while so many other nameless and faceless people remained trapped, many under detention and in jail, Fang acknowledged that the thing he was most concerned about was that "there are still so many people in prison. This is the most urgent matter, and one that I regard as my moral responsibility. China's record of human rights is, of course, very bad. As to human rights activities, in these I will participate directly."

Admitting that China was very different from Eastern Europe, he said that he nonetheless believed that "democratization is the trend of the modern world," and expressed a faith that finally

China too would progress in this direction. "To say that one cannot have democracy because one has not had it in the past, is a point of view contrary to history."

When pressed on how he intended to respond to those many Chinese democracy movement activists who had been waiting for his release with such high hopes for guidance, Fang seemed to bridle at the presumption that he could or should become more than a "spiritual" leader.

"If Chinese are waiting for the appearance of a superhero, I am not that man," he said emphatically. "Moreover, I think that this expectation is in itself an unhealthy one. Chinese too easily tend to put all their hopes on the next leader, only to become disillusioned. I do not mean that I want to avoid my responsibility, because I do feel a responsibility, especially after my experience during these last few years. But that does not mean that I want to be a leader."

What then would Fang advise those who look to him for leadership to do?

"If you ask me what should happen next in China . . . well, it's very difficult for me to answer," he said tentatively.

What Fang Lizhi's future would be as a public political figure was still unclear when he arrived in Cambridge. When he arrived in the U.S. in January 1991 to take up a position at the Institute of Advanced Study in Princeton, New Jersey, he reaffirmed his commitment to working to better China's human rights situation, but seemed as reluctant as ever to assume an organizational role in his county's exile democracy movement. Although he eschewed the comparison, one could imagine at some point in the future his being drafted, like Czechoslovak president Vaclav Havel, to serve his country in some official capacity. For the bitter truth of China today is that it has been almost completely defoliated of credible leaders. And should the Chinese Communist Party collapse, as Communist parties have in so many other socialist-bloc countries, it is hard to imagine to whom the country might then turn for leadership. But, on the other hand, one can also imagine Fang as reluctant to assume any such role particularly if it meant giving up science, a vocation that is clearly of enormous importance to him both as an intellectual and as a human being.

Some may find a certain ingenuousness in the tenacity with which he clings to theoretical astrophysics and researches into the beginning of time when there is so much at stake in his country's here and now. After all, they may claim, did he not make all those speeches, write all those articles, give all those interviews, get into all those high-visibility scrapes with authority, and, in effect, create a whole galaxy of political expectations in others?

These arguments have a point. To ignore the ever present reluctance toward political involvement that has manifested itself throughout Fang's life would be to misunderstand a very important aspect of the man. Whatever people's expectations, the fact of the matter is that Fang has never viewed himself, much less proclaimed himself, as the leader of an organized political opposition. Nor has he ever sought to define himself in purely political terms. His most important contributions to the Chinese political dialogue have, in fact, always come from his role as an independent outsider—as a scientist in search of truth. Like Havel, Fang is one of those rare public figures whose sense of himself does not derive from politics alone, and whose notoriety as public person has arisen almost *malgré lui*. While Fang has undeniably become a figure of significant political importance for China, one of the things that is most singular and compelling about him is precisely his reticence to become a "politician." Each time he has appeared in the limelight, he has been thrust into it more by circumstances than by any obvious eagerness to capitalize on it for his own gain. In a way that strikes one as almost Taoist, the limelight seems to have gravitated to Fang, rather than he to it.

And, in this day and age when megalomaniacs and publicity seekers who believe in nothing but their own self-promotion and celebrityhood are thick as flies, such reserve and reluctance can be, in a cryptic way, both rare and reassuring.

While some may see weakness and lack of political commitment in Fang's reticence, others will be heartened to see a real man, who though poised on the edge of the acid bath of politics has not recklessly plunged in; a man who, given the opportunity to write himself ever larger, cautiously continued to struggle not to lose himself, his intellectual bearings, or his integrity in struggles for political power. And, while there is no guarantee of what the future will hold, or even that Fang Lizhi will not become extinguished like so many other intellectuals in whom China has invested its hopes in the past as they momentarily streaked across the political sky, restrained political ambition sometimes emits its own special magnetic power, one that is often far more persuasive than the clamoring egos of politicos, the force of official propaganda, and even the firepower of a People's Liberation Army.

PREFACE

The publication of these works in English compels me to add a postscript to my earlier preface, for between the publication of the Chinese version and the appearance of the present volume stands the year 1989—a year that marks the passage of an era.

Strictly speaking, 1989 was the end of an historical period in Europe, especially Eastern Europe, but not so in China. Future historians will certainly classify the years immediately prior to and following 1989 as part of the same period. Nonetheless, 1989 has already left an indelible mark on Chinese history.

Over the thousands of years of Chinese history, there are already too many memorable years, some of them happy and some of them painful. But the happiness and the pain of 1989 may differ from those of all previous years in one way—they will be remembered not only by the Chinese, but by the whole world. The year 1989 not only saw a profound change in the feelings of the Chinese toward their own country, but also witnessed an even more emphatic change in the perceptions and attitudes of the rest of the world toward China.

One sign of these changes is the growing recognition that the doctrine of "China's unique characteristics" in world affairs is seriously mistaken. Because of its geographical conditions, because of the racial and linguistic gulf that separates it from both the West and the South, and because of its long isolation, there are indeed many differences between China and other parts of the world. If you are looking for differences, you need not be a trained social scientist to spot them. But these obvious empirical facts have been oversimplified and extrapolated into a theory which proclaims that everything about China—its culture, its society, its politics—is absolutely unique. China is so unique, holds the theory, that none of the principles shown to be progressive and generally applicable elsewhere is applicable to China.

The theory of China's unique characteristics has been popular both in China and abroad for a long time. Whether or not it was the conscious intent of those who propagated this theory, it has contributed greatly to both China's self-isolation and the isolation imposed upon it.

It is also the basis for the double standard that many Western politicians have adopted in their China policy. Because of this double standard, human rights violations by China's rulers are frequently ignored, tolerated, and even covertly encouraged. An oft-heard proposition is that "China has a unique history and culture, therefore it should be judged according to its own standards." Violent and repressive encroachments on human rights are thus "understandable," and rulers who indiscriminately slaughter innocent people are "acceptable."

One of the impacts of the blood and fire at Tiananmen Square in 1989 is its irrefutable proof of the emptiness of the "Chinese characteristics" doctrine, and of the shameful moral bankruptcy involved in viewing such things as understandable and acceptable. China's students, intellectuals, and ordinary citizens do not accept the standard of "Chinese characteristics." Their dreams and aspirations are no different from those of any other people. Their values are no exception to the values held by the rest of the human race. And certainly, the weapons and tactics employed by China's dictators to murder their people are not at all unique; dictators of all stripes, all over the world, use just such methods.

The fact is that double standards, or multiple standards, are shortsighted politically. Right now humanity increasingly faces problems of a global nature: population, energy, environment, atmospheric warming, deforestation, and so on. But as long as there are governments in the world that can hold up the slaughter in Tiananmen Square as a glorious achievement, as long as there are dictators who refuse to be constrained by universal standards, it is hard to imagine that there could be the necessary understanding and cooperation to solve global problems. On the contrary, there have long been precedents demonstrating that the appeasement of governments which revel in slaughter is an invitation to worldwide catastrophe. Because of this, human rights are a global problem, maybe even the most important one. Without steady progress in the human rights environment all over the world, it will be very difficult to find serious solutions for other environmental problems in the global village.

In this sense, China's problems *are* global problems. The earth is a small place and getting smaller. What destroys the environment in one part affects the rest. In the same way that the meltdown at Chernobyl contaminated the atmosphere of half the planet, the massacre at Tiananmen Square contaminated the human rights environment of the whole planet. Anyone with global concerns cannot fail to be concerned about this.

I hope that the speeches and essays in this volume will be of help to all those whose concern about the world at large has led them to be concerned about China.

Fang Lizhi
June 11, 1990
Beijing

PREFACE TO THE CHINESE EDITION

It never occurred to me that the material in this volume would someday be published.

I am a physicist, and most of my time is spent in teaching physics and conducting research. I have never studied philosophy or politics or the social sciences in any systematic way, and I have little experience in those realms. All I have done is to speak my mind about the injustice and irrationality that I have personally encountered in Chinese society. My opinions on these matters are not particularly original. Many friends and colleagues share these views, and in fact many of the ideas in these talks and essays are theirs. Mindful of Albert Einstein's injunction that to be silent in the face of injustice is to be an accomplice to evil, my airing of these thoughts has much less to do with any unique insights of mine than with the need to express publicly what many people are thinking privately.

Given all this, I never even included these materials in my *curriculum vitae.* They are not scholarly papers, and I never gave a second thought to the notion that there would one day be a need for an edited volume of my collected works. However, the student demonstrations of late 1986, and the subsequent Campaign Against Bourgeois Liberalization in 1987, attracted unusual scrutiny to my speeches and essays. Some have read them in order to make political criticisms, but I think even more have read them simply out of interest and concern. Friends and strangers alike, at home and abroad, have wanted to know what it was that I

xlv

actually said. My opinions have been carried in the press, and my articles have found their way into collections compiled and published on my behalf. The vast majority of what has appeared in these publications has been faithful to my original words, and for this I wish to thank all of those involved in editing and translating my work. At the same time, there have been a few fabrications bearing my name. In light of this, I feel that there is a need for a more complete collection of my writings on philosophy, politics, and society. This will help my friends, and no doubt my critics as well, to better understand my views. Such is the motive behind this most unexpected volume.

In stressing that this book was unanticipated, I do not intend to soft-pedal my responsibility for its contents. On the contrary, I want to reaffirm my commitment to everything I have said, regardless of how it has been received. This is true for extemporaneous talks and carefully worded essays alike, for impulsive pleas on the grounds of conscience, and for conclusions based on the most deliberate and detached analysis. Whatever the verdict, now or in the future, I gladly accept responsibility for every word. My conviction in this regard stems from a fundamental difference between the values of science and religion—or pseudoreligion. The latter insists that its doctrines are infallible and must be worshiped accordingly. Science, on the other hand, assigns more meaning to the act of seeking the truth than to any claims of possessing it.

The search for truth is among our most basic human rights. There is no theory or ideology so grand and glorious that it can declare itself above all questioning; if it does so, it simply becomes another religion. If there is a common thread among my essays, it is this: Chinese intellectuals, like any others, have the right to explore such questions as they see fit within their own professional spheres; they have the right to think freely about any social or political issue that they feel demands consideration; and they have the right to challenge any belief that they find dubious, no matter how sacrosanct.

The freethinking, skepticism, and inquiry that we consider such fundamental elements of our human rights are also essential features of science itself; in both cases, they derive from the pursuit of beauty and harmony in society and the natural world. This relationship implies that respect for human rights, like respect for science, is bound to grow in China. Developments of the past year or so testify to this. A friend has suggested a passage from the eighteenth-century *philosophe* Paul d'Holbach as a description of the current situation. In the *Concise Dictionary of Theology,* Holbach's definition of "excommunication" is as follows:

> Excommunication. This is the spiritual penalty inflicted by church pastors upon the black sheep of their flock; in the past it made Princes wither away, and sometimes struck them down with apoplexy; nowadays excommunication hardly has such a marked effect, a result of the decline of faith.

Indeed, these days we rarely see anyone withering away or stricken down with apoplexy, as happened all too often during the ten catastrophic years of the Cultural Revolution; and the only consequence of current "ecclesiastical punishments" has been a further decline of faith. An era is ending. I firmly believe that when this decline has fully run its course, these overscrutinized words of mine will return to their rightful state of obscurity. May the age in which such writings are quickly forgotten soon dawn in China!

Without the help of many students and friends in transcribing and editing the manuscript, this book would never have taken shape. To avoid causing them unnecessary trouble, I must refrain from mentioning their names. Therefore I can only convey to them from the bottom of my heart my thanks, and my warmest blessings.

Fang Lizhi
March 1, 1988
Beijing

BRINGING
DOWN
THE
GREAT
WALL

THE COSMOLOGIST

Introduction by H. Lyman Miller

At first glance, it may seem strange that a volume dedicated to the works of a leading political dissident should begin with a selection of his writings on science. Yet as the subsequent essays and speeches make clear, Fang Lizhi's emergence as a dissident is intimately linked to his experiences and outlook as a scientist under Chinese Communism. Indeed, Fang's journey to the center of China's political maelstrom began with a battle over intellectual freedom within his own professional field, cosmology.

In 1972, as the chaotic decade of the Cultural Revolution reached its nadir, Fang and his astrophysics colleagues at the University of Science and Technology of China (USTC) published a paper on the Big Bang model of the universe. For so doing, they suddenly found themselves the object of vehement political criticism, which accused them of perpetrating pseudo-scientific ideas antagonistic to the interests of the working class.

Fang and his co-authors had stumbled onto the ideological battlefield where the succession struggle between factions within the Communist Party leadership, already anticipating the death of the aged Mao, was being waged. Though ultimately concerned with power, these struggles also spilled over into the realm of ideas, touching on virtually every aspect of intellectual life (even if the conflicts were frequently expressed in such convoluted forms of political euphemism as that linking the likes of Confucius and Albert Einstein together as "reactionary academic authorities"). To understand how the debate over cosmology forms a constant reference point in Fang Lizhi's intellectual universe, and the continuities that Fang sees between the Mao era and the Deng era, it is very helpful to look at the historical background behind this war of ideas—in particular that pertaining to cosmology and Marxist philosophy of science.

Philosophers in the West have speculated about the structure and origins of the universe since ancient times. From the beginnings of modern science in the seventeenth century, Isaac Newton and the founders of classical physics debated the implications their science held for these questions. Cosmology, however, acquired acceptance as a hard science only within the last few decades, when major advances in observation techniques—especially the advent of radiotelescopes—provided a basis for distinguishing testable hypothesis from irresolvable conjecture.

Einstein's special theory of relativity, set down in 1905, resolved discrepancies between classical physics and electromagnetism by linking space and time into a unified continuum, called space-time. His general theory of relativity, advanced in 1916, went further still, describing gravity itself as nothing but the curvature of space-time by the presence of matter. When applied to the universe as a whole, Einstein's general theory implied (though he resisted the conclusion himself) that the universe must be either expanding or contracting.

Observational support for an expanding universe came in the 1920s, when the American astronomer Edwin Hubble discovered the "redshift" of light from galaxies outside our own Milky Way, indicating that all galaxies are receding from each other. If the universe is thus expanding, one need only extrapolate backward to infer that this expansion began as a Big Bang—the explosion of a primordial fireball sometime in the remote past. The 1965 discovery of the so-called cosmic background radiation—a weak electromagnetic field appearing uniformly across the sky, that is generally interpreted as the relic from such an explosion—provided strong support for the Big Bang hypothesis.

The resulting "standard cosmological model" built on these findings has won wide acceptance in the world community of physicists and astronomers. According to this model, the present universe emerged from the explosive expansion of matter from an initial pointlike concentration of all the universe's energy, usually called a "singularity," some ten to twenty billion years ago. This expansion is conceived of not as the flow of stars and galaxies into an infinite and empty Euclidean space, but rather as the expansion of space-time itself. Further, if, as many cosmologists believe, the universe contains sufficient matter (and therefore, gravity) to prevent this expansion from continuing indefinitely into the future (which would cause space-time to curve back onto itself), it will begin a mirrorlike process of contraction back into a new singularity. In that case, the universe will prove to be spatially "finite but unbounded, " and will have had both a beginning and an end.

Because these ideas bring the enormous authority of modern science to bear on ultimate questions of human concern that had previously been the province of metaphysics and religion, they have provoked both fascination and controversy everywhere they have been studied. In China, the reception of these ideas proved particularly difficult because they clashed with the prevailing tenets of an intellectual *and* political orthodoxy, Marxism–Leninism–Mao Zedong Thought. The regime's legitimating ideology derives its authority in part from its claim to be based on a scientifically consistent and universally valid materialist philosophy. Under these circumstances, cosmology's assertions about issues of fundamental concern to materialist philosophy—matter and motion, space and time—were potentially challenging politically as well as intellectually.

The roots of the cosmology controversy in China go back to the beginnings of Marxism in the nineteenth century. Seeking to shore up the materialist philosophy upon which he and Karl Marx grounded their theories of political economy, Friedrich Engels attempted in the 1870s to incorporate the findings of the sciences of his day into a new Marxist philosophy of science, which he called the "dialectics of nature." The prevailing Newtonian/Laplacian view that the universe must be infinite in extent and duration was particularly useful in this regard, since it provided the means to rebut religious criticism of Marxism. If the universe is infinite in extent, it was thought, then there can be no place external to it where God may reside; and if it is infinite in duration, then there need not be a "first cause."

Subsequently, in the USSR, Lenin and Stalin established natural dialectics, including Engel's cosmological propositions of an infinite universe, as the guiding philosophy of Soviet science. The particular views received by Chinese Marxist philosophers and theoreticians—in the course of science and technology transfer from the Soviet Union in the early years of the People's Republic—represented a singularly hardened set of these principles, canonized during Andrei Zhdanov's reign over Soviet intellectual life during Stalin's last years. Though Soviet science subsequently abandoned Zhdanovite restrictions after Stalin's death, a parallel thaw in Chinese science was short-lived.

China's thaw in the late 1950s ran afoul of escalating animosities between Beijing and Moscow on the one hand, and between Mao Zedong and his colleagues in the Party leadership on the other. Since these animosities were often communicated in terms of differences over the interpretation and application of Marxist-

Leninist principles, ultimately cosmology and other modern natural and social sciences in China were caught up in the ideological polemics and politics of the Sino-Soviet split and the Cultural Revolution. While Soviet scientists began to participate in the development of Big Bang cosmology in international scientific circles, China continued to hew to Zhdanovite interpretations from the Stalin period.

During the Cultural Revolution decade (1966–76), Big Bang cosmology was condemned in China as one of several "bourgeois idealist" fields of pseudoscience, because its implications of a finite universe were considered to foster belief in God, a tool of the exploiting classes. It was thus banned as a "forbidden zone," closed to scientific inquiry. Basic sciences in general, it was believed, could be "replaced" by Mao Zedong Thought—held to be the most general, advanced, and scientific form of Marxist-Leninist theory, which could most successfully guide the advancement of applied science and its adaptation to China's development.

It was in this environment that Fang acquired his interest and expertise in cosmology and in which, inescapably, the link between science and politics was formed in his mind. (The story of Fang's surreptitious reading in a coal mine of the smuggled text that launched his career in astrophysics is recounted in Orville Schell's introduction.) Within months of the publication of their 1972 paper, Fang *et al.* came under attack by radical Party theoreticians associated with the "Gang of Four." (A short example of these polemics is translated in the appendix. See Liu Bowen, "The Idealistic Doctrine of a 'Finite Universe' Must Be Criticized.") Despite Fang's frequent protests that the relevant issue was not the infinity of the universe *per se*, but whether rigorous scientific methods were adhered to in testing this or any hypothesis, the attacks continued until Mao's death in 1976. Fang and his colleagues could do little but keep their heads down and continue their research, relying on moderate factions in the leadership to protect them from serious harm.

Mao's death, the arrest of his political allies, and the massive demolition of his policies brought about by Deng Xiaoping after 1978 radically changed Fang's fortunes. In launching his reforms, Deng discarded the fundamental premises of Mao's approach, putting forward a new ideological platform that he called "socialism with Chinese characteristics." Holding that "practice is the sole criterion of truth," Deng insisted that socialism's success henceforth be measured in terms of economic development rather than class struggle. This emphasis on development meant that science and technology, and the associated professionals, would occupy a central place in the reforms. Further, Deng's assertion that Marxism-Leninism is a methodology that guides social progress through the systematic and scientific examination of conditions, rather than a body of unchanging, eternally valid truths, meant that some previously held ideas would have to be abandoned, while new truths would have to be accommodated.

The premises of Deng's reforms licensed a broad exploration of modern thought, inaugurating a period of exuberant intellectual revival and ferment. Chinese intellectuals and scientists surveyed the entire range of world intellectual trends and ideas, from classicism to postmodernism, from Weber to Alvin Toffler, from Lukacs to Marcuse, from chaos theory and sociobiology to quantum cosmology. In this context Fang emerged as a rising star in China's scientific establishment, and he lent his voice to the throng of scientists condemning the abuses of the Maoist period and urging China to join the world scientific community at the frontiers of modern science.

At the same time, the Deng reforms also inaugurated recurrent and increasingly sharp debates over how far such exploration and importation of new and foreign ideas should go. Were all new ideas relevant to China's modernization? Would importing foreign ideas damage China's sense of identity and its cultural uniqueness? Was Marxism-Leninism indeed only a method, or was there also an enduring core of principles that must be upheld, even if its derivative conclusions had to be modified in light of contemporary knowledge? Questions such as these divided the Deng coalition of politicians and intellectuals, initially united in their repudiation of the Maoist past, into antagonists over the direction, pace, and scope of reform.

Fang's answers to these questions grew directly out of his experiences in cosmology. Above all, he felt, science requires intellectual autonomy, so that the community of scientists and researchers may raise hypotheses and evaluate evidence according to commonly held scientific norms. For Fang, this meant that Chinese scientists could no longer tolerate the abusive interventions of Party authorities into the domain of science that had prevailed for the previous three decades. In this vein, Fang wrote numerous essays in scientific books and academic journals during the 1980s, for an audience of scientists, philosophers, educators, and officials within science and technology circles. Many of these essays are popularizations of current topics in his field, ranging from the topology of space-time to the search for dark matter. While intended to educate the reader, they unmistakably serve the additional purpose of introducing contemporary scientific findings that are at odds with one or more principles of orthodox dialectics.

As the decade wore on, Fang's essays came to an increasingly blunt point: Marxism-Leninism had no "guiding role" to play in directing scientific research, nor did the dialectics of nature contribute anything to the interpretation of scientific results. To his conservative critics, in whose eyes Marxism-Leninism remained the philosophical crystallization of all the sciences (because it could synthesize the particular truths of the individual sciences into the most general laws of nature and society), Fang's views on science denied the scientific basis of Marxism-Leninism and so called into question the legitimacy of the regime itself.

Fang's essays carried another message that went beyond the relationship of science to Marxism *per se*. Science flourishes, said Fang, within cultural traditions that foster free inquiry, skepticism of established authority, tolerance for a pluralism of viewpoints, and a readiness to uphold the truth whatever the personal cost; for these reasons, the autonomy of science is best protected under political systems that guarantee basic human rights. In asserting such a linkage—as he does often in his writings and speeches—Fang inherited the "science and democracy" mantle of the May Fourth period, the Chinese liberal enlightenment of the 1920s. With his stature as an astrophysicist of recognized international standing (in a country where decades of mass campaigns had made a successful scientific career a rare achievement, and where the lack of a single domestically educated Nobel prize winner is an acute embarrassment to the leadership), and with his ready wit and outspoken intelligence, the qualities that had made Fang a powerful and effective critic of Maoist attitudes toward science also made him a natural spokesman for radical reforms—and a lightning rod for conservative animosity.

The selections that follow lead the reader across some of the bridges between science and philosophy, and between philosophy and politics, that Fang Lizhi crossed along his path from cosmologist to political dissident and cultural critic. They span the entire period of the Deng reforms, beginning with his denunciations of the obscurantism of the Maoist period, and continuing down to his reflections on the eve of the great popular demonstrations of spring 1989. In all of them Fang's commitment to an enduring core of values and ideals that he associates with the scientific spirit is apparent. They are ideals and values that he acquired as a scientist and that remain central to his identity as a scientist. They were tempered in a political atmosphere that stifled science in the name of science, and ultimately they led him to speak out with a forcefulness and energy that made him a focus of both admiration and controversy in China.

H.L.M.
School of Advanced International Studies
The Johns Hopkins University
August 1990

FROM NEWTON TO EINSTEIN

The following essay is excerpted from the foreword to From Newton's Laws to Einstein's Theory of Relativity, *a 1981 physics textbook by Fang Lizhi and his University of Science and Technology of China colleague Chu Yaoquan. Fang wrote the foreword while a visiting scholar at the University of Rome in the spring of 1979.*

History tells us that civilization would not be what it is today without the contributions of a few great physicists. No one represents this group better than Newton and Galileo, the founders of classical mechanics, and Einstein, the father of relativity. Although they lived in very different times, spanning a period in which physics itself underwent a great transformation, in looking back we see that they had many traits in common.

First of all, they were explorers who refused to be constrained by preconceptions and traditional ways of thinking. Their scientific work exposed the weak spots in longstanding and sacrosanct beliefs. The questions they asked were seen—and might still be seen today—as too basic, too abstract: What are time and space? What is relative and what is absolute? What laws govern the motions of heavenly bodies? How did the universe begin? These issues seem otherworldly, very distant from our everyday concerns. Yet the fact is, the technological progress that has resulted from such "academic" investigations could not have been achieved through any other means.

Second, they adhered to scientific methods. Although they

were concerned with abstract problems, they did not engage in vacuous speculation. On the contrary, they scrutinized every concept and every hypothesis in the light of the data, testing their theories against experiment and observation.

Finally, they were not just "scientists" in the narrow sense, but men of lofty ideals. Einstein was a great spokesman for science, reason, and democracy. He said, "Only in devoting ourselves to the good of society will we find meaning in this fleeting and dangerous life." To him it was an outrage to submit to power or to fail, out of timidity, to act like a scientist. "Ask yourself," said Einstein, "if Giordano Bruno, Baruch Spinoza, Alessandro Volta, and Wilhelm von Humboldt had been like this, where we would be today?"

It is due precisely to these characteristics that great scientists and their theories have so often been found intolerable by the rulers of the day. Galileo was put on trial by the Inquisition, and Einstein met with fascist oppression in Germany. But what is truly astounding is that even in this very decade, the 1970s, under the fascist cultural dictatorship of the know-nothing "Gang of Four," the Theory of Relativity was still under siege in China! Although this stage of history already seems to have passed like a bad dream, it is more than simply beneficial to our understanding of science to reflect on what happened—it is essential. The reason is this: If we concern ourselves only with the technical details of our disciplines and fail to grasp the scientific spirit, the living soul that makes science what it is, then we may "transplant" science to China, but we will never make it take root, blossom, and bear fruit.

The last few days I've been staying at the Accademia dei Lincei, and looking out the window I can see the school insignia, which once adorned the cover of Galileo's *Dialogue*. Although the emblem of this most ancient of all scientific institutions is now old and worn, when I write of Galileo it never fails to inspire in me feelings of deep reverence. Tomorrow will be March 14, 1979, exactly one hundred years to the day since the birth of Albert Einstein. Today I have finally completed the manuscript of this book, and thus I respectfully dedicate it to the memories of Einstein and Galileo, two men of science who will always remain true giants in the eyes of the human race.

March 13, 1979
Rome

FROM "WATER IS THE ORIGIN OF ALL THINGS" TO "SPACE-TIME IS THE FORM OF THE EXISTENCE OF MATTER"

This essay appeared in the summer of 1982 in Philosophical Research, *a journal published by the Department of Philosophy of the Chinese Academy of Social Science. It addresses a debate among Marxist philosophers of science on two questions of relevance to Fang Lizhi's field of cosmology: the nature of space-time and the infinitude of the universe. It also addresses the question of what role, if any, Marxist philosophy should play in guiding scientific research.*

There is a phenomenon that has long been noted and that continues to occur in the development of science and philosophy, namely that philosophy is constantly withdrawing from areas that were once within its domain, while natural science moves into them one by one.

When the proposition that water is the origin of all things was advanced by Thales in Greece and Kuan-tzu in China, it was very much a philosophical one.* As the structure of matter came

---

*Thales of Miletus (ca. sixth century B.C.) is generally considered the first of the Greek natural philosophers. The *Kuan-tzu* is a book on statecraft and philosophy attributed to Kuan Chung, prime minister of the state of Ch'i in the seventh century B.C. The *Kuan-tzu*'s speculation that water is the fundamental constituent of all things is typical of cosmological speculation among philosophers in China's classical period, who sought

to be studied more scientifically, the question of whether water was indeed the origin of all things became a purely scientific topic. When it was discovered that water is not a fundamental component of matter at all, but a substance composed of hydrogen and oxygen, the issue died a natural death.

That this phenomenon of "philosophy retreating while science advances" results from the progress of natural science goes without saying. But it should be emphasized that it is also a consequence of progress in philosophy itself. This began with philosophers after Thales and Kuan-tzu, who gradually broke free of the primitive use of material analogies to express abstract ideas. They no longer used the flow of water to represent motion, the indefinite shape of water to symbolize change, the ability of water to fill empty spaces to suggest interconnectedness, or the passage of water from heaven to earth and back again as a metaphor for cyclic change or evolution. Instead they came to use directly the more philosophically meaningful concepts of motion, change, relationship, cyclicity, and evolution. The abandonment of vague, antiquated concepts in favor of newer and more precise ones was of course a step forward for natural philosophy.

Next, and more important, philosophers in later stages steadily turned away from such questions as whether or not water is the origin of all things, and instead "retreated" into asking whether there is an origin of things at all, and if so how we might come to know about it. The empiricist epistemology first propounded by Francis Bacon and later refined by Thomas Hobbes, John Locke, and George Berkeley, developed precisely through this process of "taking a step back" in looking at problems. Their approach to methodology and theories of knowledge has played

---

to reduce the diversity of natural phenomena to a few basic elements—such as earth, water, fire, metal, and wood—paralleling similar thought in the classical Greek world.

a crucial role in shaping the natural sciences. The rise of modern science is in fact inseparably linked to philosophical guidance of this type, quite apart from the role played by social or technological factors or conditions of production. Indeed, philosophy has left very distinct footprints along the path from discursive natural philosophy to modern experimental science, all the way from the classical era of Newton's mechanics to the modern era of relativity and quantum mechanics. In this sense, the very reason that science has been able to lay claim to such issues as whether "water is the origin of all things" is that philosophy has already made its retreat into questions of whether, or how, such propositions make sense.

Let's move on to a more modern example. In Immanuel Kant's day, the question of whether the universe is finite or infinite was a problem of great concern to philosophers. Some thinkers dealt with the issue quite explicitly, incorporating finitude or infinitude into their philosophical systems as an integral part of their world views. Despite attempts by Newton and others to study the extent of the universe from a scientific perspective, the treatment of the question on the whole remained half scientific and half philosophical. Not until the advent of modern cosmology in the present century have philosophers really begun to back away from this issue. But like the question of whether all things originate from water, the finitude of the universe has also become a topic purely for scientific research.

The theoretical advances underlying this transition owe much to the beckoning of philosophy. Genuinely scientific methods of experiment and observation began with Galileo, whose telescope and inclined plane heralded the beginning of this development. At the outset, however, it was unclear whether such methods would allow us to understand things that could not be seen or felt directly. Until the last century there were people who objected to the study of the atom on the grounds that we cannot see it. There were those opposed to studying the chemical composition of stars because actual samples of stellar matter are unavailable. And of course, some people have objected even more strenuously to research into the extent of the universe, arguing that whether the universe is finite or infinite is an intrinsic property of the whole, while astronomical observations are restricted to a finite region.

Scientists have been moved to rebel against such viewpoints in part because of the philosophical proposition—a correct one—that matter is interconnected. Although human beings cannot enter the realm of the atom or subatomic particles, we can nonetheless determine the structure of microscopic particles from their appearance on macroscopic instruments. This is because of the relationship between microscopic properties and their macroscopic manifestations. In a similar fashion, even though we cannot see the entire universe, we can still piece together a picture of the whole from observations of finite regions. This is again because there are connections on many levels between the properties of the whole universe and the manifestations of its various parts.

This leads me to a still more recent example, regarding the proposition that space-time is the form of matter's existence.* This idea is still a standard component of our natural-philosophy curriculum. Yet it seems that philosophy must soon retreat from this position as well, because physics has already begun to suggest that time itself may not be a fundamental physical quantity. Just as water is composed of hydrogen and oxygen, time may also be a secondary measure born of something even more fundamental. This has two implications. First, the basic form of matter is not necessarily space-time. Second, the basic properties of time may

---

*In the 1880s, Friedrich Engels stated that "the basic forms of all being are space and time," and that space and time are "the two forms of the existence of matter." Marxist philosophy remains predicated on this premise.

depend on its quantitative relationship to its own fundamental constituents, much as water's basic properties are determined by its molecular structure. In light of the research currently under way in this area, the statement that "space-time is the form of the existence of matter" seems as vague and primitive as "water is the origin of all things." It may be that this notion, too, will soon be dispelled.

The progress of physics regarding the question of time may again be attributed to a "retreat" on the part of philosophy. Philosophers have long discussed the basic forms of existence, and whether "existence" or "reality" in fact requires a form at all. As in the cases discussed previously, in the question of time insights from these philosophical investigations have been a direct inspiration to natural science.

In short, the withdrawal long ago of philosophy from the proposition that water is the origin of all things, its ongoing withdrawal from the proposition that the universe is infinite (or finite), and its potential withdrawal from the proposition that space-time is the form of matter's existence, have all resulted in part from the guidance that philosophy has provided to natural science. These "retreats" are in fact real symbols of philosophical progress.

PHILOSOPHY IS A TOOL
OF PHYSICS

The following essay originally appeared as the preface to Scientists on Method, *a multivolume work on scientific methodology published in 1985, edited by Zhou Lin, Yin Dengxiang, and Zhang Yongqian.*

I am quite unqualified to write prefaces for other people's books, particularly a book like the present one devoted to the words of people wiser than myself. However, Yin and Zhang, two of the book's editors, were bent on getting me to write for them, I think because they were influenced by the present trend requiring a token "youth" of less than fifty years of age to serve as a "decoration"! But decoration is not the method of a scientist. I would prefer to make use of the opportunity to frankly air an opinion.

What I will frankly air is as follows: We should refrain from superstitious belief in any so-called "supreme philosophical principles guiding science."* Appeal to "supreme principles" is not a scientific method. To be sure, when initiating a research project

---

*As one authoritative Party spokesman has explained it, "Marxist philosophy . . . is the theoretical system of a worldview comprehensively synthesized from every scientific discipline. It is applicable to every field and every thing, and is the ultimate methodology guiding all of our endeavors and all scientific research. . . . Practice continually proves that the guiding role of a Marxist theoretical framework cannot be denied or superseded. If we depart from correct Marxist guidance, our enterprises of revolution and reconstruction will be doomed to disruption and failure, and our scientific and other work will never attain their proper level of achievement." Jin Lin, "No Science Will Ever Supersede Marxist Philosophy," *Beijing Daily,* May 5, 1986.

everyone needs and hopes to find some guidance, to find a potential point of departure or line of investigation. Hence the guidance sought by a researcher is essentially a research method or path. "Guiding principles" are just those which provide such a method or path, and as such are clearly necessary in any research. The problem is in the reference to "the supreme." All of us have had direct experience of "the supreme," so we treat it with great care.

One often hears it said that "philosophy provides the guidance for scientific research." If this sentence is taken to mean that philosophy can offer effective methods, is a useful tool of scientific research, then I support it. If it means that the relationship between philosophy and science is that between the leader and the led, I disagree. If it is further held that there exist "supreme" philosophical principles to direct scientific research, this is even more mistaken.

It is mistaken in the first place because it is not in keeping with the facts of history as regards scientific progress. In the development of physics, many different philosophical schools contributed; its progress was not due to any omnipotent "supreme principle." Kepler sought the harmonies of planetary motion, an inspiration derived from the Pythagoreans. Newton upheld empiricism in developing his theories, imparting a realist coloring to the research methods of classical physics as a whole. The achievements of quantum theory should be attributed to positivism. The creation of the General Theory of Relativity very clearly bore the stamp of rationalism. And today's physics is pursuing super-symmetry and grand unity, seemingly in a return to Kepler's pursuit of harmony. We can see that when physics was in search of a philosophy to serve as a tool and a methodology, it never became mired in any "supreme philosophy." For the value of a tool lies in its application; the criterion of physicists is to use whatever philosophy can offer in the way of useful methods. This relationship between philosophy and physics was vividly described by Einstein:

> From the viewpoint of a systematic theory of knowledge, he [the physicist] must appear to be a shameless opportunist: Insofar as he strives to describe a world independent of cognitive functions, he resembles a realist; insofar as he sees concepts and theories as free inventions of the human spirit, he resembles an idealist; insofar as he holds that his concepts and theories hold good only to the extent that they provide logical connections between sensory experiences, he resembles a positivist; insofar as he treats the viewpoint of logical parsimony as an effective tool, indispensable to his research, he even resembles a Platonist or Pythagorean.

We can see that for the physicist, philosophy is a tool, just as mathematics is a tool. Physics takes in a diversity of contributions from mathematics, but there is no "supreme" mathematics; the contributions of many schools of philosophy are comprehended in physics, but there is no "supreme" philosophy. In fact no genuine science ever styles itself "supreme."

I greatly appreciate the work of the editors of this volume, who have provided us with some rare sources in scientific methodology, a most valuable collection of historical materials. In part their value lies in demonstrating that the methods not only of physics, but of other sciences as well, embrace the creative output of humanity down through the ages and are not the consequence of guidance by some "supreme principle."

We hope the third and fourth volumes will appear soon and provide still more historical evidence that one of the maxims of scientific methodology is never to blindly trust in some omnipotent "supreme." The statement that "Marxist philosophy is the supreme principle and methodology guiding scientific research" is itself inconsistent with Marxist principles. It is a form of blind faith and ignorance. Marxism too is the product of an age; it cannot substitute for the whole of scientific creation prior to Marx's time, despite the fact that it absorbed many of the products of this creation. Nor can it encompass all of the science of today. The essence of science is development, creation, constant self-transcendence, and Marxism is no exception.

—Translated by David A Kelly

PHILOSOPHY AND PHYSICS

This essay originally appeared in Natural Dialectics Research, *No. 5, 1986. It later served as the introduction to* Philosophy Is a Tool of Physics, *a 1988 collection of articles by Fang on scientific subjects.*

People often ask me, "How do physicists—both researchers and teachers—look at philosophy?"

There is no simple answer to this question. Certainly most people who study physics are interested in philosophy to some extent—what is physics, after all, but natural philosophy? Anyone who has taught physics knows that sprinkling in a bit of methodology or epistemology during a lecture not only livens up the class but also aids the students in their comprehension of the subject matter. At times, such digressions are not only helpful but essential. For example, in a discussion of quantum mechanics, it is difficult to avoid touching on the philosophical dimensions of what it means to "measure" something, or even what it means that something "exists."

This stems in part from the vital role philosophy has played in the history of physics. Kepler's search for harmonies in the motions of the planets was inspired by the Pythagoreans. Newton's insistence on empiricism in the development of his theories injected a realist coloring into the research methods of all of classical physics. The success of quantum theory was closely linked to positivism, while the origins of general relativity clearly bear the stamp of rationalism. Now we are pursuing super-symmetry and grand unification theories in an apparent return to Kepler's pursuit of harmony. Philosophy is obviously useful to physicists, both in teaching and in research. We are interested in philosophy precisely because it is useful.

Unfortunately, in China that interest has been abused. My first intense encounter with such abuse came in the early 1970s, when my colleagues and I were switching into cosmology. Our motives were simple. With the discovery of the cosmic microwave background radiation in 1965, questions about the nature of the universe began to fall more and more within the province of physics, and physicists around the world were increasingly attracted to the field. We in China went into it for the same reasons as everyone else.

Yet this purely scientific interest on our part led to us being accused of "serving religion," "promoting pseudoscience," and other terrible things. Born of the grossest ignorance, this meddling under the guise of philosophy led to a drastic change in my conception of the subject. I had always held philosophy up as a wise and noble pursuit, but I soon grew to despise it. I had to dispel all notions of it, as if I were brushing away flies, before I could have the peace of mind to do my work.

The cosmology affair took place during the "ten abnormal years" [the Cultural Revolution, 1966–76]. Since everything else was "abnormal" as well at that time, I thought our problems with the philosophers were just another transient bit of abnormality. Bad philosophy stupidly applied in an attempt to direct physics had produced predictably bad results. Yet after thinking long and hard about this, I knew that I didn't really accept the "abnormality" explanation. The fact is that every single "philosophical" intervention in the natural sciences since the founding of the People's Republic [in 1949] has been a huge mistake.

Actually, the problems began even before Liberation. [Lenin's] 1908 book *Materialism and Empirio-Criticism* was an explicit attempt to employ [Marxist] philosophy in directing scientific research, and featured criticisms of Ernst Mach's theories of space and time.* We should have the courage now to admit that from the standpoint of physics, the ideas in this book are quite mistaken. All they really demonstrate is that the author of this presumed "guidance" did not know physics. I should emphasize that his ideas are mistaken not only by present standards but by the standards of the day.

This example should teach us a lesson. No matter how good your philosophy, when it is placed in the role of a judge, dispensing criticism on the specifics of research projects and telling physicists how to conduct their research, the outcome is not going to be pretty. Philosophies, at least those with some depth to them, are useful to physics. But being useful does not mean sitting in judgment. Mathematics is extremely useful to physics, but it does not presume to judge physics; likewise with formal logic. Philosophy, like mathematics and formal logic, is no more to physics than a useful tool.

· · ·

In 1981 I attended an international conference on cosmology at the Vatican. The participants received a statement issued by the Pope, which touched on the relationship between religion and science. It said, in part, that "Cooperation between religion and science is mutually beneficial to both, so long as the independence of neither one is violated. Religion demands the freedom to worship, and science demands the freedom to inquire." The Pontiff went on to state that the Church had wrongly judged Galileo precisely because it had disregarded the autonomy of science.

His words left me deeply thoughtful. The advance of science

*See Glossary, *Ernst Mach.*

had, in the end, forced the Church to admit that theology has no authority over science. Science won its independence, and the days of "science is the handmaiden of theology" are long gone.* Yet today there are "philosophers" who remain unwilling to make a similarly frank admission. Witness the recently propounded "general laws of the universe,"† offered as the ultimate criterion by which to evaluate cosmological physics. This stuff even goes under the name of Marxism, though in truth it doesn't even measure up to John Paul II's theology.

Science threw off the shackles of religion through its own actions. Whether the Church liked it or not, when science disproved the claims of classical theology, religion lost its exalted status. Today, the same treatment should be applied to philosophers (theologians, really) with a proclivity for sitting in judgment. We should tell the would-be framers of these "general laws" that their basic premises are obsolete.

What is pathetic is that these grandiose philosophical systems are nothing more than recapitulations of the so-called "three great discoveries" of the nineteenth century.‡ It is true that the two books by Friedrich Engels, *Anti-Dühring* and *The Dialectics of Nature,* were based on these discoveries. But astronomy and physics have come a long way since then. Engels's conclusions have to be brought up to date, like anything else. To enshrine these ideas as inviolable precepts for practicing physics today is an abomination in the face of Engels's original intent.

To be sure, the new "grand philosophies" come with the latest

---

*A famous remark by the scholastic philosopher and theologian Thomas Aquinas (1225–1274).

†This refers to a major revision and systematization of natural dialectics by Zha Ruqiang, head of the Office of Natural Dialectics Research, which was published in the premier journal of the Chinese Academy of Social Science in September 1985.

‡The scientific discoveries held by Engels and subsequent Marxist philosophers to epitomize the dialectical laws of nature: the conservation laws of physics, the existence of cells as the basic constituent of living organisms, and biological evolution.

in scientific terminology, which lends them a modern façade. But because the authors lack a real understanding of modern science, this jargon merely sits atop the same old classical framework. The result is atrocious. For example, in discussing time and space we find a full presentation of Engels's premises about space-time set alongside such fashionable-sounding ideas as non-Euclidean geometry and Einsteinian space-time. Yet the former and the latter are altogether incompatible; Einstein's view of space-time could not possibly be accommodated by that of Engels. If Engels's works nonetheless express the gracious harmony between classical physics and classical philosophy—not unlike the *Mona Lisa*—then the latest in "grand philosophies" conjures up the image of a Chinaman with a long pigtail, clad in a Western suit.

The old guard is bemoaning the fact that students' interest in "philosophy" is dwindling. Personally, I find this situation altogether agreeable; the students' choice has my blessing and full support. They have no need to follow a brand of philosophy that will lead them only to confusion.

Over the past two years, I have discussed some of my own philosophical views with the students in my graduate seminar. One of my aims is to help them to recognize the true character of this latest theology. Among the relevant propositions we have explored are the following:

1. That the physical world is not always "dialectical" in nature.
2. That the infinite can be bounded, and the finite unbounded.
3. That the proposition "matter cannot be destroyed" is not universally valid.
4. The possibility of existence in a time-free state.
5. The creation of the universe from nothing, and the nature of "first cause."

6. The nature of "heat death."
7. Whether the objective can be distinguished from the subjective in quantum phenomena.
8. The physical basis of free will.
9. A scientific understanding of the "immortal soul."
10. [Einstein's view that] "the most incomprehensible thing about the universe is that it can be comprehended."

In sum, physicists show a willing interest in philosophy, especially in frontier issues like the ones just mentioned. What we do not welcome is "philosophy" that promotes pretentious nonsense under the banner of universal truth. I would venture to predict that such pretense will not soon disappear, and that its perpetrators will continue to do as they have done in the past. Physicists are familiar with this experience: wrong ideas persist until the passing of the old generation, and correct ideas must wait for the arrival of a new one. As James Clerk Maxwell said: "There are two schools of thought about the nature of light: the particle theory and the wave theory. We are now more inclined to accept the wave theory, simply because all those who believed in the particle theory are now dead."

Or as Max Planck said: "A new scientific theory does not triumph by convincing its opponents and making them see the light, but rather because its opponents eventually die and a new generation grows up and is familiar with it."

I believe that in our country the era of grand philosophical systems presiding over physics is nearing an end, because those who would perpetuate this state of affairs are indeed beginning to die off. And because a new generation is growing up, with the awareness from the beginning that we need a philosophy that is a useful tool, not a supreme authority.

A NOTE ON THE INTERFACE
BETWEEN SCIENCE AND
RELIGION

The following essay appears in Robert J. Russell, ed., John Paul II on Science and Religion: Twenty Reflections on the New View from Rome (Geneva: Vatican Press, 1991). Fang's observations on the role of culture in the development of science draw on two lectures he gave in the fall of 1986: "Modern Cosmology and Traditional Chinese Culture" and "Starting from Fang Yi-chih." The essay was written in September 1989, during Fang's stay in the U.S. Embassy in Beijing.

The relationship between science and religion is a difficult topic for anyone, myself included, who grew up in Chinese society. In twenty-five hundred years of Chinese literature there has been little written on this subject, and even less on whether the relationship is one of conflict or mutual support. Many historians would point to this as further evidence of the absence of a strong religious influence within traditional Chinese culture.

Yet religion has been an important component of that culture. Taoism is an indigenous religion that evolved from one of China's most celebrated schools of philosophy around the sixth century B.C. Christianity entered China by at least the seventh century A.D., and Buddhism and Islam gained varying numbers of adherents in China at about the same time. Indeed, the average number of religious structures built in China per person, including churches, temples, monasteries, convents, and mosques—one measure of the status of religion within a society—is probably comparable to the figure in Europe or the Middle East. Almost all Chinese emperors took part in some sort of religious activity. Therefore, it would not be correct to say that religion has been absent from Chinese culture.

What *is* true is that, historically, religion has had singularly little influence on Chinese thinkers. Religion has affected only the philosophical ideas of intellectuals, rather than their personal beliefs. For instance, even though Taoism was quite popular among the ordinary people of the Tang Dynasty (A.D. 618–905), the Taoist cosmology—such as the belief that the universe originated from nothing—never became a matter of religious orthodoxy among astronomers, as did Aristotle's cosmology in medieval Europe.

This uniquely Chinese phenomenon did not change with the arrival of modern science. The Jesuit Matteo Ricci [1552–1610] was the first to bring European astronomy and other other aspects of Western science to China, along with the missions and churches he established in Guangzhou and Beijing. The astronomy Ricci introduced was ultimately accepted by Chinese astronomers and used to replace traditional methods in the preparation of calendars. Nevertheless, Catholicism itself never gained much popularity among scholars. The contrast between this situation and that in the West reveals a prevalent attitude toward religion among Chinese thinkers, rooted in the Confucian tradition, which puts primary emphasis on ethics and ignores ontological questions. Confucius once said: "Respect the gods and spirits, but keep them at a distance." Thus, although the Chinese have also debated the existence of God, there has been little intellectual dialogue on the subject. A typically Confucian view is contained in the proverb "We have so little understanding of man, how can we possibly understand the gods?"

If we were concerned only with direct interactions between science and religion in China, we could probably stop here. But if we want to know about the relationship between science and religion more generally, then Chinese history provides a useful case study. Because the laws of science are the same everywhere, differences in the way science has developed in different locales lead us to look at differences in cultural context. Some light may be shed on the interactions of science and religion in China by comparing the historical development of science in China and the West.

It is generally acknowledged that science cannot be conducted in the absence of basic assumptions or presuppositions. These are the foundations from which generalizations are made, and by which one decides what data to consider. Such assumptions can be neither proven nor deduced, in the rigorous sense, from the data itself; they are very much a function of the cultural environment in which their holders live. It is through this interface that religion plays an important role in the development of science.

Perhaps the most critical assumption underlying all the sciences is that nature is capable of being understood, and therefore that it is possible to find answers to questions about the natural world. Such an assumption may seem trivial in most cases, yet in terms of some questions rather distant from our day-to-day experience, the very first task is to assume that the problem has a knowable answer. In this regard, whether or not the assumption of under-standability is made can be quite significant.

For example, a key issue in the history of Western thought was how the moon, the stars, and the planets remain suspended in the heavens and do not fall to earth as nearby objects do. This topic was studied, debated, and variously resolved by thinkers from Aristotle's time to Newton's. Of course, from the perspective of modern physics, all the pre-Newtonian answers are incorrect. What is noteworthy, however, is that all of those early thinkers believed that one could find the answer to this question. Faced with the problem of how celestial objects stay in the sky, the scholars of the West assumed understandability.

The situation in China was quite different. According to a Chinese story of the third century, people in the city of Qi were worried that the sky would fall. But in contrast to the West, their concern never attracted the serious attention of Chinese thinkers. The predominant response to the question was skepticism that one could find any believable answer at all. As the famous Tang poet, Li Bai, wrote: "Why waste time worrying about the collapse of the heavens like the people of Qi?" Since then, in Chinese, "to worry about the collapse of the heavens like the people of Qi" has become a derisive expression for people preoccupied with meaningless problems. Confronted by the problem of celestial bodies, Chinese thinkers chose to assume nonunderstandability.

This clearly suggests that the assumption of understandability or nonunderstandability is culturally dependent. But why were the presuppositions so different in China and in the West? Religion plays a key role in creating precisely these kinds of cultural differences. Even though religious propositions are in general quite different from scientific ones, Western theology nonetheless also assumed understandability, even with regard to such transcendental questions as the existence of God. Given such attitudes on the part of theology, it was only natural that few were skeptical that a solution to the more mundane question of how celestial objects stayed aloft could be found. The assumption of understandability was due, at least in part, to the Western religious tradition. The assumption that problems remote from direct experience or even transcendental in nature could nonetheless be understood was a consequence of a beneficial interaction between science and religion.

A second contrast between the ancient astronomies of China

and the West concerns the motions of the planets. The apparent orbits of the stars are regular and circular. However, the five planets visible to the naked eye are an exception to this, as seen from the earth. The planets appear to move irregularly across the sky, at times more slowly and at times more quickly, sometimes moving backward or seeming to stop altogether. Their motions were recorded with about the same precision by both Chinese and Western astronomers. Both astronomies had their own methods to predict the planetary movements, including the retrograde motion and the pauses as the planets changed direction.

A major difference between ancient Chinese astronomy and its Western counterpart was that the latter was always concerned with *explaining* the apparent irregularities and anomalies in the motions of the planets, while the former was not. A key issue in Western astronomy was to develop a model showing how the motions of the stars and the planets were, either actually or intrinsically, uniform and harmonious. The search for uniformity in celestial motion was a common pursuit among Western astronomers. This was the impetus behind Copernicus's development of the heliocentric theory, in which all celestial objects move regularly along circular orbits, with the various progressions and retrogressions of the planets being not their own, but a reflection of the motion of the earth. Confronted with differences between the motions of stars and planets, Western astronomers assumed uniformity.

In contrast, Chinese astronomers were untroubled by phenomena that departed from the norm, and in fact were quite taken with them. The astronomical records of ancient China are far more replete with such unusual occurrences as meteors, comets, sunspots, novas, and supernovas than those in the West. Chinese astronomers were content to expect diversity and nonuniformity in the heavens. It was thus quite natural that they did not consider differences between the motions of stars and planets to be of crucial importance.

The different responses to this problem by Chinese and Western astronomers probably also resulted in part from the different religious traditions in their respective cultures. Judeo-Christian doctrines affirmed that the entire universe was the work of a single Creator. Such a view may well have fostered the theory that the heavens were uniform. Taoism provides similar support for uniformity in the universe at large. In the *Tao Te Ching,* for example, it is written that: "The One begat the Two, the Two begat the Three, and the Three begat the Myriad Things." Taoism, however, never became the dominant mode of thought in China.

The assumption of uniformity is thus a second important interface between science and religion. While their absolute faith in uniformity may have caused Western astronomers to fail to record some unusual celestial phenomena, with regard to unraveling the mystery of planetary motion, the assumption of uniformity was very positive.

The concept of relativity provides a third example of science-religion interactions. A well-known passage in Galileo's *Dialogue Concerning the Two Chief World Systems* [1632] states:

Shut yourself up . . . in the main cabin below decks on some large ship. . . . Have a large bowl of water with some fish in it. . . . With the ship standing still . . . the fish swim indifferently in all directions. When you have observed . . . carefully . . . have the ship proceed at any speed you like, so long as the motion is uniform. . . . You will not discover the least change . . . nor could you tell . . . whether the ship was moving or standing still.

This passage is generally recognized as the first mention of relativity in the history of physics. Indeed, it played an important role in the establishment of Galileo's principle of inertia, Newton's mechanics, and even Einstein's relativity.

It is therefore extremely interesting to note that an almost identical statement can be found in the Chinese literary work *Shang Shu Wei,* which preceded Galileo's *Dialogue* by more than a thousand years. According to the *Shang Shu Wei,*

> The Earth is constantly in motion, while man feels nothing, like a passenger who stays in a moving cabin.

The aim of this statement appears to be identical to that of Galileo, who was responding to those who asked why we feel nothing if the earth is moving at high speed. This idea in the *Shang Shu Wei* did not, however, have any impact on the development of physics in China. A famous scholar living at the time of Galileo, Fang Yizhi, wrote the first Chinese book introducing some of Galileo's results, entitled *Essay on Physics.* In his book, Fang Yizhi mentioned the *Shang Shu Wei* comment on relativity only as a minor footnote.

The difference in responses to the idea of relativity in China and the West is related to the absence of the concept of universality in traditional Chinese science. Without a belief in the existence of universal principles, and thus with no motivation to find universal laws in nature, the *Shang Shu Wei* remark about "feeling nothing in a moving cabin" was of no special significance, no more than an analogy limited to explaining why the earth's motion is not felt. Galileo's argument, on the other hand, was based on an implicit assumption of universality: that the laws of physics are "on earth as they are in heaven." By Galileo's time, the history of physics already contained many examples of the derivation of general laws from the analysis of specific analogies;

such successes were predicated on the assumption of universality. We cannot say that this idea derives exclusively from religious traditions, since the concept was already splendidly developed in Greek philosophy. Nevertheless, Western religion did promote belief in the existence of universal principles, and in the quest for their discovery.

Any claim that science and religion have little to do with each other is less impressive in this light. They clearly interact at the point of forming and evaluating very basic assumptions involved in the scientific process. Indeed, human civilization is an inseparable whole, in the sense that each part in this whole inevitably interacts with all the others and contributes to their development. If one looks carefully at the construction of scientific theories, it is evident that collaboration and interaction among the various components in human civilization, including science and religion, are both important and necessary.

CHINESE DEMOCRACY: THE VIEW FROM THE BEIJING OBSERVATORY

Fang Lizhi wrote this essay, translated here by Geremie Barmé, in April 1989, as the demonstrations in Tiananmen Square were just beginning. It commemorates the seventieth anniversary of another great popular protest movement that began in Tiananmen Square, the May Fourth Movement of 1919. Fang writes from his research post at the Beijing Astronomical Observatory of the Chinese Academy of Sciences, to which he was reassigned in 1987 following his dismissal as vice president of the University of Science and Technology.

There's no denying that China's reforms are in big trouble. Modernization and democratization have come to a halt, unable to move forward even though the road back is cut off. All around us, societies of similar racial and cultural background are racing to join the ranks of the developed nations, while on the Chinese mainland time passes with little progress to report. Seven decades have slipped away since the May Fourth Movement began.* How many more years will pass before decisive changes take place? This is a painful and depressing question for many people.

But I don't mean to be overly pessimistic on the occasion of this commemorative essay; therefore I won't dwell on the question of democracy in China. Instead, I'd like to present an over-

*See Glossary.

38

view of the last three centuries as they relate to the Beijing Observatory.

The greatest contribution of the May Fourth and New Culture movements was to promote the absorption by Chinese culture of democracy and science, two things it has in short supply. In the case of democracy, the process of absorption began and ended with the May Fourth period. But in 1919, the clash between Chinese traditional culture and modern science was already coming to an end.

The Beijing Observatory is intimately linked to the introduction of Western science over the last three centuries. Western science made its debut in China with the arrival of Matteo Ricci in 1582. (Ricci's tomb can be found today on the grounds of the Party School of the Beijing municipal government.) Modern science ran into strong resistance from the very start. Leng Shouzhong and others in the late Ming Dynasty opposed using Western methods for the formulation of the Chinese calendar, insisting it could be based only on the Song Dynasty neo-Confucianist text *Huangji jingshi;* this was the first historical appearance of the theory of "Chinese characteristics." As a result, the court continued to use the old Datong and Islamic calendars.

In 1610 and again in 1629, the traditional methods led to erroneous predictions of solar eclipses, whereas the Catholic Mandarin Paul Xu Guangqi made wholly accurate forecasts using Western methods. At this point the Chongzhen Emperor accepted the use of these methods, and the Chongzhen Calendar was prepared based on them. But because of the opposition of the traditionalist [*shoujiu*] faction, the calendar was never actually used.* The scientific treatise on which it was based was published only after the collapse of the Ming, during the reign of the Qing emperor Shunzhi [1644–1662]. Bearing the title "The New

*See Glossary, *Calender debates.*

Western Calendar," it was used to formulate the official calendar. This was in all likelihood the first time that contemporary Western science had become a part of Chinese life.

But the good times didn't last. As soon as Shunzhi died, antiscience forces came into power once more. The eminent Confucian Yang Guangxian memorialized the throne: "It would be more preferable for China not to have an accurate calendar, than for it to tolerate the presence of Westerners." This expression of antipathy toward both Western people and their methods qualifies as the second time the theory of "Chinese characteristics" was expounded. Once this attitude prevailed at court, Li Zubai and five other people who'd been involved in calculating the calendar according to Western methods were put to death, making them the first people at the Beijing Observatory to sacrifice their lives for the sake of China's modernization. (Throughout history, astronomers have often been punished or executed as a result of official intolerance.)

During Kangxi's reign [1662–1723], the situation improved, and the Imperial Calendar was once again calculated according to Western methods. Of all the emperors, Kangxi was the one most interested in science; as a youth he even studied Western astronomy with the missionary Ferdinand Verbiest. The *Lixiang Kaocheng* and the Kangxi Calendar *(Yongnianli)* were scientific works that set the world standard for their time, and are representative of that enlightened period.

The ascent of the Yongzheng Emperor to the throne [in 1723] marked the beginning of a period of over 100 years in which science would again be shunted aside. China shut its doors to the world, cutting off scientific exchange in the process. The Qing school of textual criticism, which represented the academic mainstream of the day, was concerned only with research into the classics and had no interest whatsoever in science based on observation. As late as the nineteenth century, the leading Confucian scholar Ruan Yuan still refused to accept the theory that the earth revolves around the sun. He wrote: "This theory, which turns things topsy-turvy and confuses movement and stasis, is heretical and rebellious in nature; it must not be taken as the norm." The only norm that Ruan Yuan would accept was one based on the theory of "Chinese characteristics."

After the Opium Wars [in the mid-nineteenth century], this way of thinking fell into decline. The astronomer Li Shanlan refuted Ruan Yuan, saying, "If one neglects to make careful observations, and instead carelessly interprets the classics, devising preposterous theories, it will be a meaningless exercise." In 1868, Li Shanlan took up the post of chief instructor in astronomy at the Tongwenguan [Interpreter's College] in Beijing, and once more China began the systematic introduction of Western astronomy. Yet even still, scientific methods for calculating the calendar were not officially adopted until after the 1911 Revolution and the establishment of the Republic of China. At that point the Imperial Institute of Astronomy was renamed the Central Observatory and assigned the task of working out the calendar. While it was being prepared, the old calendar was used during the first two years of the Republic. Only in the third year was the calendar based completely on contemporary astronomy. It has never changed back. Even when "bourgeois science" was attacked during the Cultural Revolution, bourgeois science remained the basis of the calendar.

In explanatory notes to the first Republican calendar, Gao Lu and Chang Fuyuan wrote, "This calendar has been calculated on the basis of methods current in both the East and the West." The key expression is *"methods current in both the East and the West,"* for this signaled that Chinese society had finally acknowledged that the laws of science were universal; there were no "Chinese characteristics" when it came to scientific laws. This is how the clash between the Chinese tradition and modern science was resolved at the time of the May Fourth Movement. It started and ended at the Beijing Observatory.

This chapter in the history of science can perhaps help us to see the problems of democracy in China today in a longer-term perspective. First of all, there's no need to be overly pessimistic about the future of democracy in China. It's only been seven decades since the May Fourth Movement began, compared to the three centuries that it took for science to be accepted, so there's no call for complete despair. Second, the basic principles and standards of modernization and democratization are like those of science—universally applicable. In this regard there's no Eastern or Western standard, only the difference between "backward" and "advanced," between "correct" and "mistaken." Third, the chief obstacle to the modernization and democratization of Chinese culture lies in the same erroneous idea that kept science out of China for so many years: the theory of China's "unique characteristics," in all its variations.

The Beijing Observatory celebrates its 710th anniversary this year. Since ancient times, China's emperors have governed according to heavenly portents. After the Yuan Dynasty moved its capital to Beijing, the observatory served the successive courts by interpreting the Will of Heaven. It no longer had to serve this function after the May Fourth period, but its long history still has important lessons to teach, especially to those in power. It's my hope that this history will provide a useful reference for our present rulers.

The Beijing Observatory gives us an excellent vantage point from which to observe the affairs of men. From here you can see the movement of the stars and the turning of the Wheel of the Law. The dharma wheel of science has already come rolling into China, and that of democracy is starting to turn as well. The problems we face today are merely the creaking sounds it makes as it begins to roll. This is the basis of my confidence and strength.

THE COSMOPOLITAN

Introduction by James H. Williams

With Deng Xiaoping's consolidation of power as China's supreme leader in December 1978 came an abrupt end to decades of Maoist national isolation. In pursuit of the new goals of modernization and economic growth which had replaced class struggle, the Deng regime dispatched thousands of scholars and specialists abroad to obtain new skills and trade agreements. Among those in the first wave of scientists to travel overseas was Fang Lizhi, who at forty-two was China's youngest full professor and a leading figure in the field of astrophysics.

This section contains essays and personal letters composed by Fang about his experiences and observations on his travels abroad from 1979 to 1988. They are reminiscent of writings by Chinese scholars in an earlier period: the late nineteenth and early twentieth centuries, when China's doors first opened and many of her best and brightest citizens ventured abroad in a similar search for the keys to national wealth and power. Like his predecessors in late Imperial and early Republican times, Fang looks to foreign cultures as a distant mirror in which to view the problems of his own society, raising long-standing questions about China's identity and direction.

The material in this section was, for the most part, originally intended for a limited audience of friends and colleagues, or the readership of small newspapers and experimental magazines. As a consequence, these writings have an informal flavor that makes for entertaining reading: Fang makes his points more humorously and impressionistically than he does in the essays on science in the previous section (though it must be said that some of the humor is so deeply embedded in a Chinese context that it almost defies translation, an example being Fang's facetious use of political slogans from the Cultural Revolution).

At the same time, these informal and often irreverent essays address serious questions with which Fang and many other Chinese intellectuals were preoccupied in the early stages of Deng's reforms: What are the goals of modernization? What is the proper role of intellectuals in the modernization process? How will Chinese culture be affected by contact with the West? Fang's opinions on these matters, and the official responses his views provoked, demonstrate the close linkage between political and cultural issues in Deng's China.

On the question of modernization, the Deng regime stated its goals in the Four Modernizations policy: the modernization of industry, agriculture, national defense, and science and technology. To this list was added, in the early 1980s, the goal of quadrupling China's per capita gross national product (to U.S. $2,000) by the year 2000. As the first two selections below, "Written at Midnight, After Praising the Lord" and "A Hat, a Forbidden Zone, a Question," make clear, Fang challenges these goals as too narrowly technocratic. In Fang's views, without the attainment of a much broader goal—the enlightenment of Chinese society generally—even narrow goals such as scientific modernization are in jeopardy.

Such assertions were politically double-edged. No doubt Fang's bitterly satirical depictions of life during the Cultural

Revolution—whether of the imposition of medieval dogmas over the sciences, or of the political study sessions that he lampoons as "oriental-style worship services" in "Written at Midnight"—were in some sense congenial to a Deng regime hoping to justify its radical policy turnaround by debunking Maoist fanaticism. At the same time, when Fang pointed to European history—now given visceral meaning by his presence in Cambridge or Florence or Rome—to suggest that China needs to import a new value system more than it needs foreign capital, equipment, or expertise, he found himself skating on thin political ice. In the essays below and in his later public stands, Fang poses humanistic values such as free inquiry and tolerance of unorthodox views against "all deities, pseudodeities, and their spokesmen." That Party conservatives took such questioning of authority paradigms as a serious challenge can be seen from the Campaign Against Spiritual Pollution of 1983, which vigorously attacked the notion of a humanism that transcends class interests.

Attempts by the Party to separate beneficial technological imports to China from other foreign influences deemed morally corrosive or politically objectionable have been a characteristic feature of the Deng era. Such tactics are not without precedent in China. Modernization efforts by Qing Dynasty officials of the late nineteenth century were carried out under the rubric of "taking Chinese learning for the essential things and taking Western learning for the practical application" (*Zhong xue wei ti, Xi xue wei yong,* abbreviated *ti-yong* in Chinese). Beyond expressing the desire to protect the essence of Chinese culture while building a powerful modern state, the *ti-yong* formulation also reflected the profound ambivalence felt by many Chinese toward the Western countries, whose technical achievements and military strength they envied, but whose colonial aggression they deeply resented, and whose culture and morality they viewed as inferior to their own.

Fang considers the legacy of *ti-yong* policies in "A Letter from Japan" and "Arashiyama Memoir," both written in November 1981. In these essays he expresses characteristically Chinese mixed feelings toward Japan: a grudging admiration of Japan's success on the one hand, a continuing suspicion of its motives on the other. But Japan serves also to mirror China's own problems of modernization. Fang observes that Japan has had vast success despite its history of unselective imitation, first of China itself and subsequently of the West, while the Chinese insistence on "taking the essence and discarding the dregs" has helped to keep China isolated from the world and thus contributed to its continued backwardness. Paradoxically, Fang suggests, it is the Japanese who have been at least partly successful in maintaining the forms of their traditional culture, whereas under the cultural stewardship of the Chinese Communist Party came a Cultural Revolution assault on traditions so indiscriminate and devastating that—as Fang notes with bitterness in "Written at Midnight"—"one could only lament the depths to which Chinese civilization had fallen."

In his reflections on World War II in "Arashiyama Memoir," Fang echoes his predecessors in the May Fourth period, suggesting that the real source of China's weakness in addressing foreign challenges has been dictatorship at home, which has sapped the creative resources of the Chinese people. (Interestingly, student demonstrations in 1985, held on the fiftieth anniversary of a famous protest against Japanese encroachments prior to World War II, also linked concerns about Japan's growing economic power in China—"the second Japanese occupation"—to a lack of democracy.) For Fang the tragedy of attempts to protect China from spiritual pollution is thus twofold: in increasing China's isolation, and also in permitting China's rulers to exploit nationalistic sentiments in suppressing domestic political opposition. Indeed, crackdowns on liberal tendencies in the Deng era have inevitably invoked nationalism, from the arrest of Democracy Wall activists in 1979 who were charged with "aiding foreigners," to the Anti-Bourgeois Liberalization Campaign of 1987 in which Fang himself was charged with promoting "wholesale Westernization," to the aftermath of the spring 1989 demonstrations in Tiananmen Square in which Fang and others were accused of plotting treason in the service of foreign powers.

An earlier Chinese who (as Fang notes in "A Letter from Japan") once stood in Fang's shoes was Zhou Shuren, who under the pseudonym "Lu Xun" became the most famous Chinese writer of this century. While studying medicine in Japan in 1905, Lu Xun was shocked to see a lantern slide that showed a Japanese officer executing an alleged Chinese traitor amid an apathetic crowd of Chinese bystanders. He subsequently decided to give up medicine in favor of writing, for he felt it was of little use to save Chinese bodies when the nation's soul was in such evident danger. His iconoclastic and bitterly satirical stories, in which China was epitomized by the character of the hapless and self-deluded Ah Q, assaulted the backwardness and complacency fostered by the traditional culture in an attempt to shock the Chinese into awareness of their plight.

The similarities and contrasts between Lu Xun in the May Fourth period and Fang Lizhi in the 1980s are instructive. Both deplore moral cowardice and see China's weaknesses arising from feudal traditions of submission to authority. Fang is an open admirer not only of Lu Xun's ideas but also of his writing style, and clearly models many of his essays on Lu Xun's pattern. Yet Fang has not given up physics to doctor the soul of China, which in part indicates the differences in the times each has faced. In a China confronted not by foreign military domination, but by the challenges of development, Fang seeks not only to call for a national awakening, but also to set a personal example in the creation of an independent civil and professional sphere, in which problems can be addressed openly and with (as Fang concludes in "Return to Capri") a "clearheaded wisdom."

Fang's ideal of a diverse and open China begins with its citizens. By suggesting, as he does in "Galileo and Milton: Physics and Poetry" and "My Feelings About Art," a unity of purpose between science and art, Fang calls for a return of the full life of the mind that he sees denied to Chinese intellectuals confined within their niches as technical specialists or propagandists. In so doing, Fang rejects the role of intellectuals as "cog and screw in the revolutionary machine" laid down by Mao, and challenges the peremptory claim of the Party to be the sole legitimate source of intellectual synthesis in China. Going a step further, Fang holds that since both science and art require freedom of the mind, it is incumbent on intellectuals of all persuasions to fight for it. Fang's oft-employed image of Galileo defying Church doctrine offers an implicit but obvious contrast with a figure familiar to all Chinese: the soldier-martyr Lei Feng, held up throughout the Cultural Revolution (and again in the aftermath of June 4) as a model of selfless service and unquestioning obedience to the Party. What a modern society demands of its citizens, and above all its educated members, argues Fang, is not obedience but critical intelligence and intellectual courage.

Fang Lizhi's cosmopolitanism is not one of worldly sophistication. In the writings below, we see a man deeply immersed in his own culture and its problems, struggling to make sense of the outside world. What *is* cosmopolitan about Fang, however, is his commitment to see the world from a global perspective, and his struggles to transcend his own limitations, breaking through self-serving Marxist stereotypes and depictions of life abroad to see the world with fresh eyes, whether the subject is Maxim Gorky or the Protestant Reformation. As Fang told students at Shanghai's Tongji University in 1986, "The change in many people's outlook, including my own, came from seeing the out-

side world. We discovered our backwardness and were enlightened." In the selections that follow, Fang reports his findings.

J.W.H.
Energy and Resources Group
University of California at Berkeley
November 1990

WRITTEN AT MIDNIGHT, AFTER PRAISING THE LORD

Fang Lizhi wrote this essay in December 1979, while he was a visiting researcher at Cambridge University. Originally a letter to a friend, it records some cross-cultural observations that follow Fang's attendance at a church service in King's College Chapel. It first appeared in China in 1980 in a small experimental journal, Life, *which was subsequently shut down by the authorities for having published this article.*

On the evening of December 2, 1979, I attended a church service in Cambridge, England. It was a genuine Christian ritual, and it left me with some very strange impressions.

December 25 is Christmas, the birthday of Jesus Christ. According to tradition, a special service is held on the fourth Sunday before Christmas to celebrate the Advent of Christ. The rector of King's College Chapel invited me to take part in this service, offering me a ticket that allowed me to attend as a member of the chorus. I accepted his invitation.

At first I was unaware of the significance of the occasion. But when some of my British friends learned that I had been given a ticket, they were quite envious. I was told that only faithful church members and their special guests were able to obtain tickets to this once-a-year ceremony. Only then did I realize that this was to be an important religious event.

This led to some misgivings on my part. Would my attendance mean that I had violated yet another taboo? Would I not be the only Communist Party member anywhere attending foreign church services? Perhaps I would even be accused of believing in God! After all, everyone knows in principle that belief in the Big Bang leads directly to religious conversion.

But then I recalled that this was by no means my first experience of the religious life. When had a year gone by during the Cultural Revolution in which we were not required to participate in rituals celebrating the advent of "our Lord"? And yet after taking part in all those oriental-style worship services, I had still been suspected of lacking faith in Him! Looking at it this way, I realized that no one would accuse me of being a true believer in Jesus just for attending one Western-style service.

The service was to begin at 8:30, but members of the chorus were supposed to be seated at least twenty minutes earlier. I arrived at the chapel (a famous Cambridge landmark) at eight o'clock sharp, and people without tickets were already lined up outside the door, hoping for a chance to get in. There were many people participating in the service in one way or another. The full celebration called for readings and recitations, solos and duets, ensemble vocals and a mass chorus. The solo and ensemble vocals were performed by members of the choir, while the large choral parts were the task of our mass chorus, which numbered some three or four hundred strong.

On arrival we were all given hymnals with complete lyrics and instructions regarding when to stand and when to sit. You can well imagine how nervous I was. I had rarely sung in a big group at home, much less one in which I was surrounded by Europeans! But it is not to no avail that China has such a long history. Being a resourceful Chinese, I needed only to adopt one of the classic "thirty-six stratagems" for getting out of a tight spot: pretend to know what you're doing and act like the other members of the group. (I dare say that one could find many members of our country's "collective leadership" who employ this technique.)

The service lasted for an hour and a half. During this time our chorus rose to sing only three or four times; most of the time we simply sat and listened. Having the lyrics in hand was a great help; even though the songs were in archaic English, I was able to follow the essence of most of them. It was a wonderful musical experience. The choir was comprised solely of men and boys. The boys' voices were emphasized, perhaps to suggest a sense of the newborn Christ. Their singing was exquisite, their voices so different from those of Chinese children that initially I assumed they were women. Enhancing the effect, their songs echoed down from the chapel's vaulted ceiling as if emanating straight from heaven. In terms of evoking a worshipful awareness of the spiritual world within the congregation, the architects had done a masterful job. I have heard hymns accompanied by organ on previous occasions, but this was an experience of a different order. It could not help but make one realize the paramount importance of religion in Western culture.

Those around me in the chorus, none of whom I knew, were quite earnest. When it came our turn to sing, they pronounced each word distinctly, not missing so much as a final "s." I could only stand in respectful silence. In fact, the melodies were not very difficult. Even one with very little musical aptitude—such as myself—could have managed with a little practice. But it was not hymn-singing that I was thinking of as I stood there.

Instead, an old question kept going through my mind: Why has Christianity exerted such a powerful influence on the West? Cambridge is without doubt a place where science matters a great deal; so why are so many students and scholars here drawn to a religious ritual? This is a question that has puzzled me deeply since I first arrived in Europe. East Asians, and especially China's scholarly class, have never shown much interest in religion, instead obeying the Confucian maxim "Honor the gods and spirits, but keep them at a distance." Western science and Western religion arrived in China at about the same time. Yet while science has had immense repercussions for Chinese thought, the same has not been true for Western religion; it has never been accepted or appreciated by China's intellectuals. Science and religion would seem to be so fundamentally at odds—how can Europeans simultaneously accept both? This evening, as the chorus built to a crescendo, I was more keenly aware of this question than ever. But I think perhaps I have already realized part of the answer.

Chinese intellectuals know something about the Renaissance, but very little about the Reformation, or else they tend to emphasize the former and discount the latter. This attitude arises from a lack of understanding of Western history. The Reformation was certainly no less influential than the Renaissance, and in fact the two are inseparably linked. In Heinrich Heine's comments on the history of Western thought, the first person to be discussed is Martin Luther. No doubt this had something to do with Heine's emphasis on Germany, but there is also no question that religious reform has been an inspiration for new ideas in the West.

Humanism was the spiritual banner of the Renaissance. Yet the forms through which this spirit was expressed were those of a religion undergoing profound change. Much of the art of such Renaissance masters as Michelangelo and Leonardo da Vinci was closely linked to religious life, as seen in works like the *Pietà* and *The Last Supper*. Yet what these depictions of religious events embody is not divinity, but human nature. This was a strange juncture in the paths of history and tradition. Although these masterpieces contain many portrayals of deity, the emotions they express—friendship, a mother's love, pity, compassion—point to something altogether human, rather than to the power and majesty of God. In this sense, one might say that religious reform represents the spirit that transformed the Church of the Middle

Ages, claimant to both temporal and spiritual authority, into one that could later co-exist with "liberty, equality, and fraternity." This is perhaps one of the main reasons that religion has persisted in the West until the present day.

There was a hymn sung by a child tonight that fully expresses the beauty of classical Renaissance art. I was so moved that I couldn't refrain from translating it into Chinese:

> A pristine rose has blossomed,
> Sprouting from its slender roots,
> The fruit of ancient prophecy,
> The newborn foreseen by Jesse.
> Rays from its tender bloom,
> Light up this cold, cold winter
> This dark, dark night.*

Isn't the feeling inspired by this hymn not so much one of venerating a divine Christ as it is a celebration of the birth of a human infant? I should say here once again that I do not believe in God. But for the work of the Renaissance masters in turning gods into human beings, for the humanist spirit that animates their art, I have nothing but admiration. Their work stands among the crowning achievements of civilization.

In contrast, there is the Cultural Revolution. Proclaiming itself to have far surpassed the Renaissance, it tried to turn a human being into a god. In those hymns we sang year after year, praising the coming of our great Lord, who would have dared to liken Him to a tender rose? To have done so might have diminished His godlike grandeur. As far as our "hymns" were

*Lo, How a Rose E'er Blooming, music by J. S. Bach. "A noble flow'r of Juda / from tender roots has sprung / A rose from the stem of Jesse / as prophets long had sung / A blossom fair and bright / That in the midst of winter / will change to dawn our night."

concerned, with their braying tone and imbecilic lyrics—"The Cultural Revolution is good, oh it's good"—one could only lament the depths to which Chinese civilization had fallen.

Although China has never been under the control of a formal religion for any extended period, who would deny that we have been dominated by a de facto religion for far too long?

A HAT, A FORBIDDEN ZONE, A QUESTION

This essay appeared in the Beijing Science and Technology News *on October 19, 1979. It is one of several articles on the cultural and political context of scientific modernization that Fang wrote during the early years of the Deng reforms.*

I made two trips to Italy this year, during which I visited a dozen astrophysics institutes in as many cities. Since my return, colleagues have been asking me about the state of astrophysics research there. They especially want to know what the Italians have that we don't, and how we can borrow it and put it to use in our own work.

The material gap between ourselves and the Italians is readily apparent and easily acknowledged; one can even ascertain it from the literature. But there is another gap that is not evident at a glance and whose role is harder to admit, involving the cultural traditions and mental habits governing scientific work. A discussion of our shortcomings that fails to touch on these aspects is, at best, incomplete.

Italy has an illustrious history when it comes to the physics of heavenly bodies. Copernicus studied there; Galileo taught there; and Giordano Bruno was burned at the stake there. Most of the struggles that broke the stranglehold of medieval religion and turned science into *science,* in the real sense of the word, took place in Italy. For Italian scientists this is a cherished legacy. In the university museum at Padua one finds the lectern at which Galileo once stood; on display at the Research Institute for the History of Science in Florence are bits of human finger bone, evidence of the persecution of scientists by the Inquisition. In those days the penalty for upholding the truth was mutilation, imprisonment for life, and ultimately the fire.

Such scenarios are now things of the past. But this heritage has left an imprint on Italian science, indeed on all of modern science, that cannot be replaced by any material object: the conviction that a free mind is the ally of science, and that deities, pseudo-dcities, and their spokesmen are its mortal enemies.

This spirit is quite evident in many Italian scientists, one reason for the high standards of their research. The difference between their situation and our own is undeniable. If we focus only on the details of research findings and fail to comprehend the environment in which those findings are obtained—from the philosophy that inspired the research to the spirit that guided it to completion—then we will be badly misled. Research results are often inseparable from the conditions that produce them. We may be able to bridge the material gaps between ourselves and the rest of the world through purchases and acquisitions, but not so with shortcomings in our traditions, our attitudes, and our philosophical outlooks. What we need more than anything else would seem to be humility, the humility to learn about these things from others.

But at this point we encounter a hat that people are often forced to wear, namely the label "great scientist but inconsequential philosopher." It is habitually asserted, in concurrence with the [Marxist] classics, that scientists from the time of Mach and Poincaré on have had little of value to say about philosophy. At best, they "make unconscious use of dialectics." While their scientific results might be useful, their traditions and attitudes and philosophies are not worth mentioning. Far from approaching them with humility, we are told to approach them with criticism and condemnation.

But can it really be said that there is nothing about the philosophy of any scientist since the late nineteenth century that merits our humble consideration? To even raise this question is to enter a "forbidden zone."

The time has come to enter the forbidden zone and take a scientific and nondogmatic look at this issue. In point of fact, whatever guides science in its thinking or its methods is a philosophy, a philosophy of science. If someone obtains good results in his or her research, by what right do we label the ideas behind that work "inconsequential"? What is preposterous is the whole labeling process itself.

Recent scientific history shows ample evidence of the harm it has done. Let us take the case of Mach. The standard Marxist philosophical treatment of Mach starts by ridiculing his ideas on the nature of space and time. It then declares the classical Newtonian position that space and time are absolute to be a "materialist viewpoint."* Newton's ideas are certified as ideologically benign, which in essence means they are correct. This has effectively put a stop to any scientific criticism or further development of the field. Has this "critical" philosophy helped or hindered physics? It's time for a fresh appraisal.

One day we were chatting with an old Italian man, who mentioned the existence of an unwritten law in some parts of Europe: that a garden without a Chinese flower is not considered a good garden. I sighed, wistfully, at the thought; why shouldn't a Chinese flower occupy the same honored position in the garden of international science? But the nurturing of such a blossom

---

Materialism is a general term for philosophies that emphasize the existence of matter as the ultimate source of reality. Marxist philosophy holds materialism to be a correct viewpoint and idealism to be incorrect.

takes more than material support; it demands spirit, and ideas, and commitment, and integrity. These may not be sufficient, but they are certainly necessary.

Three centuries ago, back in the infancy of modern science, the criteria for determining scientific truth were already established. Yet here and now in China, this issue remains unsettled, the topic of wearying debate. Doesn't this alone demonstrate that as far as science is concerned, our cultural shortcomings are far more serious than our material shortcomings?

A LETTER FROM JAPAN

Fang wrote the following letter to a colleague while a visiting researcher at Kyoto University in the fall of 1981.

Lao You,

I've been in Kyoto for five days, and everything is going well. Kyoto is actually a replica of Xi'an,* so the layout of the city has been easy to master. Even without knowing Japanese, it's been easy to get along, because everything is written in Chinese characters [*kanji*]. The only thing I haven't liked is that I'm always being mistaken for a Japanese! People come up to me and bow and nod their heads and speak Japanese—I have no idea what to say! So, I've taken to wearing my Mao jacket and doing everything I can to draw attention to the fact that I'm a foreigner.

Visiting Japan is different from visiting other countries. One is strongly aware that we Chinese are the ancestors of these people, at least in a cultural and spiritual sense. The Japanese copied Chinese culture to an amazing extent; you could even say that it was only under our tutelage that they became civilized at all. It has been very interesting to discover the Japanese attitude during their period of borrowing from China: "Whatever is good enough for the Great Tang Empire is good enough for us."†

---

*A city in the north China province of Shaanxi, in ancient times called Chang'an ("Eternal Peace"). Situated along the silk route, Chang'an was the capital of China during the Tang Dynasty (A.D. 618–905).

†Besides contrasting with the Chinese attitude of "taking the essence and discarding

For example, the names of shops are mostly in Chinese, including such exalted archaic titles as "The Grand Immortal," "The Princely General," and "Taoist Pleasure." At the same time, you also find shops bearing such derogatory names as "The Mountain Bandit," "The Southern Barbarian," and "The Japanese Pirate," all painstakingly inscribed on their signs in the most formal characters. Looking at these I don't know whether to laugh or cry—but it is evident that during Tang times, the Japanese were content to take even Chinese epithets aimed directly at them as valuable instruction.

This sounds very funny, but how can we not respect it? Their attitude toward learning from abroad does not seem nearly so discriminating as our slogan of "taking the essence and discarding the dregs." But perhaps China has been a little too discriminating when it comes to absorbing modern culture from the West.

The extent to which Buddhist superstitions are thriving in Japan has come totally unexpected to me. Not just in the Shinto shrines, but right along the street, where the offerings placed before Buddhist icons are plentiful enough to feed quite a number of "White-Haired Girls."* Last month I accompanied John Archibald Wheeler† on a visit to the Yonghe Palace, the busiest Buddhist temple in Beijing. There was no shortage of the faithful there that day, but there were still two orders of magnitude fewer than you find in Japanese temples. Even more significant was the

---

the dregs," this remark is a sly poke at Mao's successor, Hua Guofeng, who declared in 1977 that "whatever decisions Chairman Mao made must be upheld, and whatever instructions Chairman Mao gave must be unswervingly obeyed."

The White-Haired Girl was a revolutionary model opera of the Cultural Revolution era. The protagonist was a young girl whose prematurely white hair was a consequence of malnutrition caused by a greedy landlord.

†Eminent American physicist and inventor of the term "black hole." Fang hosted Wheeler's 1981 visit to China, and edited a collection of his lectures there, under the title *Physics and Austerity*.

difference in people's attitudes. Disillusionment is the hallmark of the Chinese. We don't really believe in anything, not even Buddhism. I'm not talking about the fake monks in their genuine cassocks; I mean those who have truly come with a burdened heart to make vows and cast divining sticks. Even they see their belief as a means to an end, as a tool. When their business in the temple is finished, they can't help but mutter a derisive *"and here's one for your mother!"* to themselves. Maybe the famous mantra of the Flower Garland School, "Nor has the [mind's] bright mirror any frame," is just a slightly more elegant expression of that sentiment.*

The atmosphere in a Japanese temple is completely different. It's hard to describe in words, but when you see a Japanese, especially a Japanese woman, kneeling in supplication, with that fatalistic expression, that earnest look in her eyes, then you finally understand what piety and a sincere belief in the will of heaven mean. In Western churches, the tone is one of sanctity and worship; in Japanese temples, the comparable tone is one of supplication and fatalism.

The intrinsic features of the Japanese can be seen more readily in the women than in the men, because the women have less contact with the outside world. In their dress, in their bearing, and in their spiritual life, they preserve even more of the traditional ways. In many ways, they seem completely different from

---

*Hui Neng, the sixth patriarch of Chinese Zen Buddhism, is said to have composed the following verse criticizing an opponent who emphasized the formalities of religious practice:

> "The tree of wisdom is originally no tree
> nor has the bright mirror any frame
> Buddha nature is forever pure and clear
> where is there any dust?"

Here, Fang jokingly offers part of Hui Neng's verse as an example of the general skepticism of the Chinese toward religion.

Chinese women. Or perhaps, turning it around, you could say that in comparison to Japanese women, all Chinese women seem like Sun Erniang. This may not be such a flattering comparison, so Lin Daiyu might do just as well.* Although these two women are quite different from each other, whatever it is that they have in common appears to be missing altogether in Japanese women.

Seeing such things, you have no choice but to ask yourself: How did a society like this ever manage to modernize? And modernize to the point of becoming "Number One" in the whole world, at that?

This question led me to some wayward thoughts. Consider: The United States achieved modernization while championing the free market; the Scandinavian countries realized modernization while advocating democratic socialism; the Soviet Union upheld the banner of meat-and-potatoes and at least became a powerful country; and the Italians have prospered by embracing indolence. And of course the Japanese, busily engaged in preserving the forms of tradition, have also modernized. It would appear that modernization is a communicable disease that infects countries at the slightest contact, no matter what "ism" they espouse. Only China has avoided this worldwide plague, not suffering the slightest infection over the last three decades. This is a rare and difficult accomplishment.

I don't really mean this to disparage China, but I think our people must have some truly unique qualities. These might be bad, but then again they might be good; after cursing them bitterly, you have to love them. Lu Xun† said that the mixed

---

*Sun Erniang and Lin Daiyu are two famous female characters from Chinese literature. Sun Erniang is a magician and member of a band of gallant brigands in *Outlaws of the Marsh,* while Lin Daiyu is the aristocratic heroine of *Dream of the Red Chamber.* While Sun is a physically robust figure and Lin rather feeble, both manifest an independence and assertiveness that Fang is suggesting are less evident in Japanese women.
†See Glossary.

feelings of love and hate for the Chinese that characterize *The True Story of Ah Q* emerged while he was living in Japan. I am in Japan now, and perhaps through these experiences I am gaining a firsthand idea of what Lu Xun was talking about.

Talk again soon. Please write if you have time.
Best regards.

November 9, 1981

ARASHIYAMA MEMOIR

The selection that follows is excerpted from a letter that Fang wrote to his wife in November 1981, while he was at the University of Kyoto. The essay was never published in China, as censors felt it was overly critical of the late premier Zhou Enlai.

Arashiyama is the most beautiful spot in Kyoto, resplendent with cherry blossoms in the spring and fiery maple leaves in the autumn. Standing in front of the Moon Crossing Bridge above the Great Weir River, with the pristine water flowing amid exquisite mountain scenery and elemental clouds floating through the still air, it can seem that one is standing on the banks of the Fuchun River near Tonglu rather than on alien soil. Only the sea gulls that have accidentally wandered upstream serve as reminders that one is not in the land of our ancestors, but on a foreign island.*

I was in Kyoto for almost three weeks before having the opportunity to visit this place, which lives up to all my expectations. Premier Zhou Enlai was generally not one to wax poetic over the wonders of nature, but he was nonetheless moved to compose these verses:

> Arashiyama in the rain
> water flows beneath the Moon Crossing . . .

*Tonglu is a scenic spot near Hangzhou, in Zhejiang Province, China.

The penning of these lines in 1919 by the young Zhou was yet another noteworthy occurrence of that eventful year, a connection that lends Arashiyama an even richer historical flavor for Chinese people. Yet my Japanese friends never took me there. This can't be due to lack of time, because they showed me many other sights. And it can't be that they don't realize the historical significance of the spot for the Chinese, because Premier Zhou's poems are well known in Japan. What, then, is the reason?

Today being a holiday eve—November 22, 1981, the day before Japan's Labor Day—I took myself to see Arashiyama. I went there for the fun of it, but also to seek the answer to my question.

Though 1981 seems a far cry from 1919 and the momentous times that followed, after visiting Arashiyama I am unable to share the contentment of Premier Zhou with the tranquillity of nature. Is this because Arashiyama has lost its beauty? Not at all: Arashiyama is still extraordinarily beautiful. But in the midst of its beauty there is something deeply unsettling—the Arashiyama Museum of Art. This place is not at all what its name suggests, an exhibition of fine art with Arashiyama as a scenic backdrop. Instead, it is a violently explicit exhibit of World War II in the Pacific. I went to see it.

The first display consists of weaponry used by the Japanese army during the war, including .38-caliber rifles, 91-millimeter howitzers, light tanks, Zero fighters, and Sea Dragon [*Kaiten*] torpedoes, the type navigated by live kamikaze pilots. I was upset as soon as I saw these things, because they immediately brought me back to the days of the "Greater East Asia Co-Prosperity Sphere." Yet as a guest there, I felt I had an obligation to look on my hosts objectively.* Such displays are permissible, I decided, because the weapons themselves are not the war. Putting together

---

*In Chinese, "objective" *(keguan)* literally means "from the perspective of a guest."

such a collection and researching the history of the weapons can be considered just another part of the historian's job.

Next, I came to the Monument for the Peace of the Soul, a stone tablet honoring the Japanese soldiers killed in the Pacific war. Around its sides were accounts of the exploits that led to the "glorious sacrifice" of various units. As I stood before the altar with incense smoke coiling around it, I could scarcely suppress my revulsion. Yet again, if one tried hard to think of this objectively, then the humanitarian perspective says that the desire of loved ones to commemorate the fallen, regardless of their misdeeds, is not incomprehensible.

However, what I encountered in the third section of the exhibit *was* absolutely incomprehensible to me. Displayed there were more than a hundred giant photographs of scenes from the war, bearing such titles as:

"Front Lines of the Japanese Army at Marco Polo Bridge"
"Unit XX Entering Fengtai"
"Entrance into Peiping Along East Changan Avenue"
"Crossing the Yellow River"
"Marching Through the Suburbs of Shanghai"
"Pressing Forward Through the Mud of Nanchang"
"Surprise Attack on the Nanjing–Hankou Railroad"
"Occupying the Fortifications of Humen"
"Amphibious Landing in Sweltering Chaozhou"
"The Imperial Army Taking Hainan Island"

Next to the photographs, written in red ink, were the words: "We Love the Fatherland. Veterans Association of the Japanese Army."

• • •

At this I lost my patience and my "objectivity," along with any residual respect that a guest might have had for his hosts. I was outraged. If I had held a bomb in my hand at that moment, I would certainly have blown up the exhibition hall. I needed badly to vent some of my anger, so even though photography was not permitted, and in order to fix in my mind the memory of this place, I defiantly ignored their "dwarf bandit"* regulations and proceeded to take all the pictures I pleased. I think that any Chinese would have approved of what I did. (Although even in saying this, I know there have been exceptions. Among the exhibits in the museum was a banner declaring "Peace in East Asia," given to the commandant of the Japanese garrison in Nanchang by a man named Hu, who chaired the local puppet organization. His full name did not escape my camera.)

The point that really demands our attention is that, despite the many initial victories of the Japanese army in places other than China, only China is featured in this photographic exhibit. There is, for example, not a single picture of the successful sneak attack on Pearl Harbor. Does this reflect a private assessment of World War II on the part of some Japanese, that provoking a war with the United States was a strategic error, but that invading China was a good policy?

Concluding the exhibition was a statement that explained its purpose:

> Although Japan lost the Pacific War, thirty years later when we commemorate the illustrious battle record of the Imperial Army and its undying great spirit of the Japanese race [*Yamato Damashii*], people are still moved beyond restraint. Let those young people who think only of pleasure be awakened by this great spirit.

*Dwarf bandit *(wo kou)* is a Chinese pejorative term for the Japanese.

On the way back from Arashiyama, the train rocketed through the late autumn of the Kyoto plain. At this point, I was in no mood to appreciate the scenery. While I stared out at row upon row of squat Japanese cottages, festooned with flowers, my mind's eye was on the Beijing plain at this time of year, with its lanes of spacious adobe houses, flanked by piles of corn. I was struck by the feeling that, like our houses, the Chinese people are too open and generous. Within our country, a tyrant needs only to display a little false smile and the people will never doubt his sincerity. Outside our country, we are equally given to trusting the counterfeit goodwill of foreign aggressors.

The poems of the young Premier Zhou manifest just this kind of good-hearted openness. Yes, Arashiyama is beautiful, and expressions like "Moon Crossing" and "Great Weir" are full of emotional appeal to the Chinese. But these things made it all too easy for a well-meaning person to forget that even at that time in Arashiyama, murderous designs against China were already in the works.

After the war, Japan was due to pay China over 100 billion yen in war reparations. Premier Zhou agreed to write off this debt with a stroke of his pen. No doubt this was a correct thing for the premier to do, and it demonstrates again the generosity of the Chinese people. However, we must not allow our generosity to continue leading us into deception at the hands of fake smiles and phony friendship.

Across the river from the Arashiyama museum there is a large stone monument with five very carefully inscribed characters on the front: "Japan, China: No More War." On the back side it describes the unhappy history of China and Japan since the Sino-Japanese War of 1895. I am sure there are many decent Japanese people who genuinely desire peace, and who are committed to achieving it. Perhaps the reason my Japanese friends did not take me to see Arashiyama is that the contradiction between the two sides of the river brings up feelings that are difficult, or painful, for them to share. I know that Kyoto University has always been an antimilitarist center, from before the war right on up to the present.

But are there also people in Japan who make a hypocritical pretense of "no more war"? I think there are. With wars for the purpose of establishing outright colonies now passé, aggression has taken on new forms. And for this reason, when we hear such propaganda slogans as "One language, one race" or "Mutual support and guidance," we would do very well to consider the underlying motives.

Once, a Japanese friend took me into her confidence. Because she is a woman and understands firsthand what the "great spirit of the Japanese race" really means, and because she works in the United States, she could explain things very frankly. She told me, "The Japanese have some very unsavory customs. If you are Japanese, and people see that you are doing something wrong simply because you don't know how to do it, they will berate you for it."

Because of this, she recommended that I not speak Japanese on the street. "You look Japanese," she said. "If you speak a few words of the language people will mistake you for one, and then you might get scolded for not understanding something. Better to not speak any Japanese. Then people on the street will assume that you are a complete foreigner and put on a pleasant appearance for you."

A pleasant appearance—but what lies behind it? I've learned something about that from my trip to Arashiyama. Arashiyama is beautiful, but beneath its beauty lurks a predatory intent.

November 22, 1981
Kyoto, North White River Hostel

SUPPLEMENT

On November 27 I went to Hiroshima to see some of the history of the first atomic explosion. Near the epicenter of the blast there is now a peace-memorial park, encompassing the remains of the lone building left standing by the blast, and a peace-memorial information center.

The information center painstakingly reconstructs the horrifying aftermath of the explosion with artifacts, pictures, models, and taped explanations in Japanese, English, French, and Chinese. The event itself staggers the mind. Six-thousand-degree temperatures, a nine-kilometer-high blast column (the city itself was not more than six kilometers across), extreme high pressures followed by negative pressures. A fire that burned through the night, black rain, and a cyclone triggered by the fire. In all, 260,000 people died—from burns, from the shock wave, from radiation. Some died then, and others died later. Even today, thirty-six years after the event, there are survivors and offspring of survivors in a living hell, halfway between life and death. Such a spectacle can only evoke heartfelt pity, and leave people feeling that this hideous slaughter was an utterly inhuman act.

Even normally gregarious Americans fell silent at the end of the exhibit. They couldn't help but put a little money into the donation box in front of the Comforting the Soul Memorial, because they felt remorse over this great calamity that America has visited upon Japan. Every year there is a ceremony held on August 6, an international event with many Westerners participating. The ceremony includes a memorial service for the dead, and a prayer for peace.

But for myself as a Chinese, I cannot accept the concluding line of the narration. It says: "You can't commit mass murder in the name of war." There is certainly nothing wrong with this sentiment, but there are some Japanese who have no business saying such a thing, especially to the Chinese.

Beginning in the Meiji period, Hiroshima steadily evolved into a base for waging war. It had the Japanese Inland Sea's largest naval port and shipbuilding facilities, and was one of the command posts of the Japanese navy. The first time that the naval high command was moved from Tokyo to Hiroshima was in preparation for the 1895 Sino-Japanese War. Because Hiroshima was closest to the combat zone, it was called the "forward command post." Committing mass murder in the name of war, especially the mass murder of Chinese, started right here. This is a part of the history of Hiroshima prior to August 6, 1945. Its destruction, to borrow an expression from Buddhism, was a consequence of bad karma.

It goes without saying that the lot of the innocent people who perished in this "karmic return" is profoundly tragic. Facing the sculptures of *Mother and Child in the Mad Storm* and *Teacher and Pupil,* so full of compassion, the men lowered their heads, and the women's eyes welled with tears. The last struggles of those innocent lives are simply too pathetic for words.

But be that as it may, if you were to call Hiroshima the place that has suffered most from the calamity of war in the last hundred years, the place most deserving our sympathy—to the extent of designating it the Mecca of Peace, the Humanitarian Holy Land—I would have to shake my head "no." The reason is this: I have seen the remnants of the air-raid shelters in Chongqing, where ten thousand people suffocated during the Japanese bombing. I have seen the still-visible imprints of the bullets on Nanjing's China Gate. It is really *China* that has suffered the most from the last century of warfare, whether in the quantity or the quality of the misery.

But in all of China there is not a single peace-memorial park.

There is no annual day for commemorating the dead in a big international event, no eternal flame to comfort the soul, and certainly no donation box in front of the eternal flame. Can it be that the souls of China's dead need no memorial and no comfort? That they need no one to relate the pathos of their final hours? I find this mystifying.

But perhaps a whole people can resemble an individual, in that for the deepest grief there are sometimes no tears, and no words. Or is this only a characteristic of the Chinese? They don't complain about their bad luck, even when their misfortune is the greatest. They don't speak of their suffering, even when their lot is the most tragic. And they are too embarrassed to set out the donation box, because they're afraid that accepting any help or sympathy at all will seem like begging.

Are these traits good or bad? Don't ask me. But either way, it seems they will always be with us, everlasting features of the Chinese race.

November 28, 1981

GALILEO AND MILTON: PHYSICS AND POETRY

This essay appeared in 1985 in the University of Science and Technology campus newspaper, to which Fang was a frequent contributor.

I like Italy. I like Rome. I like the culture, so rich in the spirit of scientific inquiry, and I like the science, so profoundly steeped in culture.

I am a physicist. In China and many other countries, physics—and science generally—is often taken to be nothing more than technology, or some kind of tool that serves technology. Not so in Rome. Whether or not you know anything about the origins of modern science, in Rome you will be struck by a pervasive sense of the interconnections between science and culture. This is because modern science itself grew out of the Renaissance, thus making it a fruit of the genius of Italian civilization. It is this heritage that has lured me repeatedly back to Rome.

I have been a visitor at the University of Rome eight times now, on visits ranging from a few days to several months. One thing I am particularly fond of at the university is a sculpture in the physics building that shows Galileo together with John Milton. Galileo and Milton, physicist and poet; their meeting symbolizes beauty in physics and reason in poetry.

And indeed Galileo and Milton did meet, in 1638. That year the thirty-year-old Milton made the long journey from London to Italy. He paid a special visit to Galileo, already an old man of seventy-four, who had been placed under house arrest by the Church several years earlier. The brash young poet and the aged prisoner, still intent on his studies of nature, became instant friends. Their friendship sprang from the innate human longings they shared: to explore the workings of creation, to strive for the wholeness of body and soul, and to uphold their belief in freedom and reason.

It is precisely this common striving that the sculpture evokes. The aged Galileo sits holding a model of the solar system, as if explaining the laws of planetary motion, and perhaps how he suffered in holding fast to his theories. The young Milton stands at his side, holding a book and listening intently. He appears to be grappling with the heliocentric theory, while wondering how its advocate could have met with such a fate; stirring in him already was the seed of his famous remark "Give me the liberty to know, to utter, and to argue freely according to conscience, above all liberties." And it was thus that the physicist and the poet, far removed in age, became one in their pursuit of the freedom of the mind.

In *De Rerum Natura,* the Roman poet Lucretius integrated physics and poetry. Since Lucretius's time, few have been similarly blessed by both Minerva and the poetic muse. Yet the cultural roles of science and poetry remain similar: to cleanse society and to purify the soul. It is in this sense that physics today still has a poetic beauty. In the realm of the spirit, physics and poetry exist in harmony and interdependence, like the two giants of civilization depicted in the sculpture.

I am moved by this harmony. That is why I am so fond of Rome, where the symbiosis between science and culture is everywhere in evidence.

MY FEELINGS ABOUT ART

The following is taken from a talk given by Fang Lizhi at the opening of "Toward the Future," an exhibition of avant-garde art held in Beijing in 1988. Fang's talk appeared in China Art News *in August of that year.*

For someone like myself, who knows only physics, the world of art seems very alien. Yet even across this divide, I am aware of its presence.

It seems alien because over the years I would visit museums only on chance occasions, either for Chinese or Western art's sake. Now, at the invitation of the "Toward the Future" exhibition organizers, I am actually attending a formal art opening in China, a first for me.

I'm aware of its presence primarily because I've been abroad. Despite not spending any great length of time outside the country, I've been to see art (I realized as I added my visits up) much more often overseas than I ever have in China, even to the extent of being an official guest at more than one exhibition opening.

This is not because I am partial to foreign art galleries, but because the circumstances are different abroad. Science and art are not nearly so isolated from each other as they are in China. It is not uncommon to find scientists interested in art and artists interested in science. This is what has forced me into contact with that alien world.

Such attitudes are only to be expected in France. Had I gone to Paris and failed to visit the Louvre, my French colleagues in astronomy and physics would have regarded the omission as a grave insult to their culture. But consider the United States, which is sometimes said to lack culture. On one occasion I was being escorted around Washington, D.C., by a member of the National Academy of Sciences. We were only halfway through the Air and Space Museum when she expressed a most urgent desire to cross the Mall and see a new exhibit of Impressionist paintings from the Soviet Union at the National Gallery; for me not to go along would simply not have done.

As for Italy, the whole place is one big art gallery. I have been to Italy a dozen times, and on most of these occasions I have been introduced to artists and critics, or been invited to artists' studios for coffee, or been led on a stroll through the art market in Rome's Piazza di Spagna, or been taken to see Raphael murals not generally open to the public. And on some occasions I have witnessed artists taking part in scientific activities as well. I remember that in 1985, at a symposium on general relativity in Rome, a piece of art was presented to the Pope in the audience chamber adjacent to the Sistine Chapel; the work had been inspired by our discussions of cosmology and black holes, in which the artist had participated.

I must admit that none of this has improved my taste in art. Art has its own language, one that is beyond me; I only know the language of physics. But these experiences have made me intensely aware of a cultural atmosphere in which there is no great divide between science and art. This was perhaps most vividly brought home to me when I saw the the *Last Supper* hanging on the wall at the monastery of Santa Maria delle Grazie. Was Leonardo an artist? Or was he a scientist? It seems perhaps he was neither, that both science and art were simply the methods he employed in a more unified search for truth and beauty.

With regard to what each one strives for and sets store by,

science and art are in many ways indistinguishable. Art seeks beauty, and so does science. Art and science both advocate truth, and creation, and liberation from bondage; they esteem the works of nature and of humanity, and they also esteem that which transcends both nature and humanity. As the French mathematician Poincaré once said: "The scientist does not study nature because it is useful; he studies it because he delights in it, and he delights in it because it is beautiful. . . ." This is why, I believe, there is no lack of scientists who are interested in art.

In the Galileo Building at the International Center for Theoretical Physics [in Trieste], there hang several engravings by M. C. Escher. On one level these simply demonstrate how much Escher's "mysterious links" and the imaginings they inspire are loved by physicists; on yet another level, they seem to symbolize the "mysterious links" between science and art themselves. Here in China, science and art go their separate ways, disconnected. Is it not because we lack these "mysterious links" that we lose the strength and vitality that they engender?

RETURN TO CAPRI

Fang Lizhi wrote the following essay during a research trip to Italy in the summer of 1987, following his expulsion from the Chinese Communist Party in the Anti-Bourgeois Liberalization Campaign earlier that year. He alludes to these events several times in this account.

Capri is a small island in the Bay of Naples. In the mind's eye of the Italians, it has been perhaps what the fabled Land of the Peach Blossoms is to the Chinese: a natural place and a peaceful refuge from the world and its pollutions.

I have been to Capri twice, first in 1983 and again in 1987. My first visit was solely as a tourist. I had originally planned only to see Naples, but in two days there, our group had exhausted most of the famous sights: the Neapolitan palaces, the opera house, the monastery where Saint Thomas Aquinas wrote the *Summa Theologica*, and the ruins of Pompeii near the foot of Vesuvius. Thus contented, many people returned to Rome. But a few of us insisted on going to Capri. Perhaps I made that choice because I knew subconsciously how much my spirit was in need of balance. Too much of what we had seen in Naples, though seemingly only the relics of some ancient strife, had carried heavy overtones of ideological struggle; one couldn't help but feel a certain tension. In search of release, we headed for Capri.

The atmosphere in Capri was completely different, though it was only an hour and a half from Naples by boat. Here there were no ancient battlements blackened as if by old bloodstains; there were no ponderous and burdensome crosses; there were no signs of the frenzied depravity of Pompeii; and there were no statues of heroes, swords drawn, glaring disdainfully down at you. There was only wind, water, and sun; and in the sunlight, colorful sails so still that they appeared almost stationary. All sounds had gone into retreat, and even the tourists were quiet, as if they could not bear to disturb the tranquil air. You could hear only the rhythmic pounding of the waves, and a few notes of distant singing. Across the sea one could faintly make out red roofs amid green foliage; that was Sorrento, the home of "O Sole Mio" and "Santa Lucia."

When I returned to Capri in 1987, it was not to seek spiritual balance—although it was true that this visit also followed a "tour" of too much ideology, modern ideology this time. We had come to Capri for the sake of astronomy. It turns out that there is a small observatory on the island, dedicated to solar research, for the sun is bright there, and the dark spots on the solar surface are that much easier to distinguish. The observatory was owned by Germans, but because it was inconvenient to maintain, they wanted to close it and sell the land. The Italian Ministry of Education was interested in buying it, and so had asked the International Center for Relativistic Astrophysics [in Rome] to give their evaluation. As a member of the center, I joined the evaluation team.

The Capri observatory was in many ways similar to Capri itself—small and unpretentious, yet with fine features, an enjoyable place to be. It had no high observation dome, and it was not even built on a mountaintop; rather, it was housed in a villa overlooking the sea, not much different from the neighboring villas, with small white buildings scattered around the grounds and down the wooded hillsides. The helioscope, also white, was set amidst a grove of trees. The sense of solemn tranquillity about it reminded one of a cemetery. The German astronomers who worked there must have often been reminded of the inscription on Kant's tomb:

> Two things fill the mind with ever new and increasing admiration and awe, the oftener and more steadily they are contemplated: the starry heavens above me, and the moral law within me.

It was a holiday, so we did not get to meet the astronomers. But the caretaker, even though he knew no astronomy, went to great pains to show us around the facilities and explain what the living and working conditions were like. He also informed us that a certain country-style restaurant not far from the observatory was the best on the whole island.

When we went there to eat, we found tables set out on the grass under shady trees, with insects buzzing around in the nearby bushes. An Italian friend casually remarked, "Everything is so congenial on Capri. All of these little creatures and flying insects, and not one of them is harmful to human beings. There aren't even any poisonous plants." I was struck by this, and it led me off on a train of thought: While the Capri observatory might not be anything extraordinary in the academic sense, it wonderfully exemplifies the spirit of astronomy. There are many areas of research within astronomy, but none of them does any harm to human beings. Astronomy is not vain, and pursues neither power nor glory; it seeks only to comprehend the "starry heavens" and be blessed by their inspiration. Of all the scientific endeavors, astronomy is most like the island of Capri itself—lofty and unsullied, deeply moving to the human spirit.

Of course, astronomy is not so detached as to be out of this world altogether. On the contrary, the more you comprehend and the more inspiration you derive, the firmer the ground you stand on; there is a certainty to this faith that cannot be obtained from any other source. As if cleansed and purified by the winds and waters of Capri, one's awareness of "the moral law within" is steadily heightened.

Looking down from Anacapri, the highest peak on the island, you find that the pounding waves shrink into insignificance, and the sea becomes like the ideal plane in mathematics—level and expansive, without boundaries. The whole world should be like that, expansive and without boundaries. At such moments all the barbarities, the allegiance to totems, the habitual lies, and the worship of things that don't exist evoke in you not only abhorrence and disgust, but pity. Now at last I understand how Galileo must have felt when he muttered under his breath, "But the earth *does* move":* pity for a world so full of ignorance. What else could one feel but pity, when having seen so clearly precisely how the earth moves—or how the universe evolves—one is confronted by those who still cling to primitive dogmas. The age of Galileo is behind us, yet not entirely.

At night, these thoughts became even more intense. Capri at night is so quiet, so close to nature, that you are aware only of your own thoughts; everything else seems to disappear. This feeling was heightened because of the place where we stayed, an inn situated on a small lane called Via Mulo, halfway up the mountain. Next door to the inn was a rather elegant villa, with a marble plaque in front of its gates: "Maxim Gorky lived here from February 1911 to November 1913." That Gorky could have stayed next door for nearly three years seemed incongruous at first. In my mind, Gorky conjures up images of the hapless wanderers of the Caucasus; of the toiling Volga boatmen; of the

*Tradition has it that after being forced by the Inquisition to recant his support for the Copernican view that the earth moves around the sun, Galileo was heard to mutter *"e pur se muove"*—"but it *does* move."

red flags in his book *Mother*. How could he have tarried amid the beautiful seascapes of Capri, where there were no red flags and no anguished cries of protest?

Yet the two images of Gorky are not so incongruous after all. Consider: What is it above all else that has freed humanity from the misery of the boatmen? Yesterday's cries of protest served their purpose. But not cries based on ignorance and folly, and certainly not cries of "Don't fear spilling a little blood," used to threaten the cause of freedom.* No, what has first and foremost brought to humanity the blessings of liberty is wisdom, born of a quiet rationality. What better place than Capri to sense the beauty of a clearheaded wisdom? What better place than Capri to awaken the yearning for a free world? Gorky was right to come here.

> Deep in the night, Capri is sleeping.
> I would return once more to Capri
> to gaze upon the beauties of the sea,
> that so move my heart and soul.
> To drink my fill of nature's brightness
> and be drunk with happiness.

When I return the next time to partake of that quest for freedom, I will be singing "Return to Sorrento."

Florence
June 21, 1987

---

*In ordering the suppression of student protests in January 1987, Deng Xiaoping was said to have remarked that security forces "should not fear the spilling of a little blood."

THE DEMOCRAT

Introduction by James H. Williams

Starting in late 1978, as Deng Xiaoping was ousting Mao's appointed successor, Hua Guofeng, as China's paramount leader, there arose in Beijing and a few other large cities a brief public outcry known as the Democracy Wall Movement. Its spirit was captured by the young worker Wei Jingsheng, whose wall poster "Democracy: the Fifth Modernization" warned that no meaningful reform of the Chinese economy or society was possible without a simultaneous overhaul of the political system. The Democracy Wall Movement was suppressed in early 1979 on Deng's orders, and many of its leaders were arrested and sent to prison, where Wei Jingsheng remains to this day. Composed primarily of disillusioned young urban workers, the Democracy Wall Movement received little overt support from that small but influential stratum of Chinese society, the intellectuals.

Ten years later, Chinese intellectuals overcame their reluctance to speak out and played an important role in the spring 1989 democracy movement. In the selections that follow, we can see much of the story behind this galvanization of Chinese intellectuals, both in Fang Lizhi's perspective as one of their number, and in the catalytic role that he personally played in their collective psychological transformation.

The background to these dramatic developments is, of course, Deng's reform program itself. The old guard that had been restored to power following the political demise of Mao's radical allies faced enormous challenges: regaining a measure of credibility for the Communist Party in the eyes of a weary and cynical public; overcoming economic stagnation even as China's East Asian neighbors boomed; and confronting the disturbing prospect of China being left behind in a new global technological revolution.

In response, Deng drastically reversed Maoist policies, directing a program of reforms under the rubric of "socialist modernization." Repudiating such Cultural Revolution—era formulas as "a socialist train behind schedule is better than a revisionist train on time," Deng abolished the rural communes and encouraged private agricultural production; reintroduced economic incentives for industrial workers and sought to decentralize and professionalize industrial management; streamlined and modernized the military; and mandated the acquisition of foreign technology and training through improved trade and diplomatic relations with Japan and the West.

Central to the success of such policies were the technical expertise and managerial skills of China's intellectuals (as the less than one-half percent of China's work force with a college education are called; the term thus connotes not only academics and artists, but also engineers, doctors, and schoolteachers). Consequently, the Dengist leadership sought to enlist the active participation of this demoralized group, whose systematic brutalization during the mass campaigns of the previous three decades was symbolized by their humiliating Cultural Revolution label of "stinking ninth category." Intellectuals were reclassified by Deng in a 1978 proclamation that declared them to be part of the working class, and promised dramatic improvements in their private and professional lives.

Intellectuals were thus indebted to the Deng regime for such fundamental gains as the opportunities to travel abroad for study and to pursue their careers in relative peace. Even when the suppression of the Democracy Wall Movement shattered the early euphoria surrounding Deng's bold opening to the outside world, many intellectuals remained guardedly optimistic about the prospects for steady improvement under the banner of reform and modernization. Despite Deng's promulgation in March 1979 of the "Four Cardinal Principles" (a declaration that China would remain steadfast in its adherence to socialism, Marxism–Leninism–Mao Zedong Thought, proletarian dictatorship, and Communist Party rule), many found in the regime's simultaneous calls for "democratization" and "emancipation of the mind" hopeful grounds for long-term political change. Indeed, the Deng regime's basic charter—a flexible interpretation of Marxism-Leninism under the pragmatic slogans "seeking truth from facts" and "taking practice as the sole criterion of truth"—was ambiguous enough to allow limited political exploration within the context of policy debates that opened up among the leadership and segments of the bureaucracy and intelligentsia.

It was within these policy debates of the early 1980s that Fang Lizhi rose to national prominence. Fang's scientific reputation and popularity as a teacher brought him academic positions of increasing importance, culminating in his elevation to the vice presidency of the University of Science and Technology of China (USTC) in 1984. Fang was also elected by his peers to leadership positions in several professional societies and to committee membership in the prestigious Chinese Academy of Sciences. In these positions, Fang became a participant in the elite debate over reforms affecting science and technology, education, and intellectuals. His rejection of the intrusion of Marxist ideology into scientific research and curricula, as seen in the previous essays and in the speeches below, may have been irritating to some conservatives, but found substantial backing among leaders concerned with promoting scientific and technological development. Likewise, Fang's calls for improving the abysmal living conditions of Chinese intellectuals (an example being the poverty of his own former teachers at one of Beijing's premier middle schools, described below in "Reflections on Teachers' Day") contributed to a chorus of official concern over issues such as "income inversion" (the higher the education, the lower the pay) and an unusually high mortality rate among middle-aged intellectuals.

At the same time, Fang used his privileged position as a scientist and Party insider as a platform from which to question the basic premises of Deng's reforms. An early example is the first selection below, "The End of Old Thinking," a 1980 speech to a scientific conference in which Fang challenges both the idea of a technocratic solution to China's development problems and the validity of Marxism as a guide to reform. Fang was visited shortly after this speech by Fang Yi, then vice premier in charge of science and technology, who warned him against making such statements in public. Yet Fang did not cease to speak out; instead his critique steadily broadened as, like Sakharov in the Soviet Union, he used the prestige of science to ferry ideas from beyond the margins of political permissibility into the general discourse on reform.

Despite conservative opposition in the Central Committee Secretariat that delayed his approval as USTC vice president for three years, Fang's final confirmation in 1984 put him in a position to preside over an unprecedented experiment in academic freedom at USTC. (Such a pilot program had been championed by reformist leaders, including Vice Premier Wan Li, who were bent on improving the educational standards and creative output of the science and technology sector.) The policies inaugurated

by Fang and USTC president Guan Weiyan decentralized and
opened administrative decision-making and protected intellectual
freedom in teaching and research, making Fang a national symbol
of bold reform. As a result, he was frequently invited to speak
to formal and informal gatherings of students and professionals
around the country. Fang's speech at Zhejiang University in
March 1985 (see "Thoughts on Reform," p. 95) was the first stop
on his occasional speaking tour over the next two years. This talk
nearly resulted in his early dismissal from the Party, as members
of the leadership were angered by Fang's calls for a reappraisal
of Marxist economic beliefs, and by his open discussion of official
incompetence and corruption.

By the fall of 1986, the fault lines along which the Dengist
leadership would ultimately fracture had become increasingly
apparent. Despite progress in the rural reforms and some success
in replacing older Party cadres with younger and better-educated
ones, the failure of reforms in the urban industrial sector was
already evident. The lack of decisive steps toward political decontrol paralyzed the regime's attempts to create a "socialist
commodity economy," which greatly exacerbated existing problems of inflation, unemployment, and corruption. Moreover,
divisions among the leadership over the limits to public expressions of dissent produced a regular oscillation between relaxation
and repression within the cultural and ideological spheres. The
resulting campaigns against Westernization and liberalization in
1979, 1981, and 1983–84 progressively alienated many of those
who had earlier held out hope for the Deng program.

Fang's public statements in the fall of 1986 thus reflect a sense
of urgency over the need for fundamental political change, as
seen in the final three selections below (talks with Beijing journalists, Anhui Communist Party cadres, and Shanghai students).
The key issue facing China, Fang argues, is the question of
democracy and human rights. Without these, any meaningful

reforms will continue to be undermined by the same basic problems: the lack of accountability by public officials at all levels; the lack of economic rights for ordinary citizens; the lack of fundamental protection for dissenting views; and the lack of guarantees for long-term stability, resulting from the ever-present potential for power struggles in the top leadership.

Fang took a dramatic step further in declaring that democracy "is not a gift bestowed from above," but rather something for which individual citizens must struggle. (Vice Premier Wan Li traveled to USTC in December 1986 to challenge Fang publicly on this point.) Arguing that what China lacks is not laws or formal democratic structures so much as the attitudes and behavior that must animate these institutions, Fang lays much of the blame for this failing at the feet of intellectuals themselves. He challenges intellectuals to quit displaying the servile attitudes toward authority that perpetuate China's most feudalistic political traditions; instead they must act as an independent, critical force in Chinese society, uncowed by the leadership's manipulation of nationalism, socialist ideals, or the mythos of Marxism's scientific infallibility.

In December 1986, students from USTC demonstrated against what they felt were rigged local elections; unrest soon spread to universities all over China. Fang has subsequently claimed that he did his best to discourage such demonstrations (see "Will China Disintegrate?" p. 221), fearing reprisals against the students. His intent, he stated, had been to arouse established professionals to take a stand, not to send young people into the streets. Nonetheless, when Deng Xiaoping ordered the suppression of the demonstrations and a purge of those promoting liberal tendencies, Fang was a natural target. (Fang had already aroused Deng's ire by his public criticism of high Party officials. See p. 222.) Following his expulsion from the Party in January 1987, Fang's speeches were circulated to Party branches all over the country for criticism. This move backfired badly by making Fang's ideas broadly available, triggering an outpouring of public support (see Appendix, "Letters from the Other China") and turning Fang into a first in Communist Chinese history: a surviving and still active voice of dissent.

In the selections that follow we discover what was apparent to those reading Fang's speeches for the first time: the essential argument of Wei Jingsheng's "Fifth Modernization," but spelled out in explicit detail in the context of the reforms, and authored not by a disenfranchised young activist but by a distinguished scientist. Fang's approach combined a radical analysis, in its focus on the authority relationships at the roots of the political order, with a gradualist emphasis on consciousness-raising and steady institutional change. Whether due to the ideas they expressed or simply to their proof of his willingness to stick his neck out, Fang's words became a symbol of hope for many in China. Equally important were the messages that appeared between the lines: for the public at large, a call to a new kind of citizenship; for intellectuals, an open demand on conscience. And for the Party leadership, in its inability to accommodate Fang's critique, an ominous sign of the growing chasm between the demand to modernize and the desire to maintain a monopoly on power.

J.H.W.
Energy and Resources Group
University of California at Berkeley
November 1990

THE END OF OLD THINKING

The following is the text of a short speech given by Fang Lizhi to the Second National Conference on the Science of Science, held in Hefei, Anhui, in December 1980. Following his remarks, Fang was visited by State Science and Technology Commission director Fang Yi, who cautioned him against making public statements about Marxism of the sort contained here. This marked Fang Lizhi's first direct run-in with Communist Party officials during the Deng era.

It has been remarked that some scientists are not brimming with enthusiasm for the fashionable "three studies": human-potential studies, science of science, and futurology.* I am one such scientist.

This is certainly not due to any indifference on the part of scientists toward the future, the advancement of science, or the cultivation of talent. Quite the contrary, these are issues with which those of us in the fields of research and education are concerned on a daily basis.

But many scientists are not convinced that the "three studies"

---

*In the 1980s the Chinese leadership's policy of "opening" to foreign ideas and expertise in order to promote accelerated modernization led to an explosion of interest in contemporary Western intellectual trends, especially those that promised a scientific basis for policy formulation and management. Works such as Alvin Toffler's *The Third Wave* attracted fervid attention, as did a broad range of new disciplines such as information theory, cybernetics, and systems theory, in addition to the "three studies" Fang mentions here. These were explored with the encouragement of reform-minded leaders in the Communist Party, such as Zhao Ziyang.

will actually accomplish anything. Not only do we fail to see what these studies will do concretely for research or education, but we also question what indispensable role they will play in the society as a whole.

Interest in the "three studies" arose as a consequence of the Four Modernizations policy. These studies appear to be designed to raise the status of science in our society, and to provide a think tank for the leadership. At the bottom line, what the "three studies" seek is to promote the rapid development of science.

The presumption appears to be that science invariably benefits society. This is not always the case. Science itself and the consequences of scientific activity are two different things. If our social institutions fail to keep pace with our uses of science and technology, the results may be very undesirable indeed. To say that in the future we will have a scientific society, or a scientific culture, or a scientific civilization, paints an incomplete picture, because all civilizations are ultimately human. In looking at the future, in attempting to cultivate talent and promote scientific progress, we cannot concentrate narrowly on science *per se*. Without parallel development in the human dimensions of our society, such efforts will be illusory and futile.

There are those who want to establish a Marxist version of the "three studies." This includes another unstated assumption, namely that Marxism itself is functional. But the facts show that this is not always the case. Many standard Marxist prophecies have been proven wrong.

Right now people around the world have lost faith in Marxism. This is because Marxism has become ossified, in its rigid adherence to obsolete conclusions that have led to failure. In some quarters this credibility crisis has been called a victory for Marxism, which is enough to send a chill down your spine. We have admitted our failures and our backwardness when it comes to the material aspects of our society, but it seems that we're either afraid or unwilling to acknowledge that our failings along cultural-spiritual lines are just as bad, if not worse.

It is only realistic to predict that the crisis of faith in Marxism is going to have a profound effect on China, and especially on the next generation. In this light, the injunction to "emancipate our thinking" should not be taken to mean "restoring the original face of Marxism," nor any such thing; it means that we have to search for new theories. The real task of the present is not to create a "three studies" based on Marxism, but rather, in a forward-looking, scientific fashion, to revise and develop Marxism itself.

Marxism, in its time, grew out of a marriage of German classical philosophy, British classical economics, and French socialism. Yet one of the tragedies of its subsequent adherents has been their belief that with the advent of Marxism, the future would have room only for Marxist civilization and no other. This has led to profound alienation.

The three constituents of Marxism—philosophy, political economy, and scientific socialism—have all fallen behind the times. They must be revised. In the history of the human race civilization has passed through many stages, and it might be that Marxist culture is just another stage. But perhaps such a passing should not be seen as a bad thing, because the human race must always cast off its old ways of thinking before it is able to enter the future.

THOUGHTS ON REFORM

The following is the text of Fang Lizhi's speech at Zhejiang University (referred to here by its abbreviated Chinese name, Zheda), on March 24, 1985. The Zheda speech was the first of several talks given by Fang in 1985 and 1986 in response to invitations by student groups outside of his own University of Science and Technology. This talk was severely criticized by Communist Party officials for suggesting that Marxist economic beliefs be reappraised.

I am very glad to be with you here today to discuss a few topics of mutual concern. Just now the chairman introduced me with a string of official titles. Let me say that while these titles do mean something, I think it would be better not to bring them up in situations like this. This is especially true of the names of administrative positions, such as "chancellor"—as I've told the students at Keda, such titles reflect neither the holder's scholarship nor the correctness of his words. . . . At a recent meeting of university administrators, someone suggested that we all be supplied with uniforms. The implication was that when we wore the uniform, we would be acting in our official capacity, giving orders and so forth. Without the uniforms, we would revert to being ordinary teachers and scholars, and thus more at liberty to speak freely. But at any rate, you can rest assured that there is no direct relationship between administrative rank and how smart a person is.

Not that this matters to us today, since I have no administrative duties here at Zheda, anyway. What does matter, however, is that

I am now standing at the podium in a university lecture hall. A podium in a university lecture hall should have certain characteristics regardless of where it is located. Let me digress for just a minute before saying what those characteristics are.

The parliamentary system has been adopted by virtually every country in the world, including ours. One characteristic of the system is that while parliament is in session, its members are independent of the restraints of existing law. That is to say, if they are to enact new laws, they must in a certain respect be free of the old ones. It is only when parliament is free to criticize and change existing law that it can fulfill its responsibilities as a legislature. The National People's Congress (NPC), which is now in session, is supposed to follow this practice. Some friends of mine are People's Representatives, and they say that members of the NPC are not bound by the Constitution of the People's Republic and may speak freely—in principle, of course.

This concept should apply to academia as well. A university is a place to search for truth, both in nature and in society. Academics are not makers of law, but we are discoverers and explorers of law, of the principles of the natural and social orders. In such a pursuit we must be free to question established beliefs and challenge existing orthodoxies. This is a characteristic that a university cannot be without.

Let me digress a bit more. The university as we know it today had its origins in Europe—in England, in Italy, and elsewhere. In the beginning, universities were primarily concerned with theology, though as time went on curricula were expanded to include such subjects as law, medicine, and philosophy. The focus of theological studies was Roman Catholic doctrine. In medieval Europe there was no separation of church and state, and thus religious authority was often synonymous with political power. Theology therefore represented the intellectual orthodoxy of the day. Yet despite this restrictive environment, those studying theology in universities were able to criticize and revise existing theological ideas. Even in those days, university research transcended the limits imposed by religious canon.

Some years ago, I visited the University of Padua, one of the oldest in Italy. Many great historical figures either taught or studied there, including Copernicus and Galileo. In the Middle Ages, the Church placed numerous restrictions on what could and could not be done, a typical example being the prohibition against dissection of human corpses. Since human beings were created by God, the body was held to be sacred, and dissection was therefore considered a desecration. At Padua, however, anatomical dissection nevertheless became an authorized part of medical training. This shows what a university must be: an environment in which the search for truth is unfettered by external authority, in which there are no sacrosanct and unchallenged orthodoxies. This is the characteristic that I spoke of a moment ago. Without this characteristic, a podium in a university classroom is not worthy of the name.

This morning we had a symposium commemorating Albert Einstein. One young person made a remark that I especially liked: "In the realm of ideas, there is no preferred frame of reference." This was very well said, and reveals a perspective rooted in Einsteinian physics. There is no doctrine or way of thinking inherently superior to all others; every idea should enjoy "equal rights." We will never find the truth if we are restricted to one narrow frame of reference. If the university is truly intended to be an environment for new discovery, then it must also be the site of the greatest freedom of thought and discourse.

When I was about to become vice president of Keda, students asked me, "What can you provide for us when you become vice president?" I told them, "I came here with the shirt on my back, and not much else. If the university has housing or other resources at its disposal, I will do my best to provide them to you, though

I can't guarantee even that. What I can guarantee you, however, is greater freedom of thought." People regard universities as centers for teaching and research, but in my opinion, the essential task of a university is the generation of ideas. If a university doesn't produce new ideas, it isn't worth much. This is why universities must be places in which to question and explore all manner of ideas without arbitrary restrictions.

When I met with the campus newspaper editors at Keda, including those from various small papers as well as from the official university paper, we discussed the fact that newspapers in China are always under external control. For example, the *People's Daily* is controlled by the Central Committee and reflects its opinions, the *Hangzhou Daily* is controlled by the Hangzhou Party Committee, and so forth. Without passing judgment on these publications, I wanted to make it clear that the university newspaper at Keda belongs to the community as a whole, and should by no means reflect only my opinions as chancellor. I have my own mouth and my own tongue; I don't need a mouthpiece to do my talking for me. If I have a point of view I can try to convince other people of it, and they can try to do the same with me, and either way is fine. Newspapers should reflect the opinions of the public. Only when public opinion is truly respected will we have an environment that protects free thinking. (Of course, these ideas are nothing new. Cai Yuanpei* said such things during the May Fourth era, when he was president of Beijing University. His statements at the time also stressed the need for diversity of opinion within a university.) Anyway, ever since last year there has been an amazing proliferation of newspapers at Keda, ten or more at last count, including a women's paper. The only thing missing is a clipping service for all these papers! So it is in this

*See Glossary.

spirit that in taking the podium today I also am exercising my right to speak freely.

. . .

Now, on to the reforms. There is a question that I think is of deep concern to everyone here, namely this: Will the reforms succeed? What are the prospects for reform? This is a very serious issue for every one of you, all of whom I trust will live to see the year 2000. Will the reforms succeed, or will they fail? Everyone talks about it, even with strangers on the train, and today I'd like to share my views with you. They may not be very well thought out, but rest assured that they are genuinely mine.

If we want to know whether or not the reforms will succeed, we must first ask what "success" means. As in physics, we have to start by defining the problem. In talking with people, I've discovered that there are about as many different opinions on what constitutes successful reform as there are people. This is fine. Since people's images of what society should be like are not all going to be the same, it is only natural for them to define their goals differently. For example, one question we frequently encounter out in the real world is "When do we get a raise?" This is a serious issue, I'm not just saying it to make you laugh. Professors are quite concerned about their promotions, which are frozen at present. Students are worried about entrance examinations, and the whole arduous process of getting into a university after middle school. So, there are many opinions about what successful reform would entail. Do we have a consensus? Well, perhaps—the goal of quadrupling gross national product (GNP) by the year 2000 is one that we hear repeated over and over by the official media. But just as success can't be evaluated in terms of raises alone, or promotions alone, or improved prospects for college entrance alone, I also don't think that quadrupling GNP in and of itself is an adequate measure of success. But perhaps, if we could combine all these goals, we would then have a more complete picture of what success might look like. Given such a definition, will the reforms succeed or not? In my opinion, they may succeed, and they may also fail. This may seem like a gratuitous statement, but what I would like to stress is the uncertainty of the process: *It is by no means certain that we will succeed.*

Let me argue this case a little, starting with some remarks made by Comrade Deng Xiaoping. Not long ago, I attended a work conference on reform of the science and technology system. Comrade Deng said something which has been reported in the press, to the effect that "If we look ahead fifty years, many of the world's basic contradictions will still exist. These contradictions may be summarized in four words: North, South, East, and West." This is an illuminating statement. The East-West contradiction refers to the rivalry of the two superpowers, the question of war and peace. We can hardly expect this conflict to disappear completely within the next fifty years. The North-South issue, on the other hand, is one of economics, the contradiction between poverty and development. Five decades from now, according to Comrade Deng, there will still be poor countries and rich countries. Not all developing countries will become developed. And so within the next fifty years, China may succeed in its reforms, becoming a developed country; on the other hand, it may well remain at the developing stage. As Comrade Deng himself says, both possibilities exist for China. This should make us think long and hard about our future.

Of course, we all hope that the reforms will take off soon. But the future holds many unforeseen twists and turns, and there are definite precedents for failure. Many countries have started on the path to development, and not all of them have made it. Two recent cases stand out in my mind. One is Iran, where the Shah's modernization program failed and his government was replaced by a regime of religious zealots. Another case, and one more like our own, is Poland. Reform was introduced in an attempt to salvage a stagnant economy, but this led to massive social unrest. Although the situation has now calmed down somewhat, Poland is still unable to extricate itself from its troubles. Can China avoid going down these same paths to failure? We hope so. But hope is only that, hope. What we really need is a sober analysis of the factors that can lead us to failure. Without such an analysis, blind optimism may indeed cause us to fail.

What, then, should we do? I am certainly no scholar in this area; I'm just a physicist with a few half-baked ideas. But this has never stopped physicists in the past—they have been shooting off their mouths and getting into trouble since the days of Galileo, and so it has now become quite customary for them. And who knows, in some cases they may even be right.

So, how are we to reform our society? Of course I can't answer this completely, but one thing that is clearly indispensable is science and technology. Way back in the May Fourth period, the battle cry was to save the nation through "science and democracy." So today I'll start with science, and wend my way on into democracy.

You're all familiar with the official slogan "Stress Knowledge, Stress Talent," which basically means "Stress Science and Technology." Most of you probably couldn't care less about such injunctions; you've all been subjected to the usual platitudes. But today I want to ask if we really know how these things interact? There is no shortage of theory, but how many of our problems have actually been solved? How great is the gap between our theory and our practice? And what does it mean when I say that science and technology have much broader implications than simply their economic roles?

We are always hearing that China is *economically* backward, and it is in this context that the example of science and technology inevitably comes up. But let's be a little more specific about the problems. During our work conference on science and technology, Comrade Song Jian* reported some numbers: In a study of per-capita GNP in 126 countries around the world, China was rated "among the last twenty-odd nations." You may think this is bad, but it is even worse that the word "odd" was used! Obviously we don't even know where we rank among the last twenty countries. According to this report, per-capita GNP (in U.S. dollars) is $11,000 in Japan, $13,000 in the United States, and $17,000 in Switzerland. That means the per-capita GNP of China is only one twenty-seventh that of Japan, one thirty-third that of the United States, and one forty-third that of Switzerland. In Shanghai, per-capita GNP is $2,300. Thus, the average productivity of five Shanghai citizens is equivalent to that of one American. Of course, Shanghai happens to be the most productive region in China, a real "singularity" [in physics parlance]. But what about the nine provinces where per-capita GNP is below $100? These nine represent nearly one-third of our thirty provinces. Individually, they are probably comparable to Chad, which ranked last on the list of 126 countries. It is under these sobering circumstances that we must exert our utmost efforts over the next fifty years to develop the Chinese economy. This is the situation that those working in industry, including many of you, will face.

Nevertheless, what I want to emphasize is that the reasons for "stressing knowledge and talent," which is to say, science and technology, are not merely economic. To bring about real changes in our national circumstances, we must look beyond economics. While it is true that the economy is important—and we are putting a great effort into expanding ours—economic growth alone is not the answer. The role of knowledge, and

*Director of the State Science and Technology Commission, China's highest policy-making body in the science and technology arena.

science, and educated individuals goes far beyond economics. In China we habitually refer to science and technology simply as "forces of production," as means of dealing with technical problems. But I think this is wrong, and that there is more to it than that. The rise of Western society is intimately linked to the influence of modern science on economics, on politics, on thought and culture in general. In the West, science and technology have affected all aspects of development, not just bits and pieces of it.

What do I mean by "development"? We all know that the United States, Japan, and Western European countries are developed countries, but how would we define development in a general sense? If we relied on official pronouncements from China, we would have to say that a developed country is one in which per-capita GNP is a few thousand U.S. dollars per year. But this simple definition is wrong, or at least incomplete. For instance, there are several countries with a high per-capita GNP that are not generally regarded as developed. In the Arab world there is plenty of oil, and the per-capita GNP is high. In Kuwait, for example, it is $10,000. But these countries depend on outside technology and personnel to exploit their petroleum resources, and they just sit there and collect the money. South America also has several countries, such as Colombia and Brazil, with GNP in excess of $1,000 per capita, but which cannot be considered developed.

Coming back to our own situation, the goal of quadrupling GNP by the year 2000 may be regarded as one kind of milestone for development, but it is not sufficient: We may reach it and still fall short in other ways. Economics is not the only mark of development. In the countries I mentioned, the economy has improved but other things have not. There are many other factors which rule out calling these countries developed, such as political corruption, inequitable distribution of wealth, and social unrest.

If we emphasize only the quadrupling of GNP without regard to how we get there, we may find ourselves taking not a shortcut to development but a path to oblivion.

Consider the case of Brazil. The economy of Brazil took off within a relatively short time, but Brazil is far from being a fully developed country. Last year I visited Rio de Janeiro, and on the surface it looks very prosperous. The Brazilian economy boomed after the government borrowed heavily to build factories. But from my own observations, and from talking with Brazilians, it seems to me that life there is highly unstable. The annual inflation rate is 220 percent. I have been to hotels in many countries, and usually the hotel bill is paid upon checking out. But I stayed in Brazil for two weeks and had a brand new experience. At the end of the first week, a bill was brought to me with a note—an ultimatum, really—that said if the balance wasn't paid within twenty-four hours, the rates would go up. The owner was not trying to give me a hard time, but he was forced to do this because of inflation. He either had to collect his bills week by week, or else face losing a lot of money. Most of us have never experienced inflation, and we don't understand what it's like to live under such conditions, where you can literally see the prices rise from one week to the next. But there is little security in such a life. An economy built on foreign debt is not something we want for China.

It is also possible to fashion an economy by other dubious means. Last year I went to Colombia, where per-capita GNP has risen to more than $3,000 through drug trafficking—Colombia makes perhaps $8 billion a year from drugs. The drug trade is everywhere. Although the newspapers fume about suppressing drugs, and the government tries to police the trade, most of these efforts are only for show. Last year the government destroyed one drug center, but the real reason it did so was that the center was also used as a guerrilla base. Inflation is not so serious in Colombia, but the disparity in wealth is extreme, with classes of virtual slaves.

At one point I visited Cartagena, a small city in northern Colombia that enjoys a drug-based prosperity. (In Colombia we heard of all kinds of ways of delivering drugs, including direct air drops to the United States. Of course the United States has a good radar system, but the smugglers have developed a new technique to defeat it: The smuggler's plane flies so closely behind a commercial airliner that it can't be distinguished on the radar screen. The "Cartagena technique" thus helps to maintain the prosperity of the town.) I have encountered many different life-styles in my time, but in Cartagena I lived for a few days in the manner of an aristocracy. I do not mean simply a very luxurious life, but rather one in which I was attended by slaves. No blacks were allowed in the hotel where my colleagues and I stayed. Coming back from the beach one day, we bought some food from a stand run by local black residents. We had no money with us, so they followed us back to the hotel to collect. However, they were not allowed inside—they had to wait by the door for us to come outside and pay them. This is a master-slave relation-ship, extremely unequal. A society such as this may have a high GNP, but it is by no means developed.

These examples illustrate why economic growth is not the only indicator of progress. Progress must be all-around. So what, then, *is* the definition of development? Well, that's still not clear, at least not to me. But many people would agree that one of the best criteria of development is education. The differences between developed and developing countries in terms of educational levels are quite clear, unlike the case with GNP. Education is widely available in developed countries and not so in developing coun-tries. Illiteracy is high in places like South America and the Arab world, where the rate of illiteracy is not 1 or 2 percent, but is more likely to be 20, 30, or 40 percent. Here the contrast with the developed nations, such as those in North America, Western Europe, and Japan, is clear; they have promoted education to the extent that illiteracy is not much of a problem. In China, economic underdevelopment is an obvious shortcoming, but educational underdevelopment is even more serious. Our low level of culture generally is a primary reason for our lack of development in other spheres.

I won't repeat the stories we are always being told, about how lack of education causes problems in industry and high technology. But I would like to cite one highly symbolic example of how low our cultural level is. On June 16 of last year, the *People's Daily* ran an article, "Deep Friendship in the Water City," about the visit of Premier Zhao Ziyang to Venice. When Premier Zhao met the mayor of Venice, the latter presented him with an old map. Zhao asked: "Was this map made before or after the time of Copernicus?" Of course Copernicus is a great historical figure, whose discoveries marked a new era in our understanding of the universe, and he did study in Italy. Premier Zhao's question was properly asked. The mayor answered that the map was produced after the time of Copernicus. Premier Zhao then made a blunder: "Oh yes, were it not for Copernicus, we still wouldn't know that the earth is round." But all of us know that the greatest contribution of Copernicus is the heliocentric theory, which states that the earth revolves around the sun. The idea of a round earth is completely different from the heliocentric theory. That the earth is round has been known since the time of the Greeks, who even measured its radius. I've been to Italy twice since this event, and Italians have let me know that this gaffe was a diplomatic failing on our part, and demonstrated a low level of general knowledge. Responsibility for this blunder can't be laid solely at the feet of Premier Zhao, who presumably never studied the history of astronomy. But no one else caught the mistake either, neither the translators who accompanied him, nor the newspaper reporters who filed the story, nor the editorial staff of the *People's Daily*; and in their ignorance they enthusiastically reported this *faux pas* as an interesting anecdote.

You're all laughing, but I think it must be the laughter of embarrassment at our backwardness. Whether or not people know who said the earth is round and who said it revolves around the sun may be irrelevant to the economy, but it says something important about a culture. That is my point. If we look only at the technical aspects of science, only at its economic role— important though it may be—we will miss something essential. As I said to the physics department yesterday, physics is more than a basis for technology; it is a cornerstone of modern thought. Physics has been instrumental in the growth of human knowledge to its present stage. Development involves progress not only in the material realm but in the human realm as well. Even with the most advanced technology, without intelligent and civilized citizens no society will become "developed," and any attempt at reform will surely fail.

Why is China so backward today in so many aspects? If we take the long view, we can blame our feudal history. But if we look at the more recent past, the problem has been the orthodoxy that has held sway for the last thirty years. Since 1957, numerous anti-intellectual political campaigns have been waged, fostering suspicion and hatred of learning. From the Anti-Rightist Campaign* to the Cultural Revolution, these pogroms seemed bent on eradicating any kind of intellectual endeavor. This is one immediate reason why China's intellectual standards are so low. Moreover, although there has been some superficial acknowledg-

---

*A 1957 political campaign directed against intellectuals who had criticized the Communist Party. One-half million or more were being labeled "rightists," resulting in jail terms or lengthy periods of manual labor in the countryside. The "rightist" label made its bearers unemployable, effectively ending their careers.

ment of the importance of learning, and of the need for science and technology, things have not really changed all that much. Why?

In my opinion, the animosity toward culture and learning found in these movements originated with the ideas of Comrade Mao Zedong, which were enshrined as orthodox beliefs. His erroneous theories continue to haunt us today. If you really want to promote respect for learning and do something about our backwardness, then you have to address Comrade Mao's mistakes, which were many. Let me mention just a few.

In 1958 Mao began his misguided policy of "making intellectuals more like laborers." This was followed by his formula "the humble are the wisest, the high and mighty are the most foolish."* Mao was never explicit about who the "high and mighty" in this equation were—although such terms were generally reserved for intellectuals—and on one level there is some truth to this expression. But what Mao meant was this: The more people know, the more stupid they are, and the less they know, the smarter they are. This sentiment was made increasingly explicit as time went on. During the Cultural Revolution, the most enthusiastic statement Mao made about the usefulness of education was, "Nevertheless, we still need education in the sciences and engineering." The implication of this remark is that education is a borderline issue—to have it is fine, but not to have it is fine, too. Such opinions still exert a powerful influence; they have by no means disappeared. There are some places where these attitudes have changed, but in many other places they still govern the treatment of knowledge and potential talent and skilled personnel. If this situation doesn't change, I think our reforms will have little chance of succeeding.

---

*These slogans are typical of the Great Leap Forward, launched in May 1958. See Glossary, *Great Leap Forward*.

At our work conference, people cited numerous examples of how little respect there is for knowledge. A comrade from Shanghai told of a brain surgeon there who is paid less than a barber; it seems that he who takes care of the inside of the head gets less respect than he who takes care of the outside! You hear about such cases all the time, so I won't bother relating any more of them to you. But the inverted economic status of intellectuals is clearly a function of their inverted political status. The idea that the more you know, and the more complex the task you perform, the less you get paid, is totally inconsistent with the principles of socialism. This being the case, how could such a situation have developed? And why has it still not been seriously addressed and dealt with? I think that this problem has its origins in ideas. Whenever Mao Zedong spoke about intellectuals, it was in the context of "solidarity with the masses," "reform through labor," and "re-education." Considering this background, I think that if you want to change the status of intellectuals, you will first have to make a theoretical case for what their place in our society ought to be.

Let me try to make such a case. You can read something like it in the recently released draft report on "Reform of the Science and Technology System,"* which I helped to prepare. In working on revisions of this report earlier this year, I argued that the position of intellectuals in our society must rest on a solid foundation in Marxist theory. So what is their place? At one time, of course, they were the "stinking ninth category," but lately they've gone up in the world; they are now "old number three," just below workers and peasants! At this point, let me say that I am opposed to dividing society up into a hierarchy of classes. I'm utterly against it. But be that as it may, if someone wants to

---

*A landmark document issued on March 13, 1985, by the Communist Party Central Committee, which mandated sweeping changes in the organization and funding of research and the diffusion of technology into the general economy.

argue seriously about which class should occupy the first rank, I'll give them an argument.

Let's start from a premise that all of us will recognize: that science is a "force of production." Not only is it a force of production, it is the most advanced one. No one would deny this; we are busily employing science and technology to improve the other areas of production. On whose skills do these most advanced forces of production depend? Well, on those who specialize in science and technology, namely educated people, the intellectuals. So what place should they occupy in society?

According to the standard Marxist argument, industrial workers are the most advanced element of society, the vanguard of the working class. Why? Because at the time of Marx, industry—coal, steel, vehicles—was seen to drive the whole economy, to set the pace for all other kinds of production. Those on whose skills and labor industry depends—namely, industrial workers—were thus considered the most advanced element of the working class. This is all classical Marxist theory, so far; now let me just borrow the methodology. What is today's most advanced force of production? Science and technology. And on whose skills and labor is science and technology dependent? Intellectuals'! It is therefore apparent that intellectuals are not only *members* of the working class, but that they are the very vanguard of the working class! And yet we assign to society's most functional element the very lowest rank—this is irrational! I think this argument stands up, not only in terms of its logic—which is unassailable—but also in terms of the facts.

We know that as society evolves, different classes arise, flourish, and finally decline. The first great class was pastoral nomads, who were in turn replaced by farmers as settled agriculture developed. When capitalist industry arose, farming populations declined. In the United States, farmers now make up less than one percent of the population and no longer play a dominant role in society. More recently still, even the industrial work force in developed countries has declined. The traditional heavy industries that require manual labor, such as coal, steel, chemicals, and automobiles, are now called "sunset" industries. Their day is passing. The United States is doing all it can to export these industries to developing countries; it no longer wants to encourage this smoke-belching, water-fouling manufacturing at home. The recent accident in Bhopal, India, illustrates this point. Fewer people are working in these "sunset" industries, and their importance to the economy is declining. On the other hand, the need for workers with technical expertise is growing constantly. In the United States there are now more white-collar workers than blue-collar workers. It is the educated class that is on the rise.

Even in our country, there has been a significant drop in the agricultural population; many peasants have gone to the cities to start businesses and open shops. As the economy grows, we will also see an eventual decline in the number of industrial workers; if we don't, it will show that we have not become developed. I have already said that I deplore the ranking of different classes. But if you insist on doing it, I say intellectuals should be put at the top. Mao's idea of "making intellectuals more like laborers" was completely mistaken. Intellectuals are already laborers, the ones whose labor holds the most promise for the future. Instead, it is "making laborers more intellectual" that we need to emphasize.

The document on science and technology reform does not include this argument *per se*, because it would have offended people. But if you look at section nine, it contains the following language: "Scientific and technological personnel are the pathbreakers for new forces of production." You should all get a good grip on these words and not let them go; they are the basis of the kind of argument I just made. It will take a struggle to make our society change its views of intellectuals. It is by no means a sure thing that intellectuals are going to be allowed to play a leading role.

There is much more to the role of intellectuals than their inputs to production; they constitute an important force for social progress through the medium of thought and culture. I've discussed this point with Europeans, who tell me that far from being sequestered inside the science and technology sector, intellectuals in Europe have a far-reaching impact on all of society. Recent history illustrates this point. Prior to World War II, from Napoleon to Bismarck to Hitler, Europe was frequently at war, owing to a variety of causes, economic and otherwise. Now, however, Western Europe is virtually united. There are no armed conflicts between the nations, and even the borders between them are disappearing. During the past six or seven years I have visited Italy every year, and each time I've gone to the border crossing with France to take a look. When I first went, there were still guardhouses, barriers, and police. By the year before last, all these signs of territorial division had disappeared. In their place was a small bilingual road sign: *Italia* this way, *France* that way. The concept of national boundaries is fading fast, especially among the core countries of the European community, such as Italy, France, and Switzerland.

It is hard to conceive of these countries going to war with each other. How was such a state of affairs achieved? Was it brought about by politicians? In the end, no doubt, politicians must have signed their names to agreements. But the formation of a collective psychology that perceived the welfare of Europe as lying in community and cooperation, rather than in division and barriers, was not accomplished by politicians so much as by physicists. (There are, by the way, also nonphysicists who share this view!) It was something initiated by physicists that first suggested to Europeans that their common fate rested on cooperation, namely the establishment of CERN, the nuclear research center in Geneva. This was a first for postwar Europe, a place where scientists of all nationalities could work together for common ends, and its influence on society has been substantial.

We know that physicists do not have high political standing in China, nor are they particularly influential within our society; this is a consequence of the way our culture has developed. But the same is not true in Europe, where physics is part and parcel of their history. Especially after the atomic bomb brought World War II to a rapid close, the evident power of physics bestowed immense prestige on the physics community. Thus, the fact that physicists chose to cooperate was a great stimulus for all of Europe, prompting public opinion in favor of European cooperation in other areas.

So, intellectuals are a progressive force in production, and they can be a progressive force in society as well. If we do not play this role in China, the country will be headed for further setbacks instead of down the path of reform. This is the duty we face as Chinese intellectuals, and it is a heavy one. But without our efforts, the myriad problems that face China, both social and technical, will not be resolved, and China's attempts at reform will certainly be abortive.

I don't know if the authorities here at Zheda have let you in on this or not, but if they haven't, I will tell you a little secret. At the beginning of this semester I received a dispatch from my superiors instructing university presidents not to let the students create disturbances. So I went to the Keda students and told them, "We hope you don't create any disturbances!" This order was a consequence of the student protests that took place on several dozen campuses before the Spring Festival [Chinese New Year]. These included not only Beijing University and Beijing Normal University, but also local schools such as Nanjing University, where the trouble started. The immediate cause was probably bad food in the cafeterias; some of the students joked that they were joining the "fight against hunger." So, what I told the Keda students openly was this: "What is important here are your reasons for protesting. If you really want to make trouble, I can't stop you. But if you don't have a good cause, then it doesn't matter whether I try to stop you or not, because the protests will fizzle out all by themselves." My suggestion was that they get together and think about the root causes of the things they were unhappy about. For instance, you may complain that your cafeteria food is lousy. I have no doubt that it is—it certainly is at Keda. I have been in academia for decades and have yet to hear a student praise dining-hall food. But the real issue is not so much the quality of the food as the price, which seems to rise from week to week. There must be reasons for this, and so what I challenged the students to do is think about the underlying problems and come up with some concrete solutions. This is our responsibility as educated people, to come up with solutions. If protests will solve the problem, then protest. If protests won't solve the problem, then go back to the drawing board and think of new approaches.

Some comrades are scared to death of student protests. Not that other people don't share some of the same viewpoints as the students, or that professors aren't affected by rising prices. We are. But students are much more accustomed to expressing their opinions directly: "Look, damn it, you've raised your prices again." To me, this just means that students are sensitive to what's going on in society, which I think is extremely valuable. We need to take advantage of this kind of concern in order to go out and solve our country's problems.

Student protests demonstrate the sensitivity of Chinese intellectuals, and show that they could play the same kind of catalytic role that the establishment of CERN played in Europe. If there is unrest among the students, the question we should be asking is "Why?" And we need to look for the root causes, not just for superficial reasons like the rising price of cafeteria food. Prices indicate much more than a change from thirty cents to thirty-five cents; they are a barometer of social conditions. At the conference on science and technology reform, the general assessment of the reforms was not an optimistic one, even though this conclusion was not exactly blazoned across the newspaper headlines. But I want to tell you this: We are still facing problems of an enormous magnitude, and if we do not resolve them, the hopes for successful reform may vanish like a soap bubble.

• • •

Now I'd like to discuss some of the issues on which the success or failure of the reforms may hinge. The first big problem is that the whole reform program is without a theoretical foundation. (It may be that international relations are in better shape than other aspects of the reforms. The "one-country, two systems" solution proposed for Hong Kong is a work of genius; we promise to allow the two systems to coexist for fifty years, and whatever happens afterward is of no concern to us, at least not to the present generation. We don't need any sophisticated theory to maintain the status quo.)

However, with the economic reforms the situation is entirely different. The term we are currently using to describe what we're trying to create is "planned market economy." What does this mean, exactly? Well, it sounds as if we are going to take the best parts of a planned economy and mix them with the best parts of a market economy, resulting in a new synthesis, the best of both worlds. This is a fine idea—but can it actually be accomplished? Yesterday I ran into a comrade from the Central Party School who told me that they are not even allowed to discuss economic theory there. Yet the old theories of political economy and our current economic practices are worlds apart, and the differences between them can't be resolved by patching them together piecemeal. There are systemic incompatibilities.

The planned economy and the market economy are each complete systems unto themselves, and they are completely different from each other. Can the two in fact be combined into a new, integrated system? We hope so. But at present we have no theoretical basis for combining them. Thus we end up with regular price increases, and at the end of the year, student demonstrations. It is mismatches between the two systems that are causing this loss of consumer buying power. When the money supply increases, prices rise. At the same time, the wages of some people are increasing while the wages of other people—students among them—are not. This is guaranteed to cause trouble. The origin of the problems is clear: We used to have a planned economy, and now we're trying to create a market economy. This has worked all right in the villages, but it has led to great confusion in the cities, where the attempt to combine the two systems has produced serious dislocations. We are hoping to get the best of both systems, but if we're not careful, we may instead get the worst. Until we address this issue successfully, our economy will be unstable. That is what happened in Poland. Some wages went up, while others did not; then prices rose, and shortly thereafter the workers were out on the street, protesting. Our political climate is a bit more stable than Poland's, especially since the Gang of Four were tossed out. But societies have their own internal laws of development. We can't count on political stability if our economic problems remain unresolved. This is abundantly obvious. Signs of unrest have already appeared.

Now for the second big problem: The reforms need not only theory, but substance. The impression I have garnered from attending numerous workshops on the reforms is that our greatest shortcoming is the deplorable level of management across the country. It's apparent that no one has a quantitative grasp of what's going on. Physicists say that if you really want to understand something, you need the equations. If you want to understand the dynamics of an economy, you also need a set of equations to guide you; this way you can measure and predict its performance. The most basic requirement of management is a theoretical understanding, which we lack at the moment. The other thing we lack is even the most basic quantitative data. Our official reports are primitive in this regard, filled with vague statements like "There is too much of this" and "There is too little of that." Such language may be adequate for some purposes, but for managing an economy it is not acceptable. You have to know exactly how much is "too much." Without quantitative data, there can be no effective, scientific management. When class struggle was our motto, we didn't need any quantitative concepts; as long as we kept the number of class enemies below 5 percent, nothing else mattered! We can no longer do things this way if we want to be able to plan for the future. But at present we can't quantify anything because we lack the data.

During the 1950s and '60s, our government would say, "We've decided to emphasize agriculture, light industry, and heavy industry, in that order." A little later it was "Emphasize heavy industry first, then light industry, then agriculture." And so on, in every conceivable permutation. This is an infantile way of running an economy. You can talk in terms like "emphasize heavy industry" when you're writing fiction, but when it comes to quantitative management, this is a worthless technique.

Our quantitative shortcomings have already led to problems. For instance, why has the much-heralded pay raise not been forthcoming? (You students may not care much about this problem yet, but the professors in the audience certainly do.) What I have heard is this: that the Ministry of Labor's first calculations indicated that the salary adjustment would cost only three billion yuan, and on this basis optimistic rumors were spread. But when a more careful analysis was done later, it was revealed that the wage reform would probably cost twice that amount, about six billion yuan. I would never allow a student out of my laboratory if the results of his or her experiments were off by a factor of two! What kind of management is that? A factor of two means the difference between two meals a day and one meal a day! But worse news was on the horizon. In December of last year, it was discovered that the wage reform would actually cost even more than six billion yuan. As a result the long-awaited pay raise for schoolteachers got shelved, and has since become a bad joke.

This story reflects the depth of our management problems, and shows us another role that intellectuals must play. There are many people studying management at Keda, and we should give them our wholehearted support. Only when qualified people learn management skills will we dispense with vagueness and minimize these costly errors. Otherwise, the people running our country will be forever oscillating between three billion and six billion.

Here's another example you may not know about. Last summer we were told that China had an enormous foreign-exchange surplus, and that it needed to be used. "Everyone hurry up and spend this money!" was the message, straight from the Central Committee. Within nine months a reserve of ten billion yuan dropped to six or seven billion, resulting in a sudden crisis. More infantile management. In Western societies where regulatory systems exist, if credit is too tight or too loose, you adjust it by changing the interest rates. If you have too much of a surplus, you lower the interest rates to encourage borrowing. You don't use a bullhorn to solve the problem; that should be reserved for class struggle and frontal assaults on enemy lines. But the fact is, even though we've been told our "central task" is now economic development, we are still using the methods of class struggle.

． ． ．

There is one more thing I want to discuss, which is the problem of our long feudal tradition. Even thirty years after Liberation, feudalistic ways have not disappeared at all; in some areas, they're thriving. One of the most obvious characteristics of feudalistic behavior is the existence of special privilege. Although privilege is attacked during our so-called "democratization" drives, it always reemerges as soon as our attention is diverted elsewhere. This is a persistent situation in China. The problem is not one of just a few individuals or bad practices, requiring only a few specific reforms to clean the situation up; it's not that simple. What we've been calling "ultra-leftism" seems to have been essentially feudalistic. But do such things still exist? Of course! And if we are not vigilant, they will become as virulent as ever.

Previously I mentioned our failures in combining a planned economy and a market economy into a single working entity. Some people are now exploiting this mismatch for illegal gain. We know from thermodynamics that if you have heat sources at two different temperatures, you can construct a heat engine. Our two economies are like two heat sources, and some people have built an "engine" by circulating between the two. This kind of profiteering will not build our country but destroy it. What is going on right now is the creation of a new class of compradors, of bureaucrat capitalists. Some may think that's too harsh a thing to say, but the phenomenon exists nevertheless.

Lately there have been press reports about this. Take what's happening in our banks, for example. Under central planning, when a factory or school needed money for purposes authorized in the plan, the bank would move credits around, and no money had to change hands. Now banks are operating in a live market, with the discretion to make loans outside of the plan; this is a necessary thing. But as a result, those responsible for making loan decisions have been endowed with extraordinary power. In the worst cases, the bank gives loans to whomever it pleases, and the loan officer becomes the "boss." If he wants to refuse a loan, he cites the plan as an excuse. But when it pleases him, he can also approve loans, claiming the market economy. Thus those in charge of loans can take advantage of the gaps between the two economic systems to make enormous illegitimate gains. When people gain such power over economic decisions through their positions in the economy—or in politics—to my mind, this is called bureaucratic capitalism. In addition, since our country is now open to foreign trade, those who work as purchasers can also make huge profits in similar ways. You students probably aren't very aware of such things; I didn't used to be myself. I've been in the university behind closed doors, thinking about the nature of the universe. But these practices are out there, and not in any small measure, either. "Cadre capitalism" [*guan shang*] really exists.

How we will stop it, how we will even slow it down, is not clear to me. In previous Party rectification campaigns against corruption, the biggest problem was usually the unfair distribution of housing. Now, though, inequity in housing distribution is trivial compared to these other problems. The question is not one of who gets to live where, but rather of wholesale appropriation of public property. We've even heard reports that the use of military ships and airplanes in smuggling operations is not unheard of in China. So why are new types of corruption emerging before we can even get rid of the old ones? I think it happens because our society its still feudalistic. Some people still regard political power as a tool with which to obtain special privileges. This is a feudalistic mentality. We are far from establishing a spirit of democracy. There is no oversight by the people. In the West, although personal finances are private, once people aspire to public office they must reveal their finances. We haven't yet reached this point in China. If you try to investigate the finances of a public official here, you're going to run into some big problems. Only through democratic methods can this issue be dealt with. And democratization is a long process—it may take another generation before these problems can really be solved.

REFLECTIONS ON TEACHERS' DAY

The following article appeared in the University of Science and Technology campus newspaper on September 12, 1985. As an educator and member of the Chinese Academy of Sciences, Fang frequently voiced his concerns about education policy, including the issue of low wages and poor living conditions for teachers.

Chinese holidays are traditionally times of celebration. One aspect of them is that we always say a few propitious words to demonstrate our warm feelings toward whomever the holiday is meant to honor. Today being Teachers' Day, therefore, it is time to express our best wishes to all our teachers, past and present. Yet I find that all the appropriately cheerful words seem to be sticking in my throat, as if a fishbone were caught there.

This is by no means because there is nothing worth remembering about my early education, or because I don't cherish with deepest gratitude the memory of my primary- and secondary-school teachers. As was the case for many others, my youth was a time of dreams and visions. This was especially true during the two thousand or so days I spent at Beijing's Number Four Middle School, from 1946 to 1952. I was so absorbed with the daydreams that my teachers aroused in me there that at times I would walk right into utility poles on the side of the road. So hard did I bump into them, in fact, that I can still remember the numbers that were written on those poles.

The teachers who inspired such visions in me appear frequently in my thoughts. Although I was interested in science right from the outset, both the science and humanities teachers left lasting impressions on me. Between them they made me who I am today.

This year I received a letter from my Chinese-language teacher at Number Four Middle School. The letter carried me back thirty years. At the same time, it pulled me up abruptly in the present, and for a long time after I read it, I was very disturbed. The letter read, in part:

> Since the price of newspapers went up, I now subscribe only to the *Beijing Daily*. At the beginning of every month I go to the school library and read the previous month's *People's Daily* and other papers. Thus it was only today that I read in *People's Daily* that a paper of yours has been awarded First Prize by the Gravity Research Foundation.* I am extremely happy for you, and for the fact that there is scientific research in China that is first-rate by international standards. Although I know not a thing about gravitational theory, I warmly congratulate you. . . .

His congratulations evoked for me a feeling from long ago, of sitting in his class and bristling with pride when he praised my writing. Middle-school students all want to be the best at what they do, and I was certainly no exception. Though I had already made up my mind to pursue physics, I could not resist being drawn into my language teacher's orbit. He convinced me that there was more to being a well-rounded person than just excelling in physics; I was determined to impress him with my language skills as well. In my composition classes, I went so far as

---

*Fang Lizhi and Sato Humitaka (of Kyoto University) shared the 1985 First Prize of the Gravity Research Foundation (U.S.) for their paper "Is the Periodicity in the Distribution of Quasar Redshift Evidence for a Multiply-Connected Universe?"

to start writing poetry, and even a novel! Sure enough, this teacher was the first to compliment my writing. It is hard to put into words how good that felt. For a youngster, what feeling can compare to words of praise from a teacher he idolizes?

The reason his letter disturbed me so much was not that it brought back memories of my youth. No, what bothered me was the one sentence, "Since the price of newspapers went up, I now subscribe only to the *Beijing Daily.*" That's just it. The price of newspapers has indeed gone up, as have the prices of many other things, and so my former teacher can afford to buy only *one* *newspaper.* Our teachers' hope was that their students would go out and struggle to build a better world. Yet these same teachers today can't even afford to subscribe to newspapers. Under these circumstances, whether I did first-rate work or not, the congratulations of my teacher brought me little pleasure.

Last year I went back to Number Four Middle School to have a look. Most of my old teachers were no longer there, of course. But the room where teachers prepare their classes is the same one as thirty years ago, only more crowded and dilapidated. I also went to see my old physics teacher at his home, which was also still the same, only it seemed smaller and gloomier. An old man in an old house, with the one remaining newspaper that he can afford. Is this the better world for which our teachers taught us to strive?

Number Four Middle School, like other schools, has produced many alumni who are profoundly grateful for the education they received there. Among my fellow members of the Academic Council,* there are three former students. But what of those who have nurtured so many through their teaching? They are still waiting, bitterly, for all the empty talk about higher wages to

---

*This refers to Fang's membership in the Academic Council of the Chinese Academy of Sciences.

produce some tangible results. As we say, "They burned themselves out in lighting the path for others." Today, our teachers
apply this phrase to themselves in self-mockery. How can we, as
their former students, not feel deeply ashamed of their plight and
indignant at the injustice of it? How could the celebration of
Teachers' Day not be fraught with bitterness? Our society seems
to have little respect for the labor of teachers, especially when you
consider the policies that have created the current situation. The
prevailing disrespect for teachers in the classroom, which has even
come to include beatings of teachers, can scarcely be dissociated
from these policies.

Perhaps the idea behind Teachers' Day is to show a genuine
desire to change these policies, and a genuine respect for teachers,
at least in spirit. But the question is not really one of moral
support and the outward trappings of respect shown one day out
of the year. The question is, when will teachers' lives be improved
for 365 days a year, so that they can afford more than one
newspaper a day?

Yet on the whole, Teachers' Day seems to be a good thing.
Our wishful greetings may bring a smile to the face of our
teachers, even if that smile is a forced one.

A NATURAL SCIENTIST VIEWS THE
REFORMS

This selection contains questions and answers that followed a talk by Fang Lizhi to the Chinese Journalists Association on September 3, 1986, in Beijing. It was first published in the Shanghai newspaper Society *on October 28, 1986.*

Question: Please tell us your views on political reform.

Fang: I must start from cosmology in answering this question. Even today there are those who persist in calling cosmology a "pseudoscience," an instrument of "objective idealism." The minds of some of our philosophers are still frozen at the level of the "Three Great Discoveries"* of the nineteenth century; they know very little about contemporary science. At the recent international conference on cosmology hosted by China, Qian Xuesen† asked me, "Have you invited any philosophers?" I said, "No, we didn't invite anyone from philosophy, the people here are all members of the International Astronomical Union." Qian responded, "You should invite them to come listen, because we can't just let them go on talking nonsense forever."

Last December, Comrade Hu Qiaomu‡ wrote a letter criticiz-

---

*See Glossary.
†American-educated physicist and father of China's ballistic missile program.
‡Conservative Politburo member and leading authority on Marxist-Leninist ideology.

ing quantum cosmology. Then on May 5 of this year, the *Beijing Daily* published an article* using the same kind of language to criticize cosmology that was used during the Cultural Revolution. But the fact is, cosmology is a hard science, and trying to attack it with political labels just won't work anymore. The only thing these attacks demonstrate is that some of our philosophers have no inkling of what's going on in science or how modern science came to be what it is.

Over history, new cosmologies have more than once led to the downfall of orthodox beliefs. The kind of thinking done in cosmology is just what is required to foment a revolution in ideas. It seems to me that in China today we are badly in need of such thinking.

For decades, our promotion of Marxism has been accompanied by a narrow-minded exclusion of other points of view. It has been this way even in the sciences. Marxism was built on a distinct set of cultural and scientific foundations, yet we've tried to give people the impression that nothing prior to the arrival of Marxism was of any value. When we read about some great historical figure, we will inevitably find a disclaimer tagged on to the end: "Due to historical limitations . . ." What this really means, of course, is that nobody's achievements can match those of Marxism. But in reality, don't we all have limitations? Marxism is certainly no exception to this. Yet because of our exclusiveness, we've been unwilling to acknowledge that others do anything worthwhile. Of course we have made some contributions, but why shouldn't we acknowledge the contributions of others? This is a very backward mindset.

At the same time that we have tried to open our country up to the outside world, we have not significantly changed our

*Jin Lin, "No Science Can Ever Replace Marxist Philosophy," *Beijing Daily*, May 5, 1986.

century-old attitude of "using Western methods but maintaining the Chinese essence."* I personally advocate a complete and thoroughgoing openness. In this era of global exchange of goods and ideas, the world's cultures can and should be colliding head-on with each other. We shouldn't be setting limits in advance, fearing that the good will be lost. I believe that our encounters with the world will sift out the undesirable and leave the desirable behind. We'll learn from others, and others will accept the good things we have to offer. Therefore I say we should be completely open, and join the mainstream of internationalization. This is the way things are headed.

Question: What is the key factor in political reform?

Fang: Looking at it as an educator, I'd say that democratization is the most important thing. Without democracy, the academic community will make no progress.

Right now there's talk about "loosening up." This very phrase suggests something bestowed on us by superiors. It used to be two feet, now they'll loosen it up to three feet. This is not a very good description of what we want. I would much prefer to speak of democracy. "Loosening up" implies the setting of limits in the same breath, whereas democracy refers to the rights of citizens.

On this score, the overseas edition of the *People's Daily* is not a bad newspaper, but there was an article in it recently that betrayed an utterly feudalistic attitude. A member of the Standing Committee of the National People's Congress wrote that "3,000 to 0 is better than 51 to 49," meaning that unanimous opinions are better than disagreements. This is complete ignorance of democracy. Differences of opinion are normal. How can it be "3,000 to 0" on every score? What on earth is the purpose of publishing such an article? It sets a very bad example. I am a

*See Glossary, *ti-yong.*

college administrator. When it comes to lunch, everyone raises their hands in favor, but on other issues there is always disagreement, and a vote is often required.

Demanding that the people always speak "with one voice" is a bad idea. People have their own ways of looking at things. The Theory of Relativity says that from different points of view, from different frames of reference, one sees different things. Democracy can emerge only where there is diversity of opinion. Competition among ideas has been much easier to attain in science than in politics. In areas outside of science the situation is still "3,000 to 0."

There is another question that relates to our concept of democracy, namely, whom does government ultimately serve? We have some mutually contradictory ideas about that. For example, the "Internationale" contains the line "There have never been any messiahs," yet in "The East is Red"* it says, "He is the shining star who has saved the people." On one hand we declare that "the Party is there to serve the people," and then on the other hand we tell kids, as if we're doing them a big favor, that "the Party has provided you with a college education, so you'd better study hard." Aren't these ideas a bit contradictory?

At the Party Congress, Zhao Ziyang offered a draft of the Seventh Five-Year Plan for purposes of discussion and eliciting recommendations. What happens then, but that newspapers immediately start admonishing us to "learn from the Seventh Five-Year Plan"! It was only a draft, for heaven's sake! People were supposed to discuss it and offer their insights. How did it suddenly turn into a "study object"? What does this tell us about who is the master and who is the subordinate? Frankly, what it means is that many people still don't have any idea of what kind

*A Cultural Revolution–era paean in praise of Mao Zedong, which for several years served as China's national anthem.

of attitude and behavior is required to put democracy into practice. "Loosening up" is not democracy. Democracy is not something that can be bestowed from above.

The idea prevailing among people in many developed capitalist countries is that since government is maintained through
taxation, then it must answer to the taxpayers. I lived in America
for a short time at a place called Princeton. I was obviously
neither an immigrant nor a citizen, but nonetheless I received a
report from my congressman giving an account to the citizens of
just what he'd been up to and how he had voted on one issue or
another in various committees. The legislators are responsible to
the people. In China no citizens have ever received a report from
their representatives to the National People's Congress telling
how they voted, or whether they voted at all, or what they
worked on. I think that our socialist democracy should do better
than bourgeois democracy—in both form and substance—and
that we shouldn't stop until it does.

Speaking of taxes, I'm a teacher, and so I'm effectively paying
taxes, too. At our school, the ratio of students to faculty and staff
is about 2:1, which means that the average output per faculty
member is two graduates every five years. Our faculty members
are paid an average of 80 or 90 yuan per month, so in five years
they make something like 5,000 yuan. These days some schools
are "selling" their graduates. This means that the unit that wants
the graduates must put up 20,000 yuan in educational expenses
to "buy" each one (and in some of our "key institutes," even
30,000 yuan). Two students thus come to 40,000 yuan; that is,
they have a market value of 40,000 yuan. Let's say that 20,000
of that is overhead and expenses. If you deduct 5,000 yuan for
salaries, that still leaves 15,000 yuan. Where does all this money
go? It is equivalent to paying a tax. We get taxed in the form
of low wages rather than making outright payments, but we are
taxpayers just the same.

Government should serve the taxpayers. Nowadays we emphasize that our leaders have a duty to serve the people, but in practice many of them still act as if they're doing something out of charity. In the past I have done ideological work among students and said things like "The Party is giving you a great educational opportunity, you should work hard." But on reflection I decided that this isn't exactly right. It's fine to tell students to study hard, but it's wrong to tell them that "the Party gave you this opportunity." A citizen has a fundamental right to receive an education. It is the right of a taxpayer, and if someone tells you it is a gift, then that person is wrong. Anyone who works is a taxpayer, but since we lack a democratic mentality, we often mistake what is due us by right for charity from above.

In ancient times there was a courtier named Wei Zheng,* who had the courage to raise his objections in front of the emperor, but this is still not "democracy." In democracy there should be room for all kinds of opinions. Whereas under feudalism only a few loyal critics dared to express dissent, in this day and age every citizen must be able to speak his or her mind.

The question of whether democracy is a right or a privilege also manifests itself in the cadre system. Right now we're trying to fashion a "Bo Le"† meritocracy, selecting the best people for each job. Although this is an improvement over the system of appointments for life, who is going to guarantee that "Bo Le" does his job? Who is going to vouch for the "prime mover" that starts the whole thing rolling? Under feudalism, it was fine to have Bo Le around to select thousand-league horses, but this is

---

*Prime minister during the reign of the Tang dynasty emperor Tai Zong (A.D. 627–650).

†Bo Le was the "celestial master of horses" in Chinese legend, able to select fine horses and develop their talents accordingly. The "Bo Le system" refers to the practice of Party leaders selecting officials on the basis of informal personal recommendations.

by no means socialist democracy. The nomination and appointment of officials should be based on the will of the people and
subject to their oversight. In the same way that there is nothing
outside the universe itself to set things in motion, there is also no
authority higher than the masses of ordinary people; it is therefore the people that must be the ultimate force. We arrive at this
conclusion just as we would in cosmology. The reform of our
political institutions must continue, but our first priority has to
be getting clear on these key ideas.

Actually, as far as rights and obligations are concerned, our
constitution has provisions very similar in language to those in
the developed countries. But our understandings are very different. Theirs involve accountability to the taxpayers, while ours
involve "bestowing privileges." Progress in cosmology requires
making conceptual breakthroughs, and the reform of political
systems does also; otherwise, we are simply fiddling around with
technicalities. Reform in many Western countries has involved
leaving appearances intact while changing the substance of things,
while in China it has usually been just the opposite. We are
endlessly hoisting new banners up the flagpole, but the feudal
essence of the thing itself has never changed.

Question: Do you think that there can ever be another Cultural
Revolution?

Fang: That depends on whether the political reforms are successful, and whether people in different walks of life are able to do
what they ought to. A key point is whether intellectuals can
develop an independent mentality. Truth is independent of who
holds power and makes the pronouncements. When we finally
learn this lesson, there won't be any more Cultural Revolutions.
We saw an example of this in the latest campaign to stamp out
"spiritual pollution."

Intellectuals should advance their own ideas. At a recent conference in Qingdao, I mentioned that in the past many people
based their writings on quotations from the leaders. If the leaders
happened to be very learned, this might be all right, but such is
simply not the case. This use of quotations is utterly worthless;
its only possible function is to intimidate people. What we should
be doing instead is searching for the truth and drawing our own
conclusions, on which the policies of the leadership can then be
based. The present situation needs to be completely reversed.
Without independent judgment and points of view, political
reform hasn't a chance. The "top-down" approach to reform has
a role to play, but it is what comes from the bottom up that really
matters. Intellectuals have a little broader perspective than many
of the leaders, are a little more sensitive, and a little more precise.
As a basis for how to proceed with our modernization, their
opinions are more reliable. Without them our efforts will lack
vitality, and our reforms will not be democratic. All we will
achieve is "loosening up"—or perhaps being "loosened up."

Question: What do you think about democratization and the
Party's "leading role"?

Fang: Democracy must begin within the Party itself. If under
feudalism an enlightened monarch could permit the existence of
a Wei Zheng, then under socialism an enlightened leadership
should also permit the existence of opposing opinions, of diverse
factions within the Party. But the pluralist mentality has been
very difficult to establish in China. The monistic view of a single
correct belief has prevailed among the Chinese since the days of
Confucius; if the two of us are discussing a problem, and I'm
right, then you must be wrong, and maybe you'll even have to
be completely eliminated. In the West it doesn't always happen
that way. If I'm right, you may also be right. The opposition has

its own way of looking at things, which may not be wrong, and it's definitely not permissible to destroy them for it. The psychological leanings of Chinese culture are deeply embedded, and in the end the idea of one correct belief always seems to prevail. This is a fundamental problem.

ON POLITICAL REFORM

The following is the text of a speech given by Fang Lizhi to the Conference on Reform of the Political Structure, held in Hefei, Anhui, on September 27, 1986. The conference was sponsored by the Center for Economic and Cultural Research of the Anhui Provincial People's Government. Following the speech are excerpts from the ensuing question-and-answer period.

Political reform is an inevitable stage in the overall process of reform, and it is only natural that the issue is being raised right now. Since the Third Plenum of the Eleventh Party Congress,* we have seen the renewal of the Four Modernizations policy, followed by economic reform, followed in turn by reforms in education, science and technology, the cultural sphere, and ethics. Now there is a clear mandate for political reform as well. This has been a natural and necessary progression.

China requires comprehensive reform. The myriad problems facing us today will not be resolved by anything short of full-scale reform in every arena. The idea that we can modify a few chosen aspects of the society while leaving everything else intact is a pipe dream. Many things go into making a society what it is; one doesn't suddenly discover one factor that accounts for everything and change only that. We have to acknowledge the reality of our situation, namely that backwardness is ubiquitous

*The Communist Party Plenum of December 1978, at which Deng Xiaoping emerged as China's top leader.

135

in China and that no aspect is exempt from the need for reform. During the Cultural Revolution no one dared to say such things, but after the Third Plenum things eased up, and people began expressing their opinions.

The first thing they talked about was the economy. There were a few economic achievements in the thirty years since Liberation, but on the whole we were not successful. Even the food-supply problem was not completely solved. Industrial development lagged behind that in many other nations. Countries and territories* that were formerly at or below our level of development were now racing ahead of us. And we admitted that we had fallen behind economically. But we did not admit our shortcomings in other areas, especially in politics. Apart from our economic problems, we still thought ourselves superior to the rest of the world.

But since the inauguration of the open-door policy, with more and more people going abroad, from state leaders on down to ordinary intellectuals and cadres, we've discovered that our problems are by no means only economic. We see, for instance, that art and literature in China do not measure up to world standards. We see that our society faces a spiritual crisis, a crisis of morality and ideals. And so forth; our athletes are doing well, but that's about it. Now we've gone a step further, by recognizing that our political system is also backward, compared not only with developed countries but with other developing countries as well. Such an acknowledgment on our part is crucial, and no comprehensive reform will succeed without it. Comrade Deng Xiaoping said recently that "Reform is revolution." Reforming our political system is indeed a revolution. The reason we need a revolution is that we see our backwardness and are demanding improvement.

So, just how are we doing when judged by world standards? This is a question not only for China, but for socialist revolutions

*"Territories" refers to Hong Kong, Taiwan, and Macao.

worldwide. We need to ask, in what ways has socialism succeeded and in what ways has it failed? Look at the Soviet Union—since coming to power, Mikhail Gorbachev has spoken quite frankly. He has found many defects in the Soviet economy and political system, and his ideas about reform are based on these frank assessments. In that vein, let me ask: In the forty-odd years since the end of World War II, how has the socialist camp fared in comparison with the nonsocialist camp? What kind of progress have China, the Soviet Union, and Eastern Europe made? We don't need hot air, here; we need to "seek truth from facts." And let's not confuse ideals with reality. People all over the world share the ideal of equality, of a society not divided into rich and poor. But the question is, does our society actually live up to these ideals? Is our society doing any better in practice than anyone else's? If we really want an answer to these questions, we must ask them in deadly earnest, and open up our eyes to look at the world as a whole.

The fact of the matter is, socialism has not been successful. We must admit this and not seek to cover it up. Over the last three decades there has been little real progress in either China or the Soviet Union. Some people say that China's backwardness stems from its large population and poor economic base, therefore China shouldn't be compared with Japan or Taiwan. There is some truth to this explanation, but it doesn't completely hold water. Take population and arable land. On average, 750 Chinese inhabit one square kilometer of arable land, while in Japan the same amount of land supports 1,500 people; Japan gets by on much less land per capita than China. If you want to talk about economic conditions, let's look at East and West Germany. The same people, the same economic base—actually, before the war, the eastern part of Germany was even more developed industrially. But no one would deny that West Germany is now far more prosperous.

In this light, using the size of our population and our prior economic conditions as an excuse for our current shortcomings is not convincing. Instead of making excuses for this, we need to soberly reexamine our failed practices of the past three decades, economic and otherwise. We must adopt a scientific attitude and admit the basic facts; without this admission, there will be no way of moving on to anything else. We have to reform. If we do not reform, other countries will simply leave us further and further behind in the dust. If we continue trying to disguise our problems with the mask of socialist superiority, then reforms cannot be implemented and will not succeed. We are still subjected to propaganda that uses abstract socialist ideals in order to justify policies that are irrational in practice or to illustrate our moral superiority over the West. Of course, Western countries have plenty of problems. But their problems are of a different order from ours, and we had better learn to distinguish between the two. If we can't even tell whether we are ahead of or behind the West right now, then realistic reforms have little chance of succeeding.

The comparison of Chinese and Western culture that has erupted so feverishly in the last year or so is very beneficial. It has been over a century since forward-looking Chinese began to acknowledge our society's shortcomings and call for learning from the West. The same thing is happening today. We are still backward, and we still need to learn from the West in order to transform our society. I sincerely believe that if we want things to change, "complete Westernization" is the most viable approach.* What I mean by "complete Westernization" is complete openness to the outside world, assimilating all of the cultural advances of the human race. Why is it that for the last

---

*The expression "complete Westernization" [*quanpan xi hua*] has been the focus of intense controversy in China for a century. One of its earliest exponents was Tan Sitong, martyred leader of the abortive "Hundred Days Reform" in 1898.

century there have always been those who insisted on "using Western methods but maintaining the Chinese essence" or something comparable? Basically, it's because they fear that the "Chinese essence" is going to come under attack, and so they try to set *a priori* limits on what can and can't be changed. This is wrong. Backward ideas are bound to come under attack when confronted by something more advanced.

I admire the spirit of the "complete Westernizers" both before and after the May Fourth period, who had the guts to call for letting foreign ideas into China, where they could challenge what was not progressive in our culture. The policy of openness and reform of the last few years has indeed resulted in our economy, culture, and politics colliding head-on with Western ideas. This has been very beneficial on the whole, which is not to say that there is nothing of value in this ancient culture of ours. But our assessment of whether a thing is good or not should be based on free comparison, rather than on *a priori* rules. Once comparisons are made, the good can be retained and the bad discarded accordingly. If we can carry on vigorous comparison and debate, we will have no need to fear that the best parts of Chinese culture will be lost. The fact is, civilization develops unevenly, and in any given historical period some cultures are more advanced than others. In the past, Chinese culture has had a great influence on other peoples: the Japanese, the Koreans, the Vietnamese, and even the Europeans. But the tables are turned today, and it is time to let other cultures have their influence on us. On the whole this will not hurt us, but help us.

Political reform demands fundamental changes in our thinking. Minor adjustments here and there will not solve our problems. I am not opposed to being prudent in our actions, so as to avoid provoking social turmoil. But we have to start changing our ideas and ideologies. It is only in recent times that Western societies could be called genuinely developed, but the conceptual seeds for these changes were planted much earlier. The Renaissance was one starting place. The Renaissance shattered the existing framework of ideas, especially those underlying feudal and theocratic rule. Starting with the Renaissance came the emergence of many great historical figures in Europe: scientists such as Copernicus, Galileo, and Newton; philosophers such as Bacon; and political theorists such as Rousseau. Under the influence of these giants, Europe experienced an unprecedented burst of new thinking about society. Liberty and democracy won the day and became great forces for progress.

There are many reasons why China, the Soviet Union, and Eastern Europe have fallen behind, but at the very top of the list is the self-imposed isolation of Marxism. The ideas that have propelled civilization forward down through the centuries have invariably entailed contributions from many quarters. Marxism is no exception. Marx and Engels took the best from German philosophy, British political economy, and French utopian socialism. They drew heavily on the physics and biology of the day, basing their theories on the most advanced scientific knowledge available. But we, their followers, placed Marxism in a vacuum and hailed it as the supreme ultimate. Any and all developments in the capitalist world were deemed worthless. This was a tragedy because the world is changing all the time. If you refuse to change with it, you will simply be left behind.

These destructive practices began in the Soviet Union. The Soviets held that Marxism reached its highest stage with Lenin and Stalin. So intent were the Soviets on denying the value of any other ideas that even the latest achievements of natural science, from quantum mechanics and the theory of relativity to cosmology and cybernetics, were dismissed as capitalist pseudoscience. This led directly to the Soviets' falling behind in science, and it turned Marxism into little more than a dry dogma. Marxism is not God; it is a methodology and a worldview. It has its own historical limitations and needs to change and grow like anything else. Engels's "dialectics of nature" was appropriate to the physics of the last century, but is totally inadequate by present standards. Setting Marxism apart and refusing to touch it has caused our natural and social sciences to lag behind and led to our current backwardness in the political, economic, and cultural spheres. It has been a great impediment to progress.

We should remember that the idea of socialism appeared long before Marxism did, and independently had a great impact on the world. The socialism in our country is of the Marx-Engels-Lenin-Stalin variety, but in fact this is only one type of socialism. We regard our version as the one true faith and utterly superior to any other, but when the socialist movement first began, there were many schools. These ultimately split into Lenin's Bolsheviks and the European social-democratic parties of the Second International. Social democrats have ruled in the five Scandinavian countries during most of the postwar period.

Socialism has many definitions, but all hold in common the belief that the disparity between rich and poor should be small, and that property should be publicly owned. If we judge by these two criteria, then the countries of northern Europe are no less socialist than we are. Their public-sector ownership generally stands above 60 percent, and the gap between rich and poor is relatively small. Sure, there are capitalists in those countries. But it is hard for them to pass their wealth on to the next generation because of the high inheritance taxes. If you invent something or you're good at business, you can get rich. But the more you earn, the higher the tax rate, which can reach up to 70 or 80 percent. The economies of these countries are in very good shape, with per-capita annual incomes of around $12,000. The standard of living is high, the unemployment rate is less than 3 percent, and life expectancy is the highest in the world—around seventy-six years for men and eighty years for women.

The big difference between the Scandinavians and us is that while we were conducting class struggle, they were busy promoting reconciliation and compromise between classes. Their reasoning is that society will always have a managerial class. If this group is removed, others will simply rise to manage production in their place. Merely overthrowing one group of people in favor of another does not resolve the basic economic issue. Managers and producers by their nature have different aims. The former must make money for their factories, while the latter are out to make money for themselves. If the factory's earnings are too high, the workers' wages will be too low, and vice versa. The point is how to achieve a balance between these interests. Such a balance may not be fully satisfactory to either side, but for the society as a whole it is the best solution. This idea has begun to appear in China. One will probably never find the perfect solution to any social problem, but what we *can* hope to find is the lesser of evils. This is the most "scientific" solution we can come up with. What the Scandinavians have chosen is to opt for the possible.

If we look at the last century, we see that socialism can take different forms. We have the Chinese and Soviet models, and the Scandinavian model, and we even have the model of capitalist countries with socialist features. For instance, the Italian Communist Party is now the second-largest party in Italy and has a great impact there. Many social-welfare programs in Italy have resulted from the influence of the Communists. In the Italian retirement system, which is much better than ours, retired workers receive pensions every month. Even after a man's death, his wife will continue to receive his pension until she dies herself. At the University of Rome I found that student meals were essentially free of charge. When we talk about "adhering to the socialist path," we must realize that there is more than one socialist path in existence. We must not believe that adhering to the socialist path means adhering to our failed practices of the past three decades.

There are socialist elements even in the most developed capitalist countries. We were always told that "Imperialism is monopolistic." But now, even the United States, stronghold of capitalism, has antimonopoly laws. The Bell Telephone Company, formerly the largest American corporation and one that used to monopolize the telephone business, was forcibly divided into eight smaller companies, which now have to compete with one another. This shows that capitalist governments recognize the danger of monopolies. Another example is Keynesian economics, which advocates government interference in the economy, and thus bears a certain resemblance to the idea of a socialist planned economy.

• • •

If we are to make progress, we must learn from what has been proven to work elsewhere. We have admitted that class struggle is a mistake. Can we then learn from the experience of the Scandinavian countries? What I have observed about them is that they make a thorough study of their social problems, and through repeated adjustments have arrived at a fairly good balance, which has enabled people throughout society to find their niches and make the best of their abilities. Can our society also make such adjustments? There is no question that adjustments are absolutely necessary, though they need to be based on careful research. For instance, socialism calls for both social stability and rapid development, yet social stability and rapid development can be contradictory. When "eating from a big pot," society is very stable but development is slow. On the other hand, completely unfettered market competition promotes development at the cost of stability. We must diligently study how to balance these. But one thing is certain: We need to discard the old framework and chart a new course.

To carry out political reform we need openness, not restrictions. We have to permit free discussion of different approaches to solving our problems. This requires freedom of expression. Without freedom of expression, academic freedom can't be protected. Only with freedom of expression can we debate about what is right and reasonable, and thus inform our decisions. The success of China's reforms depends on democratization, and democratization depends above all on guaranteeing freedom of expression. This doesn't entail making new laws, because freedom of expression is already stipulated in our Constitution; what it entails is strict compliance with the existing laws. But be that as it may, only when we have democracy and freedom of speech will it do any good for us to go on and talk about anything else.

Right now many good policies are yielding bad results, and the basic reason is a lack of democracy. The separation of Party and state functions, the removal of enterprises from state control, and the system of individual responsibility for profit and loss by factory managers have been poorly implemented. The appointment of younger, better-educated people to leadership posts has also been mishandled. Democratization is the key to such reforms. We used to say that bourgeois democracy is false democracy. But false democracy brought down the American president in the Watergate scandal. If what we have in China is real democracy, then Chinese citizens should also have the ability to expose unethical practices on the part of their leaders and remove those who have violated their trust. If we had really reached this point, China would have a self-regulating political system. But we have not. The people have no way of controlling corruption, other than to hope that the top leadership will take notice and put a stop to it. Democracy is the core of reform, and everything else is secondary. Only through democracy will we begin to move in a healthy direction.

I would like to say a little about the relationship between citizens of a country and their government, in terms of who is supposed to be serving whom. At one time Communists were very keen on this issue, but it is now in capitalist countries that people have the clearest understanding of how the relationship should be viewed: The people maintain the government—concretely speaking, through their taxes—and therefore government ought to serve the people and represent their interests. The taxpayers have the right to control their government. I worked for four months this year in New Jersey. One day I received some material from a congressman, setting out what he had been doing recently and how he had voted on various bills. Every citizen of that district received the same materials. People could find out what the congressman had been up to, and if they didn't like it, they could vote against him the next time he ran for election. This is theoretically the case in our country, but it is not the case in fact. People's Congress representatives are supposed to represent the people, and they ought to be accountable to those that they represent. But the truth is, we haven't the foggiest idea of what our representatives are up to. We certainly don't receive any reports from them in the mail. All we get is propaganda telling us how benevolently the government is caring for the people.

We must start realizing that a government does not bestow favors on its citizens, but rather that the citizens maintain the government and consent to allowing certain people to lead on their behalf. We constantly hear talk about "extending democracy," but this is very mistaken, because it suggests that democracy is something that can be "extended" from the top down. In a democracy, the power rests with each individual. I fulfill my obligations as a citizen of this society, and in turn I am due my rights. These rights are the basis of my political power. I have the right to mind my country's business, and to demand the dismissal of unfit leaders. This is really just common sense, but the idea has not yet caught on in China. Many Chinese still believe that blessings are bestowed upon them by the government, as opposed to being the consequence of their own hard work. A new attitude in this regard is essential.

I think that some of the ideas that emerged in the early stages of capitalism were extremely progressive, especially the concept of humanism. We need to expand on these ideas and imbue them with new meaning, rather than disparaging them. We must respect the humanity of each individual. We are not going through the process of reforming our political system just so we can treat people as obedient tools of the state, no differently than they were treated under feudalism. We are doing it in order to enhance their dignity, to empower them, and to give them the opportunity to freely develop their human potential.

Question: How do we evaluate the organizational and cadre reforms of the last few years? Some people say that the system of lifelong tenure for cadres has not been abolished at all, and that actually a system of essentially hereditary posts has emerged. Reform has gone astray because people with selfish motives have been in charge of the "redistribution of power." Is this correct?

Fang: Organizational reform and cadre-system reform are good ideas that are aimed at overcoming the rigidity of our current system. But there are serious problems with these reforms right now, stemming from the absence of a democratic environment. Without democracy, even good ideas such as the emphasis on younger and better-educated officials will produce bad results. The cadre system has some intrinsically feudalistic features. For example, the "Bo Le system" of personal recommendations is fine for nominating potential cadres, but not as a primary method of appointing people to official posts. In Western countries a would-be official needs a number of recommendations prior to being nominated, and then the nomination must undergo general scrutiny. Relying solely on the recommendation of cronies is not acceptable. Besides which, in our system who gets to choose those who do the recommending?

Question: In recent years people across the country have lost their enthusiasm for politics and started to complain about things. How should we look at this?

Fang: This is a healthy phenomenon. The appearance of complaints is much better than their absence. There are many problems in this society. If no one complained in the past, it was not because there were no problems, but because no one dared to bring them up. One way of quantifying how much democracy you have is to look at the range of things people are permitted to complain about. The smaller the range, the less democracy there is. Nowadays people have much greater latitude for airing their grievances, and this indicates a great improvement over the situation of a decade ago. Every country has its problems. If people are allowed to talk about them, it might even help the problems get solved.

Question: Excessive concentration of power in the hands of a few is the main cause of the political corruption that we have right now. But excessive *decentralization* of power is also a problem. How are policies from the center to be carried out when local authorities oppose them?

Fang: This problem also stems from the lack of democracy. In a democratic society, the people can freely express their views, which are reflected in the legislative aspect of government. At the same time, for administration to be effective, orders must be followed down the chain of command. These two requirements go hand in hand. That is why the principle of separation of powers has existed in the West since the time of the Greeks. With the bourgeois revolutions, this idea was put into practice with the tripartite division of administrative, legislative, and judicial powers. In this system, the operation of the executive branch is based on command, and the operation of the legislative branch is based on democracy.

But since we lack democracy, we also lack effective centralization. We do not have the smooth-running machinery of a democratic system. The Party and the government control everything. Monolithic leadership can be neither democratic nor efficient in administration. Consider how often Party committee first secretaries also head the discipline committee, and how inappropriate this is. What do you do when the Party secretary does something wrong? Nor should administrative leaders be allowed to control the auditing departments. Legislative, administrative, judicial, and auditing bodies should be mutually independent. Only then will there be both democratic expression and effective administration. If everything is under the control of a single leader, the results will not be good.

Question: Please talk about how to achieve intra-Party democracy, and how to achieve democracy for the people as a whole.

Fang: If we want to prevent political and policy blunders by Party leaders, wouldn't we do well to follow the example of ruling parties in developed countries and permit the existence of factions with different points of view? This allows for public criticism and debate under the premise that beneath any conflict there lies a deeper unity of purpose. When serious conflicts arise, the different factions have to negotiate with each other, and sometimes the Party leadership will even wind up being replaced.

The fact of the matter is, there have always been divergent opinions within our Party. Chairman Mao himself acknowledged that this had long been the case, though the disagreements were never made public, and differences of opinion were tolerated only within a small elite group, which highlights the lack of democracy. The more democratic things are, the more transparent. At present we have no idea what our leader thinks, because he doesn't do anything in public or talk about his positions. This is a "nontransparent" political system. The influence of Lenin on Party organization has been profound. Leninist organization may have served its purpose at one time, but it no longer serves us well today. A Leninist party cannot cope with the problems of modern society.

As for democracy among the people as a whole, we should at a minimum begin by making People's Congress delegates represent the people. Right now, people's representative is considered some kind of honorary post—become a model worker, and they'll make you a people's representative. This is wrong. The People's Congress should become a legitimate legislative body and vehicle for public opinion. If the bourgeois system is false democracy, at least it has accountability to go with it. In Britain, every week Mrs. Thatcher has to go to the parliament, sit in a certain chair—rather like our criticism sessions of times past—and try to answer any questions the members may ask. The Cabinet sits with her, and if, say, defense issues are raised, the Minister of Defense is supposed to give straight answers on the spot. If the ministers don't answer satisfactorily or have done their jobs poorly, they can be sure they will face the music in the next day's newspapers. Cabinet members thus take their responsibilities quite seriously.

Why can't we exercise similar oversight over our government? Since our government is there to "serve the people," why can't it regularly report on how it has been serving our interests? Right now there are 3,000 delegates to the National People's Congress. It should be reduced in size and made more professional. When a person is elected to the congress, his or her main duty should be to represent constituents. In the United States, Congress allocates a substantial sum of money to members to pay for studies or to do research themselves. Once they've done their homework, they go to Congress and have their say. This is not a burden on the government, but rather a great benefit for both the government and the people. If we did things this way, we wouldn't need to change our political structure, or abandon Party leadership, or leave the socialist road.

Question: How should we go about involving the people in politics?

Fang: In China, channels for popular participation exist in theory but are not treated seriously. The key is in the People's Congress' doing what it's supposed to do. Not long ago, when I was in the United States, I read an article in the overseas edition of the *People's Daily* by a vice chairman of the National People's Congress, which received a negative response abroad. The article remarked that issues in the NPC are usually decided by a vote of 3,000 to 0, which is far better than in foreign countries where they have votes of 51 to 49. This viewpoint betrays utter ignorance of what democracy is about. Under democracy, groups of people from different nationalities and occupations and conditions of life come together to work out a balance between their diverse needs and interests. It is only when votes are not unanimous that the system is working! The vote in Western parliaments is indeed quite often 51 to 49, and this forces members to work cautiously and avoid mistakes. It also shows how much support or opposition there is for different measures, so that different sides can get together and negotiate a realistic balance. Votes of 3,000 to 0 suggest that everyone is happy, that an impossible ideal has been achieved. The person who wrote this knows nothing about democracy or politics in general.

Question: In your estimation, what kind of political system will our reforms result in?

Fang: There is nothing wrong with our Constitution. Compare it to the constitutions of Britain or the United States, and you'll see that the differences are not too extreme. But our Constitution is not seriously implemented. For instance, the Constitution stipulates a separation of powers, but in reality power is concentrated. I think I am taking a most conservative position in stating that the Constitution should be strictly observed.

Question: What is the relationship between political reforms and economic reforms?

Fang: Without reform in all spheres, economic reform will be difficult. Revitalization of the economy is closely linked to political democracy.

Question: Many people say it is more difficult to do research in the social sciences than in the natural sciences. A natural scientist may start all over again when his research fails, but if a social scientist says something wrong, he may never get another chance. This problem was worse under the Gang of Four, but it still hasn't gone away. What do you think about this?

Fang: I recently wrote an article in the *People's Daily* proposing that scientific research be judged on its scientific merits, not according to the whims of the leadership or of society. Otherwise, social science will go nowhere. Scientists must be independent, and they must not be forced to alter their results because certain leaders disagree with them. Because Marxism-Leninism has long tended to exclude all other points of view, new ideas or findings in the social sciences are often regarded as heresy. This shows the lack of even a rudimentary scientific attitude. There is also a tendency within the social sciences themselves toward pedantic, hidebound interpretations of Marxism that have no relevance to dealing with real issues. Another tendency is to quote the leaders, especially the leaders who are currently in power. Quotations from the leaders cannot form a basis for scientific work. If the leaders were scholars, it would be fine to cite their findings, but if they aren't, then we have no business doing it. In developed countries, politicians cite scholarly studies to argue for their policies, but in China we have it exactly the opposite: Scholars have to quote people who have done no research in order to justify their theories. I do not mean to insult the leaders. Leaders are organizers, politicians, and activists who are good at what they do. But quoting them doesn't prove that you know anything.

Question: In the West, newspapers can shape public opinion and provide oversight in political affairs, whereas our newspapers mostly promote the views of those in power. Should this be reformed?

Fang: As I have said, open expression of public opinion is a key indicator of democracy.

Question: Both the May Fourth Movement and the Cultural Revolution were opposed to tradition, except that the latter came from an extreme left-wing position. What difference do you see between these two antitraditional movements?

Fang: There is a fundamental difference between them. The May Fourth Movement was antitraditional in all ways. It introduced new natural science into China and absorbed the latest social theory from the West. Art and literature underwent drastic changes, humanist thought was influential among intellectuals, and feudalism was dealt a serious blow. The achievements of the

May Fourth Movement were tremendous. New thinking prospered from May Fourth right on up to the War of Resistance against Japan, as anyone who has studied modern Chinese history can tell you. But as a result of the Japanese aggression against China, the tide turned, and the study of Western culture was cut short. People began to distrust the earlier cultural and economic ties with the West, thinking that Western countries aimed to use these relationships to invade China. At this time the old culture enjoyed a resurgence, and intolerance of new cultural influences ensued, persisting right through the Korean War. This history should not be regarded as a failure of the May Fourth Movement, but rather as a consequence of the powerful grip of tradition.

The Cultural Revolution, on the other hand, was by no means antitraditional in all ways. It propagated feudalism under the guise of Marxism, to the extent of hailing our leader as we would an emperor. Some people say that the Cultural Revolution mobilized everything that is negative about China, and there is some truth to that.

Question: There are reports that the coming Thirteenth Party Congress will retain certain venerable old comrades in important posts. What are your views on that?

Fang: When Reagan ran for the presidency, some people said that he was too old to be president, and this became a topic of debate before the election. The majority of voters thought he would make a good president, and so he was elected. Moreover, he won many more votes than his much younger rival. Age is not an absolute barrier; what is important is the will of the people. Reagan became president because he was elected by the American people—as they say, he got the nod. On the other hand, through what channels Chinese leaders are chosen I have no idea. The crux of the matter is not age, but whether there are avenues for the people's voices to be heard.

Question: Does reform in all spheres imply that the Four Cardinal Principles* will have to be changed?

Fang: The Four Principles are political in nature and do not extend to every aspect of life. For instance, the syllabus of a physics course has nothing whatsoever to do with these principles. The former relates to science, the latter to politics, which are separate matters. But in fact the Four Principles themselves are evolving. Compared to the past, there has been a substantial change over the last few years in our conception of what "sticking to the socialist path" and "maintaining the leading role of the Party" might mean.

But there *are* some hypersensitive types who suspect anything that doesn't derive all its conclusions directly from the Four Principles of being subversive. This is wrong. Our understanding of the world cannot be deduced in its entirety from any set of principles, no matter how general they might be.

Question: If the fundamental premise of political reform is to democratize the system, then wasn't the promulgation of the Four Big Freedoms—speaking out freely, airing views fully, holding great debates, writing big-character posters—an exercise in democracy?

Fang: This is a very complex question. What started as a way of promoting freedom of expression in 1957 ended up being used to persecute people during the Cultural Revolution and to promote strife among the populace. From that perspective the legacy of the Four Big Freedoms is not a happy one, and thus I think it is still too early to judge its ultimate impact.

*The basic political and ideological guidelines set down by Deng Xiaoping in 1979, which call for upholding (1) the socialist road; (2) the dictatorship of the proletariat; (3) leadership by the Communist Party; and (4) the leading role of Marxism–Leninism–Mao Zedong Thought. Also known as the Four Upholds, the Four Basic Principles, or simply the Four Principles.

I do have an observation on a related point, namely that a democratic society must be pluralistic. This applies not only to governments and leaders, but also to private individuals. Above all else, in a democracy you must recognize the existence of opposing viewpoints and permit those views to be expressed. Respect for the opinion of your opponent is a crucial requirement. During elections in Western countries there are heated debates, but when the elections are over, the winner and the loser congratulate each other and acknowledge each other's existence. There is no talk of the winner annihilating the loser. Pluralism is about allowing people to have different beliefs. Society is complex. The will of the majority must be respected, but it may be that the minority turns out to be right nonetheless. This is all the more reason to insist on mutual respect.

In the West, people have the capacity to disagree strongly while still respecting each other's views. But here the protracted influence of feudal culture has instilled in the Chinese a strong sense of orthodoxy. We think there must be an absolutely correct answer to any question, and that any other answer is wrong. If we're in a debate and I claim to be right, it's tantamount to saying that you are wrong. Such an absolutist mentality has not prevailed in the West. I might be right, and you might also be right. In a pluralistic society, there is no absolute good and evil, no orthodox correct response to every question.

Many of the excesses perpetrated in the name of the Four Big Freedoms derive from this absolutist mentality. Democracy is hard to establish in such an environment. Democracy can be maintained only where there is a high level of culture; it requires tolerance and the recognition of opposing viewpoints. I welcome the expression of all kinds of views, even those I consider conservative or feudalistic. We must be equipped with such a mentality if there is to be any real hope for the reform of our society.

Question: Could you talk briefly about the theory of the expanding universe? If we admit that the universe is expanding, does this mean that it has boundaries? And does this mean that the concept of space and time in Marxist philosophy will have to be revised?

Fang: This question involves the whole field of cosmology, so I can give only a very brief response here. The expansion of the universe does not necessarily mean that the universe has boundaries. These are two separate matters. But developments in modern cosmology have indeed superseded the concepts of space and time found in the Marxist classics. In this regard Marxist philosophy is already undergoing revision.

DEMOCRACY, REFORM, AND MODERNIZATION

The following is the text of Fang's best-known speech, delivered to an audience of about three thousand students and faculty members at Shanghai's Tongji University on November 18, 1986, and the ensuing question-and-answer period. Many of the remarks in this speech were later singled out for criticism by the Communist Party as examples of bourgeois liberal thought. (A few passages that overlap extensively with material in previous selections have been deleted.)

Yesterday a few Tongji students came to find me at Jiaotong University, and started asking me some big questions—the prospects for political reform, the role intellectuals should play in the reform process, the shortcomings that college students of the 1980s must address in order to meet the challenges of the future. There is much to each of these questions, and my talk today will only begin to address them. According to the bulletin board outside, I'm speaking on "Democracy, Reform, and Modernization." Let me turn this around and discuss these topics in reverse order.

Our goal at present is the thorough modernization of China. We all have a compelling sense of the need for modernization. There is a widespread demand for change among people in all walks of life; and very few find any reason for complacency. None feel this more strongly than those of us in science and academia. Modernization has been our national theme since the

Gang of Four were overthrown ten years ago, but we are just beginning to understand what it really means. In the beginning we were mainly aware of the grave shortcomings in our production of goods, our economy, our science and technology, and that modernization was required in these areas. But now we understand our situation much better. We realize that grave shortcomings exist not only in our "material civilization" but also in our "spiritual civilization"—our culture, our ethical standards, our political institutions—and that these also require modernization.

The question we must now ask is, what kind of modernization is required? I think it's obvious to all of us that we need complete modernization, not just modernization in a few chosen aspects. People are now busy comparing Chinese and Western culture—including politics, economics, science, technology, education, the whole gamut—and there is much debate over the subject. The question is, do we want "complete Westernization" or "partial Westernization"? Should we continue to uphold the century-old banner of "using Western methods but maintaining the Chinese essence," or any other "cardinal principle"? Of course this is not a new discussion. A century ago, insightful people realized that China had no choice but to modernize. Some wanted partial modernization, others wanted complete modernization, and thus they initiated a debate that continues down to the present day.

I personally agree with the "complete Westernizers." What their so-called "complete Westernization" means to me is complete openness, the removal of restrictions in every sphere. We need to acknowledge that when looked at in its entirety, our culture lags far behind that of the world's most advanced societies, not in any one specific aspect but across the board. Responding to this situation calls not for the establishment of *a priori* barriers, but for complete openness to the outside world. Attempting to set our inviolable "essence" off limits before it is even challenged makes no sense to me. Again, I am scarcely inventing these ideas. A century ago people said essentially the same thing: Open China up and face the challenge of more advanced societies head on, in every aspect from technology to politics. What is good will stand up, and what is not good will be swept away. This prognosis remains unchanged.

Why is China so backward? To answer this question, we need to take a clear look at history. China has been undergoing revolutions for a century, but we are still very backward. This is all the more true since Liberation, these decades of the socialist revolution that we all know firsthand as students and workers. Speaking quite dispassionately, I have to judge this era a failure. This is not my opinion only, by any means; many of our leaders are also admitting as much, saying that socialism is in trouble everywhere. Since the end of World War II, socialist countries have by and large not been successful. There is no getting around this. As far as I'm concerned, the last thirty-odd years in China have been a failure in virtually every aspect of economic and political life.

Of course, some will say that China is a big, poor country, and therefore that progress is hard to come by. Indeed, our overpopulation, our huge geographical area, and our pre-existing poverty do contribute to our problems. This being the case, some say, we haven't done badly to get to where we are today.

But these factors by themselves don't completely account for the situation. For every one of them you can find a counterexample. Take population, for example. While our population is the world's largest in terms of absolute numbers, our population density is not. China has about 750 persons depending on each square kilometer of arable land, while Japan has about twice that, some 1,500 persons per square kilometer. Why has Japan succeeded while China has not? Our initial conditions were not that different; after the war, their economy was nearly as devastated as ours. Why have we not prospered like Japan? Overpopulation alone does not explain this.

Similarly, some will argue that China has done well to attain its present level of development when you consider its prior poverty. Yet this doesn't really wash either. Comparisons involving other socialist countries make the problem with this argument very clear. Consider the contrast between the two Germanys, and especially between the two Berlins. I visited East and West Berlin for two days, and the visit made a profound impression on me. There is a high wall dividing Berlin. On the West Berlin side there are few guard posts. When West Berliners want to go East, there are few formalities; we bought tourist tickets, and the lone guard at the nearly deserted border crossing languidly waved us across. On the West Berlin side there was an extraordinary abundance of goods. Then we went into East Berlin, which didn't seem too bad at first, as the architecture is magnificent; East Berlin contains the former governmental center of Berlin, with beautiful buildings such as the Reichstag and the museums. But we could see through the store windows that there was little on the shelves. The people seemed very somber, reluctant to have much to do with you. . . . On our return from East to West, it was announced that everyone had to get off the bus for inspection. Guards searched the bus inside and out, looking to see who was trying to escape by hiding underneath it. Why should a good society fear that its people are going to run away? If you're so good, people will be trying to get in, not out. This is simple logic.

My intention in telling this story is not to condemn the East Germans. However, as scientists we know that the first thing we have to acknowledge is where we have failed. If we want to see improvement, we must start by having the courage to admit our failures. And the socialist system in China over the last thirty-odd years has been exactly that, a failure. This is the reality we face. No one says it, or at least not outright, but in terms of its actual accomplishments, orthodox socialism from Marx and Lenin to Stalin and Mao Zedong has been a failure.

We need to take a careful look at why socialism has failed. Socialist ideals are admirable. But we have to ask two questions about the way they have been put into practice: Are the things done in the name of socialism actually socialist? And, do they make any sense? We have to take a fresh look at these questions, and the first step in that process is to free our minds from the narrow confines of orthodox Marxism.

When I expressed these views at Beijing University last year, it was still a dangerous thing to do, and afterward there was an uproar. But now even Central Committee directives admit the narrow-mindedness of Marxist propaganda. What do I mean by narrow-minded?

I have been in academia for a long time, so I've been subjected to a lot of propaganda. I've always had the feeling, even though we claim that Marxism embraces all contributions to civilization down through the ages, that when you really get down to it, we're saying that only since Marx has anyone known the real truth. Sometimes even Marx himself is tossed aside, and all that counts is what's happened since Liberation. Everything else is treated very negatively. Anything from the past, or from other cultures, is denigrated. We are very familiar with this attitude. When a historical figure is discussed, there is always a disclaimer at the end: "Despite this person's contributions, he suffered from historical limitations." In other words, he wasn't quite of the stature of us Marxists.

This is typical. When scholars of other races or nationalities make great discoveries, we'll say that they've done some good things, but due to the limitations of their class background, thus-and-so. In one area after another, it is made to appear that only since Liberation have truly great things been accomplished. This is parochial and narrow-minded in the extreme. What became of embracing the contributions of other cultures? We see ourselves towering over the historical landscape, but the fact is, nothing can justify such a claim. Only religions view their place in history in this fashion.

Let me give an example. Last month the fiftieth anniversary of the Long March was commemorated. The Long March was indeed a praiseworthy event in which many people suffered great hardship in their pursuit of the truth, marching from Jiangxi to the Northwest. But the propaganda about it referred to the Long March as "historically unprecedented," a deed that could not have been accomplished by ordinary mortals. Such talk evokes a counterreaction in people. One wants to ask, is it really true that in all of history there is nothing to compare with the Long March? The fact is, there *are* comparable occurrences, even in Chinese history itself. I would like to offer the example of the Long March of Xuan Zang,* in which he traveled to the "Western Paradise" to obtain the sacred Buddhist scriptures. His Long March was also in the pursuit of high ideals. Xuan Zang holds an important place in the cultural history of the world, yet in China today he has become a nonentity.

I have been to Pakistan. Xuan Zang went through Pakistan on his way to India and is held in high esteem there. After traveling all over, he finally arrived at India's greatest center of Buddhist learning. Having gone there to obtain the sutras, he studied Buddhism, and so great was his learning that he soon became the second-ranking teacher in the whole academy. At this academy, advancement in Buddhist scholarship depended not on the favoritism of superiors, but on skill in debate; if you debated well, you advanced, and otherwise you did not. I don't know if the historical records are exaggerating or not, but what they claim is that

---

*The story of Xuan Zang's journey to India (ca. 7th century A.D.) to obtain the Buddhist scriptures has long been a subject of Chinese folklore. A highly fictionalized and allegorical account of his adventures in the company of the magician-king of the monkeys was set down in the sixteenth-century epic *Journey to the West*.

Xuan Zang debated with hundreds of people there, and none could better him. This was the source of his fame.

One important historian of science says that in the history of science and civilization, every half century more or less there is one individual who can be used to symbolize the period (for example, Aristotle can be used to symbolize the period from 350 to 300 B.C.). In this scholar's history, which is recognized by both the scientific and historical communities as well written and objective, only two Chinese are offered as symbols of their respective half centuries. One is Yi Xing,* the other is Xuan Zang, who represents the period A.D. 650–700. Thus he is recognized by people around the world for his contributions. In terms of its significance for civilization, his quest was no less important than the Long March. The Long March is simply not "historically unprecedented."

Our narrow-mindedness is a consequence of feudalism and its associated attitudes: No one but yourself is legitimate or worthy of respect. We must forsake this narrow framework and open our eyes to the world. We should look with humility at what others have to offer, and what is good we should try to incorporate. Complete openness, allowing the outside world to challenge our way of doing things, is the only way to change our society. We need to take an objective look at what's really out there, and then decide what to believe and what we want or don't want. But not before then. When I saw East and West Berlin with my own two eyes, I couldn't help but be affected by it. If we could quit bolting our doors and proclaiming that everything here is wonderful, and instead open our eyes to the richly varied outside world, we would not remain so narrow-minded.

Leninism and Stalinism face grave problems and are in serious

---

*A Buddhist monk of the Tang dynasty, astronomer and mathematician. In A.D. 725 he determined the position of the ecliptic and established the imperial calendar.

need of reform. But is the whole socialist movement in the same boat? No, in fact. The socialist movement, from the inception of Utopian socialist thought on down to Marx, from the Paris Commune to the October Revolution and beyond, has included many different streams. There have been diverse approaches to socialism, some of which make a great deal of sense. Farsighted and committed people around the world have sought to study the problems of society, to initiate social movements. Some were more successful than others.

For example, this past July I went to a conference in Sweden. The Swedes say their country is socialist. And, indeed, why not? One way of defining socialism is as a system of public ownership, and another is as a system with little disparity between its richest and poorest members. Sweden meets both these criteria: more than half of all ownership is public, and the gap between rich and poor is relatively small. The level of state ownership in many countries of Northern Europe, and in fact in Europe generally, is quite high. Scandinavia and Austria are 70 to 80 percent nationalized. . . . Moreover, Sweden's GNP is very high, about $19,000 per capita. China cannot even compare to this. Sweden's social welfare far surpasses our own; it is the archetypal welfare state. The Swedes care for their citizens essentially from cradle to grave.

In ideological terms, they also profess to follow Marx (though not Lenin, which makes a big difference). I've seen Swedish art that contains "propaganda" about their party history. I went to a major art gallery and saw three big murals there. The first told how the pioneers of the Social Democratic Party went to spread their message among the workers and incite uprisings. The second mural displayed marches, strikes, confrontations with police, and so on, though the Social Democrats' ultimate success came through parliamentary struggles. The third mural showed Sweden's present way of life and its benefits: people with enough food to eat and clothes to wear, vacations from work, time to sunbathe, and so forth. They also have this kind of ideological propaganda. With the murals were oil paintings of the Paris Commune and similar themes. In another vein, Swedes think that television should be a tool of education, not of commercial pollution, and therefore advertisements are prohibited. Comparing Sweden to China, we can see that its ideology and propaganda both have a strongly socialist flavor.

The Swedish Social Democratic Party broke with Lenin at the Second International. Lenin opposed the Second International and called the Social Democrats "renegades." We have stood by Lenin ever since, holding that nothing accomplished by these renegades is worth discussing. But we need to look at what other people are doing, whether they are renegades or not, and see how they deal with their problems. Isn't "practice the sole criterion of truth"? What kind of progress have they made, and how does it compare with the socialist ideal? Have they backslid, or have they in fact surpassed us? The fact is, Swedish society is actually much more stable and developed than ours, and we should admit it.

Sweden was once a poor country, quite comparable to Russia. But, as some Swedes told me, while China and the Soviet Union were busy implementing the dictatorship of the proletariat and destroying the bourgeois class, Sweden was traveling a different path. The Swedes acknowledged the existence of classes and class conflict, but they sought to reconcile these conflicts through compromise and mediation. Half a century later Sweden also eliminated a class, but it wasn't the bourgeoisie—it was the proletariat! The bulk of its population became middle class. Does the Swedish experience have anything to offer us? I'm a physicist, and my true interest is in the distant realm of cosmology, but I know that there is something very substantial and worth studying in the Swedish example. Unfortunately we remain wedded to archaic beliefs and thus continue to see things in a very perverse light.

Much of what is wrong with socialism comes from subscribing to obsolete ideas, ideas without basis in either theory or fact. Yet we never change, because we've lived with these notions so long that we are no longer aware of them. I am like this myself. I used to think that many of our problems were just a consequence of the way things are, part of the natural order. But going abroad has changed my perspective drastically. Socialism has failed in China. Certainly there are many reasons for this failure, but beyond the shadow of a doubt, much of what we have done here is neither progressive nor socialist. On the contrary, it has been extremely backward and feudalistic.

We've talked about the need for modernization and reform, so now let's consider democracy. Our understanding of the concept of democracy is so inadequate that we can barely even discuss it. With our thinking so hobbled by old dogmas, it is no wonder we don't achieve democracy in practice. Not long ago it was constantly being said that calling for democracy was equivalent to requesting that things be "loosened up." In fact the word "democracy" is quite clear, and it is poles apart in meaning from "loosening up." If you want to understand democracy, look at how people understand it in the developed countries, and compare that to how people understand it here, and then decide for yourself what's right and what's wrong.

I think that the key to understanding democracy lies first of all in recognizing the rights of each individual. Democracy is built from the bottom up. Every individual possesses certain rights, or to use what is a very sensitive expression indeed in China, everyone has "human rights." We seldom dare to utter the words "human rights," but actually human rights are very basic.

What are these human rights? That everyone from birth has the right to live, the right of existence. From birth I have a right to think. Of course, I have a brain; a severely mentally handicapped person may not be capable of possessing this right. I want to learn, and I have the right to an education. I have the right to find a mate, to get married. And so forth. This is what human rights are. In China we talk about human rights as if they were something fearful, a terrible scourge. In reality they are commonplace and basic, and everyone ought to acknowledge them.

But perhaps we are starting to view the spiritual aspects of civilization a little differently. We are beginning to see "liberty, equality, and fraternity" as a positive spiritual heritage. Over the last thirty years it seemed that every one of these good words— liberty, equality, fraternity, democracy, human rights—was labeled bourgeois by our propaganda. What on earth did that leave for us? Did we really oppose all of these things? If anything we should outdo bourgeois society and surpass its performance in human rights, not try to deny that human rights exist.

Democracy is based on recognizing the rights of every single individual. Naturally, not everyone wants the same thing, and therefore the desires of different individuals have to be mediated through a democratic process, to form a society, a nation, a collectivity. But it is only on the foundation of recognizing the humanity and the rights of each person that we can build democracy. However, when we talk about "extending democracy" here, it refers to your superiors "extending democracy" for you. This is a mistaken concept. This is not democracy.

"Loosening up" is even worse. If you think about it, what it implies is that everyone is tied up very tightly right now, but if you stay put, we'll loosen the rope a little bit and let you run around. The rope used to be one foot long, now we'll make it five feet. This is a top-down approach. Democracy is first and foremost the rights of individuals, and it is individuals that must struggle for them. Expressions like "extending democracy" and "loosening up" would have you think that democracy can be bestowed upon us by those in charge. Nothing could be further from the truth.

The newspaper often refers to National People's Congress (NPC) representatives coming for an "inspection" tour. At times we speak sloppily ourselves, talking about "inspections." But think about it: Why should a visit from a People's Congress representative be called an inspection? We have become accustomed to talking this way, but it couldn't be more mistaken. These people are our elected representatives, who supposedly listen to us and speak on our behalf at the People's Congress, so why should their visit be called an "inspection"? Simply to use the word "inspection" reveals contempt for democracy. But of course, our NPC representatives do not actually represent our opinions, and in fact I don't even know who my representative is.

Why bother with this comparison? At one time I thought that it was perfectly natural for big officials from the NPC to come "inspect" us. But during the first half of this year, I was at the Institute for Advanced Study, in Princeton, New Jersey, doing research in cosmology. While I was there I received a mailing from our local member of Congress, explaining what Congress had been up to lately and what he had been doing during the session. He wrote quite a bit about his voting record, explaining what he'd voted for and against. He spoke about his achievements in office, how he had gone on the record for this or that, and why he had done so. In short, he was "reporting" to us. Although I was only a temporary resident, he had sent me this material, showing respect for anyone living in his district. He wanted us to know how he stood on the issues, and whether we agreed with him; if not, we could raise our concerns and he could turn around and express these in Congress. Despite representing a "false democracy," this man was clearly accounting to me for his actions.

Now what about our "true democracy"? I have never received any document telling me what issues my representative talked about, or how he or she voted at the NPC. I have never known what my representative supported or opposed, or what his or her accomplishments in office were. And the next time I have to go cast my vote for this person, I will still be totally in the dark. Our "true democracy" had better get on the ball until it can do better than their "false democracy"! I lived in China a long time without being aware of these problems. But when I went abroad and was finally able to see for myself, the contrast was glaringly obvious.

In democratic countries, democracy begins with the individual. *I* am the master, and the government is responsible to *me*. Citizens of democracies believe that the people maintain the government, paying taxes in return for services—running schools and hospitals, administering the city, providing for the public welfare. . . . A government depends on the taxpayers for support and therefore *has to be* responsible to its citizens. This is what people think in a democratic society. But here in China, we think the opposite way. If the government does something commendable, people say, "Oh, isn't the government great for providing us with public transportation." But this is really something it *ought* to be doing in exchange for our tax money. . . . You have to be clear about who is supporting whom economically, because setting this straight leads to the kind of thinking that democracy requires. Yet China is so feudalistic that we always expect superiors to give orders and inferiors to follow them. What our "spiritual civilization" lacks above all other things is the spirit of democracy. If you want reform—and there are more reforms needed in our political institutions than I have time to talk about—the most crucial thing of all is to have a democratic mentality and a democratic spirit.

An experience that I had in France exemplified the democratic spirit for me. Western Europe is now undergoing a lot of terrorist activity, and people are worried about it; there is strong public opinion in favor of a crackdown against terrorism. A Chinese graduate student in France told me that a recent wave of violence there, such as airport bombings, had led to proposed legislation requiring citizens to report anyone they suspect of involvement in terrorist activities to the police immediately. This seems natural to us in China: Sound the alarm, and put the whole country on alert. Therefore, I just assumed that the French would pass this law. But the student, to my great surprise, told me that after this bill was proposed, the National Assembly discussed it for a while and then voted it down. Why? The members obviously didn't veto it because they approve of terrorism. No, their reasoning was that such a law would create informers, and the appearance of informers is the worst thing that can happen to a democratic society, an affront to human dignity and the right to privacy. The French Assembly refused to allow its citizens to be subjected to casual suspicion.

In China, if I suspect that you harbor bad intentions, I'll just trot over and "make a report," and never think twice about it. In fact, such behavior is praised for demonstrating "a high sense of alertness," and "an elevated class consciousness." But it also runs completely counter to democracy, and it demonstrates a lack of comprehension about fundamental human rights. No one should be subjected to casual suspicion or forced to live under constant terror. But in China people have long lived in perpetual terror, afraid of someone reporting on them even when they have done nothing wrong. If I look suspicious in the least, whether I've done anything or not, you'll rush right out and report me. Democracy will never take root in such an environment. I finally grasped this when I heard the story about France and could see for the first time how backward my own ideas were. I had lived in China so long that I had become accustomed to the idea that informing on people is normal. But the French felt that the existence of informers would endanger a democracy. It is experiences like this that make us understand what a democratic society is all about.

In democratic societies, democracy and science—and most of us here are scientists—run parallel. Democracy is concerned with ideas about humanity, and science is concerned with nature. One of the distinguishing features of universities is the role of knowledge; we do research, we create new knowledge, we apply this knowledge to developing new products, and so forth. In this domain, within the sphere of science and the intellect, we make our own judgments based on our own independent criteria.

This is the distinguishing characteristic of a university. In Western society, universities are independent from the government, in the sense that even if the money to run the school is provided by the government, the basic decisions—regarding the content of courses, the standards for academic performance, the selection of research topics, the evaluation of results, and so on—are made by the schools themselves on the basis of values endemic to the academic community, and not by the government. At the same time, good universities in the West are also independent of big business. This is how universities must be. The intellectual realm must be independent and have its own values.

This is an essential guarantee of democracy. It is only when you know something independently that you are free from relying on authorities outside the intellectual domain, such as the government. Unfortunately, things are not this way in China. I have discussed this problem with educators. In the past, even during "the seventeen years" [1949 to 1966, the era prior to the Cultural Revolution], our universities were mainly engaged in producing tools, not in educating human beings. Education was not concerned with helping students to become critical thinkers, but with producing docile instruments to be used by others. Chinese intellectuals need to insist on thinking for themselves and using their own judgment, but I'm afraid that even now we have not grasped this lesson.

In physics, for example, you'd assume that the evaluation of physicists is what matters in determining the merits of one's research. But in China, the work of physicists has long been subject to the evaluation of officials who know nothing about physics, and moreover we're ecstatic if they deign to say a few good words about us. This leads to a "docile tool" mentality that is still a major problem. Things are even worse in the social sciences. Naturally, we physicists check out the latest "philosophical" writings in order to keep ourselves out of hot water, but much of the writing of philosophers and social scientists in this country is little more than recapitulation of the latest official pronouncements. If our leaders were experts in philosophy—or experts in anything, for that matter—their words might carry some weight as academic authorities. But if they aren't philosophers, what is the value of quoting them? This is a worthless enterprise and it doesn't prove a thing, but we quote the leaders nonetheless because we need the sanction of political authority before we dare to open our mouths.

The opposite relationship obtains in the West. At Princeton I met with some Chinese economists. They delved into their subject in whatever manner they saw fit, and they came up with whatever theories they found appropriate, without any interference. But contrary to our situation in China, when the American government was making policy, it requested the opinions of these academics; the government wanted to know if they had obtained any relevant results on which to base policy. What a far cry from our situation—officials needing the sanction of college professors to lend them credibility! This is what I mean by intellectual independence. Knowledge must be independent from power, the power of the state included. If knowledge is subservient to power, it is worthless.

. . .

I think that recently there has been a turn for the better, especially in the resolution on "spiritual civilization."* This document refers to the need for Marxist guidance in developing new ideals, in establishing our legal system, and in other areas, but it no longer calls for Marxist direction of scientific research. That tenet has been abolished. At the least, Marxism will no longer direct our research in the natural sciences; it has no place there. Of course it can *participate*; the policy is one of "letting a hundred schools of thought contend" within the domain of science, and Marxism is one school. But it is no longer in the position of lording it over everything else, and if anyone claims to you that it is, you can just point to this document.

Not only is such "guidance" mistaken even in principle, but in actual practice the philosophical guidance usually amounts to nothing more than whatever the leaders happen to be saying at the moment. Every single "academic critique" undertaken since Liberation has been wrong, without exception.† We currently witness much less of this kind of thing, but it still happens from time to time. We run into it sometimes in my field. I will not tolerate political interference in academic research! I work in cosmology. I am an assistant editor of *Science Digest*. Last year I published an article introducing quantum cosmology, which is a new theory. Whether this theory is correct or not is something

---

*The "Resolution on Guiding Principles for Building Socialist Spiritual Civilization" was issued by the Sixth Plenary Session of the Twelfth Communist Party Congress, held in September 1986.
†This refers to the interventions of Marxist theoreticians into scientific debates in such areas as genetics, relativity, quantum mechanics, and demography.

that we can decide using the methods of our field. We can ask whether or not it makes theoretical sense, and we can test it against our observations. We can accept it, we can revise it, and we can even reject it outright; all these things are legitimate. This is the process by which science works. Nevertheless, as a result of publishing this article, the editorial board received a letter, which came from a Very High Place. It said that our introduction of quantum cosmology was "objective idealism." They were meddling again! Of course, if a scientist wants to criticize the theory, to agree or disagree, that's fine. But today there is no longer any market, at least not in the scientific community, for the authorities to use "philosophical" labels to suppress someone's work. This was true even at the tensest moments last year.

When we received the letter in December, the physicists on the editorial board decided to ignore it. If the author had wanted to express his disagreement in a scientific paper, or to argue his case using some kind of scientific methods, of course we would have published it. But if he's going to argue philosophy, using the arrogant methods of Marxist "guidance," then we will not! We have our own standards when it comes to science, to physics, to cosmology. What does his philosophy have to do with us? Of course, the author of the letter was very high up indeed, none other than our nation's ideological generalissimo, Hu Qiaomu. Even so, we ignored him.

We have our own independent values. If you know some physics, then we can have a debate; we're more than willing to do that. But if you don't know physics, then step aside! This is the kind of spirit that scientists must have if democracy is to be safeguarded. When it comes to our fields of knowledge, we must think for ourselves and exercise our own judgment about what's right and wrong, and about truth, goodness, and beauty as well. We must refuse to cater to power. Only when we do this will Chinese intellectuals be transformed into genuine intellectuals, and our country have a chance to modernize and attain real democracy. This is my message to you today.

. . .

Question: Last summer in a speech at Zhejiang University you called Beijing Vice Mayor Zhang Baifa an idle junketer. Now they want you to apologize to the city of Beijing. Do you think you should apologize? Have you already?

Fang: Let me correct something. First of all, I did refer to Zhang Baifa by name, but it was not in a speech at Zhejiang—it was elsewhere.* I did not call him an idle junketer; I simply recounted the facts of the situation. Last October there was a conference in the United States on synchrotron radiation, attended by a twenty-five-member delegation [from China]. The University of Science and Technology of China (USTC) was one place involved from the outset, because it is currently building a synchrotron accelerator, and another place that needed to send people was the Institute of High Energy Physics. These two places should have been the main ones involved, but in fact USTC and the Institute sent only five people each. The remaining fifteen were all from other units, not from USTC or the Institute. Of course some other people, such as foreign-affairs officers, needed to go. But among the others was Zhang Baifa. All I said was that Zhang Baifa doesn't know anything about synchrotron radiation.

The next day there was a phone call to Hefei, demanding that I apologize to Beijing. I didn't take the call; it was received by our USTC president, Comrade Guan Weiyan. Comrade Guan stood right up to them and said, "Comrade Fang Lizhi has no need to apologize." Last month Guan Weiyan and I went to the

---

*Fang's remarks about Zhang Baifa came in a speech at Beijing University on November 4, 1985.

Chinese Academy of Sciences and told them why what we did was right, and why allowing Zhang Baifa to go on the trip was wrong.

Question: It was because of this that Hu Qiaomu asked, "What headquarters do the leaders of USTC belong to?" Do you think this is any kind of thing for a national leader to say?

Fang: I think that the recent newspaper articles* on democratic education at USTC were a way of going on the record about his comments.

Question: Is Hu Qili† the behind-the-scenes patron of USTC?

Fang: Not that I know of. USTC doesn't have a patron, it has itself. We have our own independent standards of value.

Question: What is your relationship to Hu Qili? We've heard that Hu Qili was chairman of the Beijing University Student Association, and that you were a department head in that organization. Is that true?

Fang: Indeed Hu Qili was chairman of the Student Association, but I was never a department head. As far as my relationship with Hu Qili goes, it was only once, during a little fracas in 1955, that he might have known who I was. The commotion happened in a Youth League Congress. Some other third-year students and I found the meeting very oppressive, just a bunch of formulaic talk. We were all "Three Goods"‡ students, doing well in everything,

---

*Refers to a series of articles entitled "Running Education Democratically at the University of Science and Technology" in the *People's Daily* on October 22, 26, and 31, and November 4 and 14, 1986.

†Politburo member specializing in cultural matters and propaganda, considered a reformist. Hu was removed from his post following the crackdown on the democracy movement in June 1989.

‡Good health, good academic performance, and good moral character.

but somehow we weren't really satisfied. So we decided to liven things up a bit.

We discussed it and decided that on the second day, when the physics department general branch secretary took the podium— of course the branch secretary was in on the plan, he was one of our classmates—he would let me go up there and grab the mike to make a statement, since I had the loudest voice. And so when the branch secretary was speaking, I sprang up, grabbed the mike, and started speaking. We really did have this one well planned.

I said, "This meeting is boring and depressing. We should be discussing how young people are being educated. I think that young people should be raised to think for themselves. The 'Three Goods' are not enough, even though we're all 'Three Goods' students. The expression 'Three Goods' itself is depressing." After I spoke, the meeting was really in an uproar, and as a consequence no one else was even able to speak. The auditorium was in pandemonium.

The next day, the first Party secretary, Comrade Jiang Longji, spoke all day. He said that independent thinking was all well and good, but what we needed right then was to calm down and get back to studying. Afterward we went through some more ideological training. Now, that was 1955, so it could be that Hu Qili still has an impression of me from that. Those of us who created this little ruckus were all labeled rightists during the Anti-Rightist Campaign.*

Question: It's said that because of your speech at Zhejiang University, you're being pressured to resign from the Party. Is that true? Did you have any misgivings about coming to talk to us today?

Fang: Nobody has mentioned my name directly, but I have heard that a major personage at the December 9 commemorative in

*See Glossary.

Beijing commented that a certain university vice president has been talking too much, and ought to resign from the Party. As far as my having misgivings goes, do any of you have misgivings about listening to me? Frankly, during the Anti-Rightist Campaign those doing the speaking were made rightists, and those doing the listening were *also* made rightists.

Question: In the final analysis, is the bourgeois class reactionary or not?

Fang: During the period of feudalism, the capitalist class is extraordinarily progressive. It is revolutionary.

Question: If capitalist society exploits surplus value, why hasn't there been any overthrow at all of the capitalist scheme by the working people in the developed countries?

Fang: Haven't we been preaching Marxism-Leninism to them, inciting them to rebel? . . . Actually, we're finding that many of our old beliefs about capitalism no longer apply. What manner of thing *is* capitalism? What is Western Europe really like, or America? People don't really know, and the old concepts from the days of Marx and Lenin no longer fit. A Chinese who had been in Sweden for some time told me that he had recently started to read Lenin's works on the corruption and decline of imperialism. Immediately, he began to wonder who it was really referring to. Which system is actually corrupt and in decline was not so clear. . . .

Question: It's said that the policy of requiring students to pay their own way abroad was promoted by senior professors who were worried that they would no longer have any assistants left to work for them. Because of this, many people lost the chance to go abroad.

Fang: I support openness. There is really no need to worry that China will run out of people. There are plenty of intelligent people in China. We know that 20,000 to 30,000 people have left Taiwan, and Taiwan's economy has not been detrimentally affected; in fact, it has flourished. Right now there are about 20,000 students from the mainland in the United States, a few less than from Taiwan. We went to a dozen schools in the United States, and what we saw bore this out, about the same number of mainland students as Taiwanese, or a few less. There is no reason to get concerned about all our talent leaving, with so many young people in China who would jump at the chance to go to school if they had an opportunity, and who would be every bit as smart as those they replaced. Wait until about three million have gone—it still won't be too late to worry.

Question: Do you think socialism or capitalism is more appropriate for Chinese conditions?

Fang: As our understanding of socialism and capitalism has become less monolithic, the meaning of this question has become less clear. . . . What is socialism? Is it the orthodox kind, the Second International kind, or some other kind? Which one is the "real" socialism? The same question applies to capitalism. There is free-market capitalism, and there is Western European capitalism, in which the state plays a major role. With all the social services and social welfare of today, capitalism is very different from the classical Marxist conception of it.

I can only say that classical capitalism and classical socialism for the most part no longer exist. We need to look at what actually exists in today's world. Societies can no longer be neatly divided into socialist and capitalist, and absolutely not into the Cold War divisions of Western bloc and Eastern bloc. There is a multitude of different economic forms, and they merit our serious investigation.

Question: Is the current emphasis on the "Four Cardinal Principles" a necessity for developing our productive forces, or a fallacy based on the personal feelings of the leadership?

Fang: I think that the Four Cardinal Principles are a political article of faith. Not long ago, in September, a newspaper ran a story on my opinions about the kind of atmosphere that should prevail in a university. I said that a university should have a spirit of science, democracy, creativity, and independence. After the reporter had finished transcribing what I had said, he sent me a note. It said, "This spirit is very good, but you had better say a little more, because people might interpret what you're saying as reflecting on the Four Cardinal Principles. There are four of them, and you mention four things—it could be a little dangerous." He said, "Maybe you could just add a couple of sentences that let people know what you really mean." So afterward, I sent him back a letter saying that I would add a paragraph.

What I advocated was that a university must possess a spirit of science, of democracy, of creativity, and of independence— four things. Now there are some people who are oversensitive about the "Four Upholds." They're always looking to see if a statement contradicts the Four Upholds. As soon as they see anything that comes in fours, they want to know if it is meant to contradict the Four Upholds. So what I added was this: "Is it possible that science, democracy, creativity, and independence are in conflict with the Four Upholds? If so, it's because the Four Upholds advocate the opposite of science, which is superstition; the opposite of democracy, which is dictatorship; the opposite of creativity, which is conservatism; and the opposite of independence, which is dependency." This was the paragraph that I added. The reporter said that it was even worse than the previous version.

I think we have to go all out in fostering this spirit. If somebody confronts you on it, ask them right back, "Do you mean to say that the Four Upholds are in conflict with science and democracy? If they are in conflict with science, democracy, and so on, then it must be because the Four Upholds advocate superstition, dictatorship, conservatism, and dependency." You tell them that, and see how they respond.

Question: Is there any difference between Mao's patriarchy and Deng's patriarchy? Mao promoted six criteria for distinguishing "poisonous weeds" from "fragrant flowers"; Deng offers the Four Upholds. Aren't these both just ways of keeping the people in line?

Fang: I don't think they are the same. Those in my generation have lived through the "seventeen years" [from 1949 to 1966] and lived through the current era. If I'd said during the "seventeen years" what I'm saying now, I would have been ground into hamburger. China has made some progress.

Question: People should have the right to know their leaders' political attitudes, their level of comprehension, how they think. Why do we have to get these things indirectly, through foreign press reports and so on? Why can't we read public accounts of Deng Xiaoping? Why should our leaders, in a "people's republic," be veiled in mystery? All kinds of scandals and ruthless power struggles elude the control of the people. Isn't this the worst kind of mockery for the citizens of a republic to endure?

Fang: Of course it's a problem. In undemocratic or insufficiently democratic countries, what goes on in politics is often unseen by the people. The more democratic a society is, the more transparent. . . . China right now is like the universe in the early stages of its evolution—in a primordial haze.

Question: The methods of class analysis provide a theoretical basis for class struggle. Now is the time to discard this instrument of backwardness and narrow-mindedness. Why are some comrades, especially certain comrades in the leadership, still clutching to class analysis, unwilling to give it up? Please analyze this morbid fixation of theirs for us.

Fang: Even before the time of Marx there were economists who used a class perspective to analyze economic phenomena. This made sense on their part. Farther down the road, the economic evolved into the political, and this also made sense. But after this, and above all during the Cultural Revolution, class struggle was expanded without limit, and applied to everything in the world. This was obviously wrong.

I'll give you an example of how absurd it can be. For the past few years, I've been responsible for the physics curriculum at USTC. Now, the use of the Four Upholds to analyze politics is all right, because the Four Upholds belong to the political domain. But when I first looked over the instructional plan for physics, I discovered such statements on the syllabus as, "According to the Four Upholds . . ." this, and "According to class analysis . . ." that. I took one look and crossed them all out. They had no business there. I don't care what class you're a member of, Newton's Laws are Newton's Laws everywhere. There is no class analysis in natural science. As I just said, it's fine for Marxism to carry out class analysis in the political sphere, but don't try to "guide" our physics. When it comes to physics, get out of the way.

I think that an all-encompassing class analysis is a very crude way of looking at the world, a grand oversimplification. The fact is, the reason class struggle became so central for these thirty-odd years is that Comrade Mao Zedong put the stamp of class on everything after the Anti-Rightist Campaign. Of course some things have a class nature, such as economic relations, but some things do not. Placing class labels on everything in the universe is wrong.

Question: Lu Xun advocated reading foreign books instead of Chinese books. Does this idea hold any significance for the present? What sort of mentality should those working for reform possess?

Fang: Lu Xun* was one of the most radical figures of the May Fourth period. He was for complete Westernization, and so he urged people to read foreign books instead of Chinese books. He opposed the entire Chinese tradition. He called practitioners of Chinese medicine "witch doctors" and roundly cursed Chinese religion.

I think the mood of those people [in the May Fourth period] was desperate, and that their wish was for China to modernize very quickly. Their spirit is still worthy of our respect and admiration. As far as reading goes, I'd agree that you should read more foreign books. To go a step further, I hope that all of you have an opportunity to go abroad and have a look for yourselves. There is a Chinese saying that has it right: "What's real is what you see with your own eyes." Say whatever you like, but then go take a look and make your own comparisons. The change in many people's outlook, including my own, came from seeing the outside world. We discovered our backwardness and were enlightened. All our attitudes were challenged. Any person with normal intelligence can look and see for him- or herself. Once you take a look, the comparisons will be obvious.

Question: Do you have aspirations of vying to win the Nobel Prize and with it glory for China? Why is it that in China, people

---

*Chinese writer of the 1920s. See Glossary.

who are just as intelligent [as people elsewhere] cannot attain this great honor?

Fang: The failure of China to win a Nobel Prize is not due to Chinese people's lacking the capacity to win one. As far as the caliber of Chinese minds is concerned, there have already been four overseas Chinese who have won the prize. But we are limited by the conditions in our society. I think this fact all by itself shows that China is backward; no matter what you say, it is culturally backward.

Question: Why haven't we produced a Qian Xuesen* in these last thirty-odd years?

Fang: I have one obvious theory about that: With so many political mass movements, how *could* we produce a Qian Xuesen?

Question: Currently there are a lot of articles in magazines and periodicals criticizing the deep-rooted negative traits of the Chinese people. What do you think about this?

Fang: Among these writings you could point to Bo Yang's *The Ugly Chinaman,* or even to Lu Xun's *True Story of Ah Q.* My feeling is that there really *are* many problems in the psychological make-up and ethical practices of Chinese people. The characteristics Bo Yang† points to really do exist, and one might even say that he didn't go far enough. What I want to know is where these traits come from. I personally think that they are the psychological consequences of a long feudal tradition. I *don't* believe they are inborn characteristics; they can be changed. If they were produced by history, they can be undone by history. . . .

Some of our negative traits are a consequence of still being

---

*Senior Chinese physicist. See Glossary.
†Taiwanese writer. See Glossary.

under semifeudal rule today. The Chinese people's lack of unity is a very serious problem. What causes this? One characteristic of feudal rule is that the rulers want those at the bottom to fight with each other. If they're fighting with each other, it's much easier to maintain your position of power. And in fact you can still find those today who are hoping for the people to fight among themselves, so they can take advantage of both sides as they sit back and survey the situation from a safe distance. I think that we can get to the root of this problem, if we thoroughly democratize our society and allow Western culture to enter.

Question: How do you evaluate members of the current and older generations?

Fang: I think that there are generational differences. The generation that came of age in the 1950s was idealistic; for them everything was ideals, the Chinese people, the motherland. The subsequent generation doesn't share this feeling, for a very simple reason: Idealism was terribly abused during the 1950s, '60s, and '70s. Anyone who acted idealistically was toyed with, his or her life ruined. So the next generation—quite naturally—felt that idealism was idiotic. While I still think that idealism has some good points, the generation of the 1950s was educated during the "seventeen years" when the doctrine of turning people into tools was also very strong. This promoted a feudalistic mindset. Whether you're a tool of the Lei Feng* variety, or some other kind, you're still just a tool. All you can do is defend feudalism, not build a modern democratic society. I think that members of the current generation tend to view themselves less as tools, that they're more independent. That, at least, is more conducive to establishing a democratic society.

As for the generation gap between older and younger intellec-

*See Glossary.

tuals, I think there might be one in some senses, but not so extreme as some would have you believe. For instance, people my age are always telling me that young people want to leave the country, while they themselves are staying put, so there must be a generation gap. Actually, if you look at this issue in some detail, there isn't any gap. Certainly young people want to leave the country; this is because of the policy toward intellectuals. Of the young faculty at USTC, more than half has left. But is it true that middle-aged and older people don't want to leave? No. They want to leave, too, but their conditions and status are different. They have families and children, and when you get to be forty or older the competition to go abroad gets fierce, so you can't stay overseas for a long period. The difference is due to different conditions, not a generation gap.

As a matter of fact, there is a flood of people leaving the country. Research conditions here in China are inferior, and wages are so low that people want to go abroad and earn a little money before coming back. . . . If somebody gets a Ph.D. abroad and comes back, there's no telling right now what his life will be like. If he gets a Ph.D. and works for two years, he can come back with twenty or thirty thousand U.S. dollars, maybe a hundred thousand Chinese yuan, more than he'll make altogether for the rest of his life. Some people think that this is bad. What they should say instead is that the pay of intellectuals is too low, leaving them with no choice but to take this option if they can.

I have encountered many middle-aged Chinese intellectuals abroad, some of them very capable. One was a very skilled surgeon from Shanghai. You all know that most Chinese doctors can't practice in the United States, that physicians must be certified by the American Medical Association. Only a very few Chinese, who've been there a long time, can practice medicine. If you can't practice, then what do you do? Well, this surgeon went to work in a medical school laboratory, killing rats. This is tragic—I think that a physician reduced to killing rats is tragic in the extreme. China has produced someone of great skill who would rather stay in America and kill rats than come back to China. I think this is a result of our policy on intellectuals. Many middle-aged and older people are reduced to doing such things. There's no generation gap in this. The outlook across age groups is identical.

Question: Surely we can't pin our hopes on the Communist Party's reforming itself peacefully and carrying out "complete Westernization"? In your heart of hearts, do you really think that the Party can remove the cancer that has spread all through it? Or do we, in the end, need another people's revolution?

Fang: I think I can answer this question. The Communist Party faces a great many problems. Behind closed doors, the assessment is that even if the reforms are successful, the Party will still be in serious trouble. Some people will ask how I can say such things in public, but I think that the Party is in a situation where it has to reform whether it wants to or not. If all of China awakens to this fact, starting with all the students, and all the young intellectuals, and finally all the other intellectuals, then things will change. And if there were no change, the country would get rid of the Party.

Whether the Party reforms itself or not won't be determined by some leader, but by all the forces of history. We shouldn't think that the Party can remain totally isolated from the masses; it's impossible. The Cultural Revolution was a disaster, it's true, but in the end there arose the April Fifth Movement* that ultimately finished the Gang of Four. These events are not independent of history.

So when you ask if the Party is going to reform itself, you

*See Glossary, *Tiananmen Incident.*

have to look at the society as a whole. Of course, if the leaders are good, that's great. But even if the leaders aren't good, as long as the masses can slowly absorb the most progressive Western cultural influences, then there will be change, one way or another. Now, as to how change is achieved: Will it definitely take violence? I think—especially after seeing both the East and the West—that there are many pathways available. As soon as we think about change, we think of political power growing from the barrel of a gun. We are conditioned by our ideology to think that any kind of change requires a gun.

But I think that in the West, many reforms have succeeded without taking such a drastic course. They have followed the path of gradual reform. Reform is not an absolute impossibility. Last year was better than the year before, this year better than last year, and maybe next year will bring still more improvement. . . . Don't underestimate the power of incremental change.

THE DISSIDENT

Introduction by David A. Kelly

In 1989, the prospects for dissent in socialist bloc countries appeared very different than they do now. Figures such as Poland's Lech Walesa and Czechoslovakia's Vaclav Havel still faced uncertain and indeed dangerous futures. At the time of this writing, one year later, Walesa contests for national leadership, not with the Communist Party but with former Solidarity allies; Havel is the president of his country. They risk now, not the tanks of the Soviet army or the secret police of its local allies, but the wear and tear of democratic conflict and compromise.

Fang Lizhi, on the other hand, is now and for the foreseeable future an exile, exerting little direct influence over the day-to-day struggles of his compatriots. Yet events have shown that Fang's break with the rules limiting political participation, particularly after 1985, has been of no less historical significance within his own country than the actions of Sakharov, Walesa, and Havel in theirs.

The political success of the European dissidents is a very recent matter. For many years the conventional wisdom held that their quixotic endeavors were doomed to irrelevance, or worse yet, to endangering the sensible attempts of others to make piecemeal improvements of the repressive order from within. It is only in hindsight that the marginal-seeming human rights movements of the Eastern bloc can be seen as indispensable catalysts in wearing down post-Stalinist regimes. We are now seeing how these movements, operating mostly through clandestine networks, opened new zones of public awareness and thereby created new political forces. In addition to the obvious facts of impending economic collapse, writes one analyst,

> The insistence on the introduction of human rights into the Helsinki process resulted in the slow but inexorable diffusion of the principle into Soviet-type politics and contributed qualitatively to weakening the legitimating force of Marxism-Leninism. In effect human rights transcended the universalist claims of Marxism-Leninism and provided the central and Eastern European opposition with an intellectual basis from which to attack and thus erode the official system.*

Although we may not expect to see events in China follow the same trajectory as those in the Eastern bloc—given the historic weakness of Chinese civil society and its frameworks of legal culture, religious and trade union organization, and so on—the relevance to China of the recent turn of events has not been lost on observers either outside or inside that country, nor indeed on the Chinese leadership itself. Thus Fang's present status as "public enemy number one" in China is a function of more than Deng Xiaoping's personal hatred. Although he had meticulously avoided making direct contact with the democracy move-

---

*George Schöpflin, "The End of Communism in Eastern Europe," *International Affairs*, 66:1 (1990), 3–16.

ment in 1989,* Fang was nonetheless named the arch-conspirator behind it. This was not merely a matter of convenient scapegoating on the part of the authorities. For the Deng regime, Fang represents more than an occasional irritant: he threatens the whole of Deng's self-legitimating power structure.

To consider Fang in the light of East bloc dissidents is not to imply that history turns only on the actions of a few "big men," and still less to disparage the role of unknown individuals and faceless social movements in the ongoing transformations. On the contrary, it is often the case that the famous dissidents owe their role to two factors: on the one hand an endowment of talent, official connections, or both, sufficient to place them in a prominent social position; and on the other, a capacity to articulate the oppositional culture which develops spontaneously within the interstices and on the fringes of the official system.†

Along the first of these axes, Fang's similarities to Sakharov are obvious and widely alluded to.‡ Both are scientists, physicists whose abilities achieved international recognition. Both took early exception to the intellectual dogma of official Marxism and only later turned their attack on other aspects of the political order. Both seek to base their oppositional politics on universal values modeled on those of science (as in the article "Patriotism and Global Citizenship," see p. 244), rather than on culturally unique moral values in the manner of Solzhenitsyn. There are of course many differences, some due to their personal histories,

---

*Perry Link, "The Thought and Spirit of Fang Lizhi," in George Hicks, ed., *The Broken Mirror: China After Tiananmen* (London: Longmans, 1990), 100–114; see p. 103.
†For a useful overview of "post-totalitarian" culture see Jerry Goldfarb, *Beyond Glasnost: The Post-totalitarian Mind* (Chicago: Chicago University Press, 1989).
‡Orville Schell, "China's Andrei Sakharov," *The Atlantic Monthly,* May 1988, 35–52; much of this story appears in *Discos and Democracy: China in the Throes of Reform* (New York: Pantheon Books, 1988).

others to the differing responses of the Soviet and Chinese regimes. Fang was never subjected to internal exile as Sakharov was; on the other hand, Sakharov never lost his Academician status, whereas Fang was removed from the Chinese Academy of Sciences during his stay in the U.S. Embassy.* Perhaps decisive have been the differences in what each perceived to be possible under his respective regime and institutions.

While Fang has often posed his moral claims in strong and even heretical terms, his view of politics has been broad enough to encompass a variety of options; these include some forms of cooperation with the reformist establishment. For the earlier half of the 1980s, Fang was himself a member of the reformist intellectual elite, no more openly rebellious than others such as Yan Jiaqi, Su Shaozhi, and Wang Ruoshui. All, as Party members, made use of the prestige of science to push for a more liberal or pluralist ideology, but retained faith in the possibility of reforming the Party from within.† Even today Fang has not completely cut himself off from this position.

It was in 1985 that Fang crossed the line into open polemics with the conservative wing of the leadership, unable to reconcile his growing sense of what is true and good in science with official cant and corruption. Fang's fiery speeches to students, particularly those given at Shanghai campuses in late 1986, were outspoken to the point of recklessness. Thanks to the curious official policy of circulating "incriminating materials" to political study groups mandatory for most of the nation, these gained wide exposure

---

*Zu Wei, *"Yiran yang tian zhang xiao—Jianqiao ting Fang Lizhi xiao tan 'chidu' si ji"* [Laughing Up at Heaven as Ever—Four Vignettes of Fang Lizhi Joking about "Macromeasurement" in Cambridge], *Zheng ming* (HK), 8 (August 1990), 16–22.
†Chris Buckley, "Science as Politics and Politics as Science: Fang Lizhi and the Chinese Intellectuals' Uncertain Road to Dissent," *Australian Journal of Chinese Affairs*, 25 (forthcoming, January 1991).

and unanticipated popular influence. His most devastating broad-side against Marxism, in the 1987 *Der Spiegel* interview with Tiziano Terzani (see p. 207), doubtless enjoyed less exposure within China, but Chinese readers would have felt no less shocked at his earlier statements.

Some of Fang's most powerful and lasting political messages are aimed at intellectuals as a group. In post-Stalinist countries, particularly in Hungary and Poland, a crucial phase in the process of democratization was the loss of support for the regime among significant sections of the critical intelligentsia. As George Schöp-flin has analyzed it,

> [T]he supporting intellectuals sustain authoritarian regimes by acting as a mirror in which the rulers see themselves reflected. It is vital that this mirror reflects a picture that is positive for the rulers, because at the moment when some other, much more realistic picture is visible in the public sphere—and the intellectuals control the public sphere through their hegemonical control of language—the rulers become confused. This confusion is then transmitted through the hierarchy, upwards and downwards, until the ruling party loses its cohesion and becomes prey to self-doubt.*

In the selections below, Fang calls on Chinese intellectuals to assert their independence and break the regime's mirror of self-legitimation. His demand that intellectuals assume greater social responsibility and affirm a common political interest has on occa-sion been misunderstood in the West. Some observers have taken this as a program of *embourgeoisement,* akin to the notion ad-

*Schöpflin, "The End of Communism in Eastern Europe," p. 6.

vanced by certain Eastern European writers that the intelligentsia would emerge as a ruling stratum in socialist society.* Thus one China scholar sees Fang "less as an advocate of democracy than as a spokesman for a group of intellectuals who are resentful that they do not have greater privileges."†

Fang's own statements provide much evidence against this interpretation. He has insisted that he never advocated that the intellectuals assume power, but rather that they "become a force which exerts influence;"‡ this influence is conditional on their acting as guardians of interests of a universal nature, not those of narrow self-interest. Regardless of how one takes Fang's arguments, it must be acknowledged that when Fang defined the intellectual as one willing to make a stand for moral and cognitive principles, it was backed up by his personal example. Indeed, Fang spent much of his time denouncing intellectuals as being unworthy of the name because of their supine political posture.

Fang has in fact moved steadily away from the elitist, technocratic assumptions common among intellectuals in the early 1980s, and from statism to an advocacy of civil society as the vital agent of change. His New Year's message of 1989, "China's Despair and China's Hope" (see p. 250), found that

> As democratic consciousness spreads, it is bound to form pressure groups that will have ever greater power to weigh

---

*See Georg Konrád and Istvan Szelényi, *The Intellectuals on the Road to Class Power* (New York: Harcourt, Brace, Jovanovich, 1979).

†Richard Kraus, "The Lament of Astrophysicist Fang Lizhi: China's Intellectuals in a Global Context," in *Marxism and the Chinese Experience,* Arif Dirlik and Maurice Meisner, eds., (Armonk, N.Y.: M. E. Sharpe, 1989), 294–315. See also David Kelly, "Fang Lizhi: Democrat on the Road to Class Power?," Proceedings of the Asian Studies Association of Australia Bicentennial Conference, ANU, February 1988 (1989).

‡Fang Lizhi, interview with *Die Welt,* Hamburg, 10 July 1990; text in FBIS CHI-90-149, 2 August 1990, 7–10; quote from p. 9.

against the authority of the leadership. In fact such groups have already begun to appear in embryo. Right now, in many trades and professions, and at all levels of Chinese society, we are seeing the growth of unofficial clubs, associations and discussion groups and other informal gatherings that have begun, in various degrees, to wield influence as pressure groups. Democracy is no longer just a slogan; it has come to exert a pressure of its own.

Many observers would point to Fang's letter to Deng Xiaoping in January 1989 requesting the release of political prisoners (see p. 242), and the open letters of support from Beijing intellectuals that followed shortly thereafter (see Appendix), as the falling pebbles that started the avalanche of the 1989 democracy movement. At last following his lead, Chinese intellectuals broke the mirror of legitimation in April and May 1989.

Yet for many this was done hesitantly and with little explicit commitment to civil society rather than the state as the engine of further reform.* Fang's recent remark that "China is where Eastern Europe was ten years ago" was made with explicit reference to the attitudes of intellectuals.† Like the magic iron headband with which the monk Xuan Zang controls Monkey in *Journey to the West,* the "superculture" of Confucianist Leninism continues to hold many intellectuals in the cheerleader role alluded to earlier by Schöpflin. They are to varying degrees aware of the ways in which they have been used and sacrificed, yet they continue to rationalize their positions.

Yan Jiaqi, prominent political theorist and until recently chair-

*David Kelly, "Chinese Intellectuals in the 1989 Democracy Movement," in George Hicks, ed., *The Broken Mirror: China After Tiananmen* (London: Longmans, 1990), 24–51.
†Interview with *Die Welt;* quote from p. 8.

man of the Paris-based Federation for a Democratic China, acknowledged this problem in a discussion with Fang in Cambridge after the latter's exile.

> Another issue is how to shake the common view of Marxism. Even though Fang has been criticizing Marxism all this time, in China almost no one dares voice agreement with him. In the past when I read his statements, I felt that Fang was extremely courageous as a man; but he did science, so he could say this where we could not! . . . Put it another way, his statements had an attraction for us, but we could not raise a real chorus of agreement; we dared not admit that what Professor Fang said was right. Something very heavy weighed on our minds, because this thing, Marxism, had already taken root among the younger generation in China and could not be shaken. When he made his criticisms of it, I felt there was reason in what he was saying, but I didn't dare let my faith be shaken . . .*

Yan's observations on Fang bear out Havel's insight that a sense of ordinariness is an important asset in cutting through the Gordian knot of official doublethink. Although a major proponent of political reform, and as a consequence suspected of intellectual subversion from an early stage, the highly gifted Yan Jiaqi remained trapped within the system, unable to admit *in the first place to himself* that Fang's views were "right."

Other writers have stressed Fang's common touch: here indeed was a model intellectual of the 1950s, of irreproachably humble background, for all his distinction.† This ordinariness is a source

---

*"*Fang Lizhi, Yan Jiaqi duitan jilu*" [Record of Dialogue Between Fang Lizhi and Yan Jiaqi] *Zhongyang ribao* (Taibei), 16–17 August 1990 (in two parts).

†Link, "The Thought and Spirit of Fang Lizhi." Note also Fang's response to a Hong

of the ecumenical role he plays in the spectrum of Chinese opposition movements. He is able to see in a charitable light those who adopt a different *modus vivendi* with the regime. This has been particularly noticeable in his public statements since leaving sanctuary in the U.S. Embassy in Beijing for Cambridge. In his meeting with Yan Jiaqi, Fang discussed Yan's suggestion that a "Chinese dissident network" be formed. While accepting the idea in principle, Fang was against establishing a formal organization that would compete with those already in existence, or take the part either of those "reforming from within" or "reforming from without":

> My view is that we shouldn't set these in opposition to each other. This development will be carried through in various forms. In fact we see that of the forms taken in Eastern Europe some were internal to the Party, some external; even Gorbachev was inside the Party. So no approach should be excluded.*

As analysts frequently noted during the days when human rights movements were extremely marginal in the East bloc, dissidents played a delicate game with the authorities, to the point where dissidence implied a certain measure of cooperation as well as defiance.† This reveals the ironies of the "dissident" label. As

---

Kong critic's assertion that he was no giant, but just an ordinary man: "This is quite correct. I agree entirely." Lu Keng, *"Fang Lizhi tan Dashiguan binan shenghuo"* [Fang Lizhi talks about his life in sanctuary in the U.S. Embassy], *Baixing banyuekan* (HK), 221 (1 August 1990), 3–7.

*"Fang Lizhi, Yan Jiaqi duitan jilu," part 2. See also the interview with Tiziano Terzani republished as "Free to Speak," *Far Eastern Economic Review*, 2 August 1990, 21–22.

†This literature is surveyed in Robert Sharlet, "Varieties of Dissent and Regularities of Repression in the European Communist States: an Overview," in Jane Leftwich Curry, ed., *Dissent in Eastern Europe* (New York: Praeger, 1983), 1–17.

Havel observed, "they do not usually discover they are 'dissidents' until long after they actually become one."* The label suggests, he writes,

> a protected species who are permitted to do things others are not and whom the government may even be cultivating as a proof of its generosity; or it lends support to the illusion that since there is no more than a handful of malcontents to whom not very much is really being done, all the rest are therefore content, for were they not so, they would be "dissidents" too . . . the categorization supports the impression that the primary concern of these "dissidents" is some vested interest that they share as a group, as though their entire argument with the government were no more than a rather abstruse conflict between two opposed groups.†

In Havel's terms, "the political organs and the police do not lavish such enormous attention on 'dissidents' because they actually are . . . a power clique, but because they are ordinary people with ordinary cares, differing from the rest only in that they say aloud what the rest cannot say." The real importance of the dissident attitude, Havel goes on to say, is that it stands or falls on its interest "in what ails society as a whole, on an interest in all those who do not speak up."‡

This clearly applies to Fang, as confirmed for this writer during a three-month research visit to Beijing in the spring of 1988. A wide variety of people expressed agreement with Fang.

---

*Vaclav Havel, "The Power of the Powerless," in Havel, et al., *The Power of the Powerless* (Armonk, N.Y.: M. E. Sharpe, 1985), 23–96. See especially 57–61.
†Havel, "The Power of the Powerless," p. 59.
‡Havel, "The Power of the Powerless," p. 60. Havel elsewhere emphasizes the role of Marxist ideology in maintaining a bridge of rationalizations between the regime and its victims.

What came as a particular surprise was that this group included respected middle-aged professionals, people with a stake in the *status quo,* who a few years earlier would have expressed political attitudes quite opposed to those of Fang. They were explicit that Fang was expressing views that they were not at liberty to air but nonetheless held privately.

The following articles represent perhaps Fang's most polished interventions in Chinese politics. They display him as a dissident in Havel's understanding of the term. He had the role of political outsider thrust upon him three decades ago, in the Anti-Rightist Campaign. He found his way to "living in the truth"* almost by accident, through his scientific work. And he retains a closeness to ordinary people with ordinary cares, for all his strategic appeals to the intellectuals. No one who has visited Fang at home can think of him as motivated by a taste for luxury or status. His status as a scientist would hardly have suffered had he played it safe; indeed, political action has cost him dearly in normal career terms. Yet he chose to say aloud with simplicity and humor what so many knew but were too intimidated, or too mesmerized, to say.

D.A.K.
Contemporary China Center
Australian National University
October 1990

---

*The fountainhead, as Havel tells us, of all opposition to post-totalitarian regimes—see Vaclav Havel, *Living in Truth* (London: Faber and Faber, 1987).

MY LIFE ON MAY 21, 1987

The following selection was written a few months after Fang's expulsion from the Chinese Communist Party. It was originally intended for One Day in New China, *a record of events in the lives of people throughout China on May 21, 1987. (This collection was inspired by an earlier volume with the same premise,* One Day in China: May 21, 1936, *edited by the novelist Mao Dun.) Fang's entry was never published.*

My contract with the publisher of *One Day in New China* says that this article is to be a record of my activities and experiences on May 21, 1987. This raises an immediate problem for me: How to define May 21? Are we talking Beijing time, or some other time zone? Since the book is about "New China," I'd better use Beijing time. But I was actually in Italy then, so I'm not sure what to do. To avoid promoting "complete Europeanization," the safest course would seem to be using Beijing time—though when you think about it, Beijing time itself isn't really Chinese in origin, either. But be that as it may, this account covers the period of May 21, Beijing time, midnight to midnight.

During those twenty-four hours, I was in Trieste, doing research at the International Center for Theoretical Physics (ICTP).* According to my diary, nothing very special happened on that day, which went as follows:

*See Glossary.

May 20

5:00 P.M.—6:00 P.M.

Discussion with Mr. Z. at ICTP

6:00 P.M.—10:00 P.M.

Dinner at S. Restaurant

May 21

9:30 A.M.—10:00 A.M.

Met with Ms. Tussa to discuss federation accord

10:00 A.M.—5:00 P.M.

Looked into cosmic strings and fractals

10:30 A.M.

Call from Mr. C. at Cambridge University

2:30 P.M.—5:00 P.M.

Calls from the U.S.:

  Mr. M. from Long Island

  Mr. W. from the University of Buffalo

  Mr. Ch. from the University of California, Campus C

  Mr. S. from California

  Mr. H. from the University of California, Campus S

(My book contract says that the names and locations referred to in this record should be real, for the sake of future reference. But with the exception of Ms. Tussa, who is quite European, I've disguised the identity of the other people to whom I refer. I regret having to do this, but the contract doesn't stipulate any guarantees that *One Day in New China* will not be used for investigations of a nonacademic nature.)

The meeting with Ms. Tussa was to request approval for an

accord between ICTP and the Beijing Observatory, which would facilitate sending young researchers from the observatory to the center in the future. Ms. Tussa agreed on the spot. Then she asked me a question, as the only Chinese member of the ICTP committee governing international academic exchange. Why, of late, had Chinese researchers not been arriving at ICTP as scheduled? People who had said they would come were either long delayed or had not turned up at all. "Is it because it's getting more difficult for your people to go abroad?" she asked. "The papers here say that China is launching a new political campaign. We've been worried about your situation for the last few months." I thanked her and her colleagues for their concern. At the same time, I was thinking, "Foreigners really don't understand. If you took the thirty-eight years 'New China' has been in existence and subtracted from it all the years taken up with campaigns, what would be left? Almost nothing! So why worry? Without the campaigns, those of us who grew up in New China wouldn't be who we are."

Besides, being the object of criticism during the current "non-campaign" has its own rewards. The owner of the S. Restaurant insisted on inviting me to dinner. Despite my dozen or so visits to Trieste, we had never really gotten to be friends, but he felt compelled to invite me because "Lately, your name has appeared more often in the Italian papers than XXX's. . . ." Well, what can I do? My infamy has even spread to the Adriatic.

Conversation over dinner centered on the wave of illegal immigration from Wenzhou.* It seems that 90 percent of the Chinese in Italy come from Wenzhou. During the last few years, a thousand or more Wenzhou natives have entered Italy illegally, to the annoyance of the Italian authorities. The result is that Italy is now making it hard for Chinese to get visas, and has also

---

*A city in Zhejiang province on the central China coast.

arrested some of these immigrants and those abetting them, and put them on trial. This matter has disgraced the Chinese already in Italy. Lawbreaking, even when it involves European laws, is a shameful thing to the Chinese.

Yet the crackdown is not stemming the influx of illegal immigrants. Scores of Wenzhou people remain in Yugoslavia and Austria, awaiting their chance to cross over into Italy. The reason is simple: They want to make a living. Back home in Wenzhou, youths who fail to get into college find it difficult to get any job at all, let alone one with a future. In Italy, despite the hardships of living in a foreign land, at least they have a fighting chance. Take the example of the S. Restaurant. It is an ordinary Chinese restaurant with a daily take ranging from 2 million lire ($1,500) on up to about five million lire ($3,800). In comparison with incomes in China, the difference in earning potential doesn't take a mathematician to figure out. The lure is so great that some Wenzhou girls, barely literate even in Chinese, brave the long journey to Italy by themselves and sneak into the country. They are so skillful at smuggling themselves across the border that the Italian police, experienced as they are in handling the Mafia, find themselves at wit's end dealing with them. "Those Chinese are so damned clever," they sigh. Who says the Chinese—especially we products of New China—lack the pioneer spirit?

Mr. W. and Mr. H. belong to a different category of would-be pioneers. After three years of post-doctoral research in the United States, Mr. W.'s J-1 visa is expiring; he had intended to return to China at the end of the year to find a job. Mr. H. just finished his Ph.D. and also wanted to return home, to visit his family after six years of study abroad. But in our telephone conversations today, both told me that they had canceled their plans because of the recent turn of events. Now Mr. W. is preparing to go to a third country to work for a while, then return to the United States. Mr. H. will be going straight into a post-doc at the

National Aeronautics and Space Administration. Even over the phone, I could sense how much they want to go home, yet dare not do so.

Mr. Ch.'s call touched on similar issues. He and his colleagues had been informed that a certain high official from a certain Chinese ministry would soon be visiting the United States, where he would discuss with the U.S. authorities the problem of Chinese students staying on after completing their studies. This official would also be addressing gatherings of Chinese students, informing them of the wonderful conditions in China and the brilliant success of the campaign against bourgeois liberalization. The students at Mr. Ch.'s university were eagerly awaiting his visit.

Mr. M. and Mr. S., on the other hand, have actually gone and become American citizens. I should be especially cautious in dealing with them, since they are now "imitation foreign devils."* Mr. S. asked me point-blank over the phone why I don't just stay abroad for good. If I stayed, he said, I could continue my research, and the working conditions would be much better. I hastened to inform him that such a move was completely out of the question.

Actually, he was not the first person to have mentioned this idea. As soon as I arrived in Rome, my Italian colleagues tried to persuade me to stay on permanently. They would let me do my research in peace and make me a professor. Thanking them warmly, I declined. This was not because I had any expectation of returning home to a headline like "Prof. X. Resolutely Turns Down Offer of Foreign Employment and Returns to the Motherland." No one like myself, who retains only one political

*The "Imitation Foreign Devil" is a character in Lu Xun's *The True Story of Ah Q,* so named by his townsfolk because he cut off his pigtail and wore Western clothes.

right—the right to confess my mistakes—will ever be thus featured.

(Besides which, even though we do see such items in the news fairly regularly, it really doesn't make much sense to report them. After all, don't we always contend that the West is in a deep crisis, a spiritual void, while New China is the finest place on earth? If that's the case, then spurning their offers and returning to China is no more than rational self-interest. What's so newsworthy about that?)

No, as far as *my* decision to return is concerned, the words of Johann Schweigger are more relevant:

> If a crippled opponent utters not a sound yet refuses to subordinate himself and be among the ranks of sycophants and lackeys of a tyrant, then his continued existence will be a source of troubles.

I hesitate to divulge what transpired during my conversation with Mr. C. from Cambridge, because it touched on the British Royal Society, Trinity College, and a letter from a certain professor to Premier Zhao Ziyang and the Chinese Academy of Sciences.* In deference to Chinese tradition, be it ancient China or New China, I wouldn't presume to question the authorities.

Despite the many phone calls that day, I still managed to make some progress regarding the pecular velocity of objects distributed with a fractional dimension. In this sphere at least, I never avoid questioning the authorities. For example, all the results of my cosmological research suggest that the proposition that the universe is infinite contained in many of our revered

---

*This refers to a letter written on Fang's behalf by Cambridge University physicist Stephen Hawking, who had visited Fang's research institute in China in 1985.

Chinese textbooks is at best an unproven doctrine. In fact, it is not much superior to the doctrine of five centuries past that the earth is at the center of the universe. There is still much to be said on this subject, but it looks like I am digressing too far from the scope of *One Day in New China.*

Well, I have written enough about one day's activities. But whether they are fit to be included or will just be tossed in the discard pile, I have no way of knowing. Amen!

July 5, 1987
Weixiu Garden, Beijing University

INTERVIEW WITH
TIZIANO TERZANI

By special permission of Premier Zhao Ziyang, Fang Lizhi left China in May 1987 to attend a physics symposium in Trieste, Italy. Former Der Spiegel China correspondent Tiziano Terzani met with Fang in Florence, where Fang wished to see Galileo's house. This interview appeared in English in Far Eastern Economic Review, *October 22, 1987.*

Question: Professor Fang, among Chinese students you are a hero. The international press has hailed you as China's Sakharov. Deng Xiaoping, on the other hand, calls you a "bad element." China's Communist Party maintains you are a victim of the disease called "bourgeois liberalism." What are you really?

Fang: A little bit of all of these. But in the first place I am an astrophysicist. The natural sciences are my religion. Einstein once said something of this sort. In the past I did not understand him. Now I know: We scientists have a belief and an aim, we have an obligation toward society. If we discover a truth and society does not accept it, this weighs us down. That is what happened to Galileo. That is when, as scientists, we have to intervene. With this mission, I step into society.

Question: What kind of mission do you have for China?

Fang: Democratization. Without democracy there can be no development. Unless individual human rights are recognized, there can be no true democracy. In China, the very ABCs of democracy are unknown. We have to educate ourselves toward democracy. We have to understand that democracy is not something that our leaders can hand over to us. Democracy that comes from above is no democracy, it is nothing but a relaxation of control. There will be a heavy fight. But it cannot be avoided.

Question: First you have attacked local Party cadres, then the Party committee of Beijing, and recently you attacked the Politburo itself. What is your next target?

Fang: Marxism.

Question: You go very far.

Fang: It is a truth that cannot be denied that Marxism is no longer of much use. In the sciences I can prove it. Most answers given by Marxism with regard to the natural sciences are obsolete, some are even downright wrong. What Marxism has to say about the natural sciences stems from Engels's book *The Dialectics of Nature.* On nearly every page of this book one can detect something either outdated or completely wrong.

Question: For example?

Fang: In the 1960s, with the help of Marxism, the Soviet Union and China repeatedly criticized the results of modern natural sciences. In biology they criticized genetics, in physics they criticized the theory of relativity; their criticism reaches from cosmology to the development of the computer. Not even once has their criticism been correct. Therefore, how can one say today that Marxism should lead the natural sciences? The idea is totally wrong.

Question: Have you ever believed in Marxism?

Fang: I surely have! Immediately after Liberation and in the 1950s I firmly believed in Marxism. When I entered the Party in 1955, I was convinced that Marxism should show the way in every field and that the Communist Party was absolutely good.

When I was expelled in 1958, during the Anti-Rightist Campaign, I made a sincere self-criticism. I was convinced that I had wronged the Party. Now the Party has expelled me for the second time, but this time I know that I was not mistaken. Therefore I refused to make a self-criticism.

Question: Deng stated in 1979 that, in conformity with the Chinese Constitution, every citizen should be guided by four principles: the socialist path, the people's democratic dictatorship, leadership by the Party, and Marxism–Leninism–Mao Zedong Thought.

Fang: Marxism is a thing of the past. It helps to understand the problems of the last century, but not those of today. The same is true in physics. Newton developed his theory three hundred years ago. It is still valuable, but it does not help to solve today's problems, such as those related to computer technology. Marxism belongs to a precise epoch of civilization which is over. It is like a worn dress that must be put aside.

Question: Hearing you talk, one must admit that this time the Party was right to expel you. Would you like to be the founder of a new party?

Fang: I have asked myself this question. But under present circumstances it would be impossible. Perhaps in thirty years' time. Perhaps then we shall be in the position in which Taiwan finds itself today, with more than one party.

Question: Are the Four Fundamental Principles a sort of straitjacket that prevents China from developing into a democracy?

Fang: Yes, if the principles remain rigid. But the leadership itself said that Marxism should develop. I read this sentence in the

People's Daily, and I picked it up. We can hold on to the principles provided they are being developed.

Question: But how can fundamental reforms be achieved within the present power structure?

Fang: One could keep the form, but change its content. The Protestants made their Reformation of the Roman Catholic church, but keep using the same Bible. In China we could do the same. In front of the shop the sheep's head keeps dangling, but inside the shop one sells dog meat.

Question: You consider it possible to reform a Communist system, but until now this has never been achieved.

Fang: It is difficult, but if any country stands a chance, that country is China.

Question: A better chance than the Soviet Union under Gorbachev?

Fang: Of course. We find ourselves in a much better position for a simple reason: In the Soviet Union the Communist Party has achieved a few successes—in military defense and in the sciences. Soviet intellectuals enjoy much more freedom than we ever had. In China, on the contrary, the Communist Party cannot boast of a single success. It has achieved nothing of value during the past thirty years. That's why leaders on all levels are worried. That's why even among the highest cadres there are some who admit that nothing of value has been achieved. This couldn't be said as easily in the Soviet Union.

Question: Is there really not a single success for China to boast of?

Fang: What do you mean by success? Sure, in Ping-Pong and volleyball we have been successful, but in no other field. That is why the need for reforms is being felt so strongly at all levels of society. Belief in the Party has vanished in our country, especially among the young.

Question: You seem to consider it a matter of course that intellectuals should be the vanguard of society. Isn't that the old Platonic ideal of philosophers' becoming kings?

Fang: Intellectuals are not kings, but still they are the main force for pushing society ahead. They should be independent and free. Intellectuals ought to play a big role.

Question: Up until now it has been the Party which decided on the role of intellectuals. During the Cultural Revolution they were forced down to the lowest, "stinking ninth" position of the "nine bad categories" of society. Today, under Deng Xiaoping, they have climbed back up again to the third position, after peasants and workers. But still they are not independent.

Fang: Quite right. Mao described this dependency of the intellectuals with the words: "The hair clings firmly to the skin." Nothing has changed in this situation. The intellectuals continue to be used as tools. Now is the time for them to show their strength. Nobody should be intimidated. That is democracy. If we fail to achieve this, China will hardly become a truly developed, modern country.

Question: Already in 1978 something similar was said. In those days, the worker Wei Jingsheng wrote on a wall in Beijing, which later became known as Democracy Wall: "Without Democracy, No Modernization!" He got fifteen years' imprisonment for it. You, Professor Fang, are still free. Is it because you are a well-known scientist, whereas Wei was nothing but an electrician?

Fang: Of course. That's how things are done in China. A worker who has done something objectionable can easily be removed.

Worker unrest does not worry the government; workers are easily dealt with. Right now there are quite a few incidents of unrest, but the public is not aware of them. Abroad one knows nothing of them, for these people have no international contacts.

Question: Are things different in the case of intellectuals?

Fang: Whenever it is students who demonstrate, the government is more concerned. It does not as easily dare to take action against the students. That is why I maintain that the power of the intellectuals is relatively great. That is why I keep telling my students that he who has knowledge also has influence, and cannot be disregarded by the government. I advise my students not to open their mouths too wide at first, but to study diligently. Those, however, who have completed their study successfully, those *must* open their mouths.

Question: What about human rights in China?

Fang: It is dangerous to talk about them. Human rights are a taboo subject in China. Our situation is far worse than in the Soviet Union. Wei Jingsheng's is a famous case, but there are thousands of others whose names are not even known. In the Soviet Union name lists at least exist. Not in China.

Question: Is democracy really a necessary condition for the development of a country? States like Taiwan, South Korea, Singapore, and the Crown Colony of Hong Kong have made enormous economic progress without being true democracies.

Fang: First of all, in the countries you named there is far more democracy than in China. Secondly, those countries are under American protection, and the United States wishes their economies to develop. In the case of China things are different. Moreover, in China it is particularly difficult to separate economic from political democracy.

Question: Deng holds a different view; he has told the Chinese: "Get rich. To be rich is glorious. The Party will take care of the rest."

Fang: In China, the Party does not want to manage only politics. It wants to control everything, including the way of life and thoughts of the people. Today factories are being managed by managers, but the Party cadres keep wielding the power. Peasants enjoy the free-market system, but the cadres tell them, "You still need our rubber stamp. You still have to buy us off!" Therein lies the root of the new corruption. In order to create a true economic democracy in China, one must abolish political controls. That is exactly what the Party fears most.

Question: Hasn't Deng Xiaoping opened Pandora's Box with his economic reforms? Doesn't Deng equally want democracy?

Fang: No. Deng's reforms are intended to stabilize the system in the short run. What Deng wants to avert is the collapse of the system. The Party is in a quandary. If it introduces reforms, then it has to reduce its power; if it does not introduce reforms, then it loses power even faster.

Question: Deng is the hero of the West. In 1985, *Time* magazine selected him the Man of the Year. The West views him as an ally on the international stage.

Fang: The West seems to have a very superficial understanding of China.

Question: Could Deng even revoke his reforms?

Fang: I don't think so. The economy would collapse, and also the Party would disintegrate. In 1962, when millions of people in China died of hunger because of economic mistakes, the country was kept together thanks to Mao's prestige. Today, nobody has such prestige.

Question: But haven't a lot of Deng's reforms been successful?

Fang: Many people, particularly people abroad, believe so. There have been some successes in agricultural production. But in the cities, in industry, reforms have not really started yet. The reform of wages and prices was unsuccessful.

Question: You cannot deny, however, that people in China are better off today.

Fang: They have more TV sets and more refrigerators.

Question: Isn't that progress?

Fang: Certainly, but the progress of a society should be all-round. The economy is an important indicator of development, but it is not the only one. The Arab countries are affluent, but their society is not developed. I believe that education and cultural standards are important characteristics of a developed society. Eating and drinking are very important, of course, in a poor country like China. But it is equally important for the human being to realize that he or she is a human being.

Question: China today is importing Western technology in order to push ahead its own modernization. Do you think this is right?

Fang: Certainly. But it is not enough to import something Western here and there, to buy a few big computers. In order to become truly modern, we have to import the spirit of Western civilization into China. Chinese civilization has gained many a profound insight, but it ignores logic. For the sake of our development, we must adopt the Western spirit.

Question: The Party has accused you of being polluted by Western ideas, and to be advocating a complete Westernization of China. Is that true?

Fang: We must open our country in all directions; then many positive things will enter it, while our own values will not be lost. I have never said that we should repudiate those Chinese traditions that are good. However, the feudal relationships of Chinese society are bad and must be abolished. True, Western morality is different from ours, but that doesn't mean it is worse.

Question: By inviting the Communists to reform the system, don't you invite the Party to commit political suicide?

Fang: One cannot ask the Party to relinquish its power. The Communists hold on to their totem pole. One must carefully consider whether there isn't a way around it. Couldn't it be that one day the totem pole vanishes all by itself?

Question: If the totem pole vanishes, China will be without an alternative power structure. Wouldn't there be a danger of chaos breaking out, of warlords taking over the country?

Fang: There is always that danger in China.

Question: What is going to happen when Deng Xiaoping dies?

Fang: In the short run we might be worse off, but in the long run, better. It's possible that after Deng's death Mao's thought will no longer be valid and that then we shall be able to radically discuss the past thirty years. That is probably what Hu Yaobang, who was demoted in January, planned to do. He once said that not one portrait of Mao should be hanging in China. Today, the last one hangs on Tiananmen Square, but Mao's thought continues to dominate us.

Question: Could the army play an important role in the future?

Fang: In our society, the army does play an important role. But it is no monolith. I, for one, have received many letters of solidarity from members of the military.

Question: How many have you received in all?

Fang: Thousands. Often they were open postcards with the name and address of the sender—a brave deed in China. On one it even said, "If this postcard does not reach its destination, then there is no democracy in China." When I passed through customs on the day of my departure, the policemen on duty in the boats stopped their work and came to talk to me: "Are you Fang Lizhi? Have you solved your problems? Are you allowed to travel abroad? That's good!"

Question: Are you sure that after your return to China you will not be arrested, or at least banished to a faraway region?

Fang: I am prepared for it.

Question: You could emigrate.

Fang: In the past I thought about it seriously. Now I can no longer do it. Should I leave now, I would abandon my students and my friends in China. I have been criticized by high cadres, yet I don't leave the country, whereas cadre children who were never criticized do go abroad to study.

Question: What happened to the students who took part in the demonstrations?

Fang: As far as I know, no student of one of the well-known universities has been arrested. However, we know that all of them have been photographed and registered by name. Later, they will make them wear narrow shoes, as we say in China.

Question: The campaign against bourgeois liberalism continues.

Fang: That campaign has shown us the strength of the resistance against the reforms. It has shown us that we badly underestimated the strength of our opponents. We have been too optimistic. On the other hand, the campaign has convinced more and more people of the necessity of reform. We do not want a revolution, which first of all is difficult to achieve, and second is not necessarily good. Therefore, the only path open to China is that of reform. Democracy, education, and intellectual freedom are its absolutely indispensable prerequisites.

LEARNING ABOUT DEMOCRACY

The following selection is an excerpt from a February 1988 letter by Fang Lizhi to a Chinese organization in the United States which had given Fang an award for promoting democratic education in China.

"Democracy" is not a new word in China. The first political association I ever joined referred to democracy in its title: The League of Democratic Youth. At that time (early 1949), not yet thirteen and only in the third year of middle school, I knew little of politics or society. Even then, however, I understood that democracy was indispensable to progress and symbolized a society's level of development.

So it's interesting that thirty-eight years later, in 1987, this idea that I grasped even as a middle-school student should meet with such a chorus of condemnation. I have done a little survey of newspapers and magazines published in China in 1987, and I find that the number of articles castigating freedom and democracy overwhelmingly exceeds the number condemning dictatorship or autocracy. It appears that the former is far more detrimental to society than the latter.

Last November, when I returned to Keda for the first time, my friends threw me a welcoming party. One colleague rose and sang a song popular during Russia's October Revolution, the "Ode to Light." This incident soon came under investigation; the reason, we were told, was that the lyrics of the song contained the word "freedom" (as in "Comrades, look to the sun, look to freedom"). This is one small example of the reception being encountered by "freedom" and "democracy" right now. It is apparent how badly we need education in just the rudiments of democracy that even a middle-school student can understand.

What *was* being said about democracy last year, and repeated *ad nauseam,* were such lofty propositions as these: (1) that Chinese students don't know what freedom or democracy is; (2) that the ordinary people don't need democracy; (3) that our current task is to build the economy, and dictatorship is more effective in this regard; (4) that considering our cultural background, the Chinese people would not know what to do with democracy even if they had it. In brief, democracy is a Western import unsuited to Chinese conditions.

These notions make me mindful of a certain episode in Chinese history. About three hundred years ago, when modern astronomy was first introduced into China, there were people who violently opposed the use of a calendar drawn up on this basis. They insisted on following the calculations of Shao Yongxian, a Sung Dynasty philosopher, to make the calendar, their argument being that Western science was not appropriate to China. We no longer find such people, because it is universally acknowledged that science has no East or West. Scientific laws apply everywhere.

I believe that those arguing that democracy is unsuited to China will someday meet with a similar fate. This is because democracy also makes no distinction as to geography, but applies all over the world. What's more, I believe that this will take less than three centuries to accomplish. My argument is based on one of the ten most important unofficial news items of 1987 in China: the defeat of Deng Liqun* in an election. This incident demon-

---

*Ideologically conservative former Politburo member and director of the Party's Propaganda Department, who was defeated in elections for membership in the Central Committee at the Thirteenth Party Congress in October 1987.

strates clearly that the Chinese people are neither ignorant of what democracy means nor incapable of using it once they have it.

Last year's events also showed that intellectuals are increasingly aware of their responsibilities to society. Among my friends, most of whom are scientists, Einstein's views on the nature of these responsibilities have started to catch on:

> In principle, every citizen should be equally responsible for defending the constitutional liberties of his country. The "intellectual" in the broadest sense of the term has, however, an even greater responsibility since, due to his specific training, he is capable of exerting a particularly strong influence on the formation of public opinion. This would explain why those who endeavor to lead us toward an authoritarian government are particularly anxious to intimidate and silence the intellectual.
>
> Therefore, under the prevailing circumstances, it is all the more important that the intellectual recognize his particular obligation to society. This should involve the refusal to cooperate with any measure which would violate the constitutional rights of the individual. This refers particularly to all investigations into the private life and political affiliations of a citizen. Whoever cooperates in such inquisitions becomes an accessory to the crime of violating or invalidating the constitution.

Indeed, in the face of last year's campaign of intimidation against freedom and democracy, many intellectuals refused to cooperate. It is on this basis that I feel hope for democracy, and for China.

WILL CHINA DISINTEGRATE?

The following interview was conducted by Li Yi, editor of the Hong Kong monthly The Nineties, *as Fang Lizhi passed through Hong Kong in September 1988 on return from a scientific conference in Australia. In it Fang discusses rising social and political tensions in China, along with some of the lesser-known background to his expulsion from the Communist Party the previous year. His remarks about nepotism and corruption among the high Party leadership are said to have greatly angered Deng Xiaoping, who reportedly spoke of suing Fang for slander.*

Li: I'd like to start by asking you the real story behind your expulsion from the Party last year. What actually happened? Some say it was because you openly criticized Beijing Vice Mayor Zhang Baifa in 1985, others say because you criticized [Politburo member and ideology czar] Hu Qiaomu in 1986.

Fang: Those were just the sparks that finally touched off the explosion. By the time I became vice president of Keda in 1984, things I had said had already attracted quite a bit of notice. As early as 1981, I had remarked that Marxism was obsolete, which met with loud rumblings from above. The authorities were unhappy with me early on. No one had previously said such things at a national conference.

Li: Perhaps the Zhang Baifa affair, by involving an actual person, was more of an invitation to disaster than just expressing dissenting views. It's reported that Keda wanted you to apologize to Zhang Baifa at the time.

Fang: That was in 1985. After I criticized Zhang, some people told the Chinese Academy of Sciences [CAS] that I should apologize to Beijing. [Keda President] Guan Weiyan paid no heed to it, and so the matter never reached me. The physics community knew all about Zhang Baifa. It was from open remarks at a physics conference that I learned about Zhang in the first place.

Li: Officials taking junkets abroad happens all the time, but it seems you were the first to raise the issue in public.

Fang: The problem was that I talked about it with student audiences, and also that I came down rather hard on Zhang. I said he should resign.

Li: Wasn't it in 1985 that Deng Xiaoping said he wanted you out of the Party?

Fang: No. In 1985 I heard that someone was suggesting I resign, but it was very likely Hu Qiaomu. The end of 1985 was a tense time. The Anhui Party Secretary came calling and said that the things I was saying were not being taken well. But they made no mention of Zhang Baifa, just of the speech I had given at Zhejiang University in March of that year. I think they did that because there was nothing they could say about Zhang Baifa—I had the evidence.

Li: According to Liu Binyan, the Campaign Against Bourgeois Liberalization was not so much about ideology as it was a response to the criticism of [high-ranking] individuals. Is that why you and the others were expelled from the Party?

Fang: I think so. Many people have said to me, "Say what you like, but don't mention any names."

Li: Yet you go on mentioning names. There is another theory, that they wanted you and Wang Ruowang to resign [of your own volition] a long time ago. Have you heard anything about that?

Fang: Of course I heard the rumors. That was also in 1985, though it might have been even earlier for Wang Ruowang. I believe that Hu Yaobang approved this suggestion, saying that they had to had to ask people to leave three times before kicking them out. Actually, I did hear that Wang Heshou of the Central Discipline Inspection Committee wanted to talk with me. I was about to take a trip to Beijing, and the Anhui Party Committee asked me to wait for a day, so that Wang Heshou could talk with me. I changed my plans and waited for a day, but he never showed up.

Li: So how many times did they ask you to resign? Is it true that Hu Qili* came to see you? Was that one of the times?

Fang: Hu Qili came with the Anhui Party Secretary to talk with me, but there was nothing said at all about my resigning from the Party. He didn't even disagree, to my face, with anything I had said. He even acknowledged at that meeting that Communism is in serious trouble worldwide. Hu Yaobang has said such things himself. But in any case, I was certainly never asked three times to leave.

Li: Was your position as vice president also in jeopardy at that time?

Fang: I knew the vice president position was shaky for a long time. Actually, when I was first nominated for the post in 1981, I was turned down by the higher echelons. It took them until

*Politburo member, considered a reformist. See Glossary.

1984 to approve me. At that point I learned that the problem was the things I was saying. I had already started to speak up before 1981; since they couldn't control me, they refused to approve the nomination.

On the other hand, they did finally confirm my nomination in 1984, and there was a reason for that as well. The Nanjing University students had just toppled their Party secretary, shouting, "Party branch secretary get out!" This was a first in China. The administration at the university was changed. Outsiders didn't hear much about it, but the incident had serious repercussions. I think the decision to make me vice president was a consequence of this. The leadership was afraid of the students, and they wanted to improve their image by appointing people the students would accept. Besides which, Keda students had asked a number of times why I hadn't been made president, since I surpassed the other nominees in terms of qualifications for the job. Besides academic performance, I was the right age and had seniority in the Party.

Li: So the reason for making you vice president was to placate the students and keep them from causing trouble?

Fang: Of course. And the previous president, Yan Jici, had strongly recommended me.

Li: So they had contradictory feelings toward you from the outset: They wanted somebody to calm the students down, but they also felt uneasy about you.

Fang: That's right. So as a result, they made me first vice president. It came down to Zhou Guangzhao,* Guan Weiyan, Fang Lizhi, all physicists. They decided to put Guan Weiyan in the top spot. Even though his ideas were quite similar to mine, he was

---

*President of the Chinese Academy of Sciences since 1987.

more of a Party man. Behind closed doors he was a harsh critic—he also criticized Zhang Baifa—but he was careful about saying things in public, especially to the students.

Li: But he didn't try to keep you from speaking out.

Fang: That's right. He didn't interfere with my speaking to the students.

Li: And so he also paid the price, later.

Fang: He was on the second list of people to be purged from the Party, along with Xu Liangying* and a few dozen others. In the end only five were expelled, the so-called "Five Gentlemen."†

Li: Given your criticisms of Marxism and the Party, why didn't you voluntarily resign sooner?

Fang: At the time I felt that even within the Party no one believed in orthodox Marxism anymore, so one might be able to accomplish something from inside. I told students to join the Party and change it from within, and I think many other people who joined the Party shared that view. Since Mao died, there hasn't been any orthodox doctrine. The Four Upholds don't uphold anything, they're just a façade.

Li: They're there to present the appearance of legality, but the real point is power.

Fang: They're for controlling the truth. What the truth consists of is subject to interpretation via the Four Upholds.

---

*Leading historian of science and translator of Einstein's works into Chinese. Xu organized the open letter of forty-two academicians in February 1989 calling for the release of political prisoners and other liberal reforms.

†The five were playwright Wu Zuguang, philosopher Wang Ruoshui, *Science and Technology News* editor Sun Changjiang, and the director and deputy director of the Institute for Marxism–Leninism–Mao Zedong Thought, Su Shaozhi and Zhang Xianyang.

Li: Was the student movement [of late 1986] another reason for your expulsion?

Fang: Of course that was part of it, along with the fact that they found it difficult to ride herd on me.

Li: From the reports we saw, the students didn't do anything radical.

Fang: That's right. On the evening before the first march, which was December 4, I gave a speech agreeing with their points but encouraging them not to march. The fact is, I was the first university administrator in the country to try to dissuade students from marching; no one else had done so. My relationship with them was good, good enough that they wouldn't completely ignore my wishes or drown me out when I spoke. In the end I kept about half the students from going, so that less than a thousand of them actually marched. I got half the students to go with me to the auditorium to talk things over; the other half insisted on demonstrating.

Li: Why didn't you want them to march?

Fang: I was afraid it would be turned into an excuse for repression. As vice president, I had a responsibility to protect the students. I told them: "If you stay on campus, I can protect you, even if someone tries to arrest you; but if you leave the campus, I have no power to protect you. You say you're not going to break the law, but if someone else breaks the law and runs you down, or burns a car and blames you for it, you're out of luck."

The Central Committee knew I restrained the students. This was the first march, very peaceful, no incidents at all. Someone asked if we should tell the public-security bureau [that the march was going to happen], and I said why not; they'll help maintain order. The students handed fliers to the police, and the police gave a courteous salute in response.

Li: Sounds good so far.

Fang: Indeed it was, as was the response of the provincial committee. The students asked if they could hold a march, and the
committee replied that they could, because it was stipulated under
the Constitution, as part of the election law. The students also
believed no harm would come of marching, because the State
Education Commission had told them it was all constitutional
and promised there would be no repercussions. So the whole
thing went smoothly.

Afterward, students from other Hefei schools marched, and
there were more people involved. On December 9, Li Honglin*
came and said that my students were marching, but I told him
they weren't involved in that march. Then on December 16, a
demonstration in Shanghai got out of hand, with the police
beating people. The Hefei students were incensed. On December
24 the Keda students went back on the street in support of the
Shanghai marchers. This time it was more confrontational. The
students held a sit-in in front of the provincial committee office,
demanding that Shanghai be asked to make a public apology.
Such a demand, of course, was not easy for Anhui to comply
with. The officials got rigid, and the students refused to leave the
office.

Guan Weiyan and I went there to mediate. We talked with
both sides and came up with an agreement, with the committee
making a statement that the beatings were wrong. It was after
midnight at that point, and if the students had continued to stay,
the committee might have taken some action against them. I
told the students that their demonstration had already succeeded,
and that they weren't going to resolve everything with one

*Prominent theorist of political reform and former president of the Fujian Academy
of Social Science.

march; there was no possibility that Shanghai would respond immediately. The students listened and soon dispersed. The next day the provincial committee commended us, saying that henceforth if there were any problems with the students, the university presidents should deal with them personally.

Li: Perhaps you were expelled precisely because the students listen to you.

Fang: It's possible. Certainly on that occasion they left after I talked with them.

Li: Why did they call you to Beijing?

Fang: I was going there for a conference. I also went because the rumors in Beijing were flying thick and fast, even as I was down in Hefei pleading with the students. Li Shuxian called me and said she had heard from many quarters that Beijing was about to purge me.

Li: Did the Central Committee know all the facts?

Fang: I don't think so. Deng Xiaoping made the final decision, but I think the Education Commission played an ugly role in the whole thing. They had their opinions about Guan Weiyan and myself early on. Keda is not under their jurisdiction; it belongs to CAS. We had climbed to the rank of number two in the country, in terms of publications and the quality of the students, right behind Beijing University. The Education Commission was jealous and wanted us purged; every time something happened on our campus, they issued a report. But when the Qinghua University students marched, they pretended not to notice.

Li: How about CAS? Did they stand by you?

Fang: Not entirely. The reason is that we had offended Zhang Baifa, and Gu Yu had allowed Zhang to go on that trip. Gu Yu is Hu Qiaomu's wife, as well as a member of CAS. So CAS was also annoyed with us. The whole thing was entangled in a mass of personal politics.

Li: It looks as if they used you to bring Hu Yaobang down. Deng's speech pointed to the student movement. The logic of the Campaign Against Bourgeois Liberalization was that the student movement had resulted from liberalism, and that liberalism had been encouraged by Hu Yaobang. You were all representatives of liberalism, so they took care of you together. Did any of the Party leaders ever come to talk with you in Beijing about the campaign?

Fang: Only to read me the declaration that I was expelled from the Party.

Li: In 1986 there were mixed messages: people urging you to quit the Party on one hand, people writing articles in the *People's Daily* praising Keda on the other.

Fang: Yes. But the latter may just have been manipulating public opinion for the Thirteenth Party Congress. There was one rumor that I would be nominated for the Central Committee. This wasn't the first time; prior to the Twelfth Party Congress [in 1982] people were dispatched to Keda to scope out the situation. They thought I would make a good model: young, yet had endured all the purges; good relations with the students; relatively senior in the Party; clean family history, no landlords, rich peasants, counter-revolutionaries, rightists, or criminals in my background [the five "black categories" of the Cultural Revolution], so my class status was good. But even if I had joined the Central Committee, they just wanted me for show, to be their tool.

Li: Li Shuxian remains in the Party, yet you've vowed not to rejoin even if given the opportunity. Do the two of you see things differently?

Fang: Not at all. As anybody who knows the two of us can attest, she's even more outspoken than I am. The situation with the Party is extremely complex. There are fine people in the Party, not just in terms of their political ideas, but as human beings. Liu Binyan is a fine person. Xu Liangying [who helped to plan a commemorative of the 1957 Anti-Rightist Campaign with Fang and Liu] said he was sorry that he hadn't been kicked out of the Party with us. He was a true Marxist in his time, and he and I argued over this. Now he says it was all a dream. The point is, there are all kinds of people in the Party.

Li: The other night someone remarked that Liu Binyan and yourself represent two schools of thought. One hopes to improve the Party from within, developing a "consultative" position from which to encourage reform. The other wants to establish an outside force to balance the Party and promote change. Which of these two approaches is more appealing to people of your generation?

Fang: Personally, I think both are needed. They have to work in concert. Outsiders think that faith in Marxism is an essential requirement for being in the Communist Party, but that's just not the case. Deng himself has refuted many of the tenets of Marxism-Leninism.

Li: Marxism is just a façade over the Party?

Fang: Just a façade. When the Party followed Marxism, they didn't need the façade; now that they don't follow Marxism, they need the façade as an excuse when they want to purge you.

Li: What's your view of one-party dictatorship?

Fang: In 1985–86, there was open discussion in China of a multi-party system. When I got back from abroad, they were even discussing it in the Central Party School.

Li: One-party dictatorship is tied up with various entrenched interests; it won't be that easy to change.

Fang: Allowing multiple factions within the Party could be a bridge to a true multiparty system. This could be an evolutionary process: the Party changing color over time. Right now the Party is running the country, and it isn't possible to simply toss it out. If all we have is opposition from the outside, and nobody inside the Party working along parallel lines, then we won't have much impact.

Li: Liu Binyan's hope lies in having good people in the Party.

Fang: For myself, I don't think we need good people so much as we need to change the nature of the Party itself.

Li: Even so, absolute power corrupts.

Fang: Definitely. We want the Party itself to become democratic. I think there are some ruling parties, such as the one in Singapore, that are not internally corrupt despite their dictatorial power over society. But right now the Chinese Communist Party is both dictatorial and corrupt. Its corruption affects the whole country.

Li: Do you think China's biggest problem is having a privileged class [*i.e.,* Party cadres]? How bad is the corruption?

Fang: I think the issue is that power inevitably corrupts. How far the corruption goes I have no way of measuring, but I hear about it more and more all the time. The stories are frightening. They even say there is smuggling—drug smuggling—going on within the military, things have gotten so bad. The motive is power and money.

Apropos of this, I have discovered a correlation: The less people understand China, the more optimistic they are. Foreigners are told things like "More houses are being built in China" and they think, how wonderful. Overseas Chinese are less optimistic, because they hear more of what's actually going on. Chinese students abroad are less optimistic still, because they had a hard enough time getting out of the country; they really have a sense of how things are. People living in China, like myself, are more pessimistic yet. But do you know what is the most pessimistic group of all? It's those who are closest to the leadership, the ones who work most closely with them, such as their personal secretaries. These people say we shouldn't believe a word the leaders say.

Li: Until recently people on the mainland were maintaining that since the fall of the Gang of Four, despite the occasional setbacks, the general trend was one of slow improvement. Since the decontrol of prices exposed the problem of special privilege so starkly, people are now saying the trend isn't positive after all. They can't see how a privileged class is going to give up its privileges. This has led to violence and unrest in some places. What is the situation with young people right now?

Fang: In general, I think young people are pessimistic. They are busily trying either to get rich or to get out of the country.

Li: How do you feel about the issue of people leaving China? With Hong Kong facing [Chinese control in] 1997, many people are trying to emigrate. But there are also those who say we should develop a nationalistic attitude and welcome 1997. What do you think about "national consciousness"?

Fang: To be quite frank, I don't support patriotism, at least not in all its aspects.

Li: You agree, then, with Einstein's remark that nationalism is an infantile disease?

Fang: I agree with Einstein's idea of world citizenship. He said, don't be narrowly focused on your own country, look at things from a planetary perspective.

Civilizations rise and fall. Even the complete extinction of a civilization is not such a remarkable thing. Some cultures disappear because they can't adapt to new situations. The Mayans are gone, and so are the original inhabitants of Mesopotamia. The disappearance of a culture is not necessarily a bad thing, and we needn't tear our hair out over it. Scientists generally have this attitude toward the future, because science has no national boundaries. Of course I don't mean to denigrate the positive aspects of national culture. But if these things are truly good, then they can stand up to pressure from the outside.

Li: Many people are critical of Chinese political culture, with its traditions of autocracy and hereditary rule. Let's consider patriotism in this light. Patriotism in many countries seems to be the theme of the most reactionary elements of society.

Fang: I think we need to build a new society. Science looks for what is true; there is no other rational starting place. We don't need to declare that we're preserving Chinese traditions or China's special characteristics. I'm not going to oppose things simply because they are Chinese, but I also won't be devastated if some of them are lost.

Li: When Liu Binyan was in Hong Kong, he was asked about emigration from China. He said that if conditions changed in a way that allowed a person to like China better, with a little more freedom and a little progress toward overcoming injustice, then people would stay, even if the material conditions were not the best. But he says he wouldn't try to talk anyone into staying under present conditions.

Fang: He didn't say that lightly. But I think if a society is no longer functional, if it's going to collapse under its own weight, you should just let it. It's better that way, it propels the world forward. If you try to prop it up, you're only preserving backwardness. This is the view of many young people in China. They still want to devote themselves to high-minded pursuits, but no longer solely for the sake of China.

Li: You say that Hong Kong lacks a nationalistic mentality, and it's true. But some people here say that if we're going to become part of China, we had better develop one.

Fang: Nationalistic attitudes are scorned abroad. My overseas colleagues have never treated me like a foreigner. Americans don't generally think in such terms. But the Chinese, even when they're not being racist, do some really irritating things, like calling foreigners *laowai* [ol' foreigner]. . . . Foreigners don't carry such attitudes, yet their national traditions persist. Good traditions don't require being held in a death grip; if we have to maintain such a grip, it just says that our traditions can't stand up to the challenge. Many young people agree with me on this point. "Patriotism" has become the Communists' final slogan, but even this one is wrong.

Li: Do you think young people on the mainland are becoming nihilistic?

Fang: I think they're at a loss about what to do. They don't know what the future holds for China, and in China the prospects for individuals are very tightly linked to what happens to the country. The individual's way of life is dependent on politics. Not like Hong Kong, or the United States; in the United States presidents can come and go, and people aren't affected very much. But not so in China. Maybe it's a little looser now than under Mao, or it's looser here in the Pearl River delta, but at least in Beijing it's still much as it was.

There are times that you think not in terms of China being liberated, but of it dissolving, falling apart because it lacks anything to hold it together. Without a doubt many people are thinking, If the culture is not working anymore, then let's just help it finish disintegrating.

Li: What about in your generation?

Fang: Of course my generation doesn't want the society to break up just yet, but if the young people want to dismantle it and replace it with something better, it's not our concern.

Li: But there are those who insist that we can't allow China to break up, that it has to be kept strong.

Fang: Such ideas have increasingly lost their attraction. Consider this: A few years ago China's triumphs in sports elicited a very narrow-minded patriotic enthusiasm in people. But lately if we win, people don't get that excited; some will even say openly that we should lose. A physics professor at Nanjing University recently said that it would be better if we lost the volleyball championship.

Li: Why?

Fang: Because victory doesn't reflect China's real conditions. The excitement is like a stimulant; it isn't real happiness, it doesn't nourish you or make you better. Also, many people don't like how much funding is going to sports. So people say openly that we should lose. Producing fine athletes is not a sign that the country in general is in good health or making progress. We are managing with great effort to produce some athletes, but this is no proof of how superior the Chinese are.

Li: If Chinese culture does break up, what will happen?

Fang: I don't know.

Li: There is news of rioting in a number of places right now. Mightn't we end up just replacing one tyranny with another?

Fang: Yes. We still haven't learned that if you use violence to overcome violence, the result is still violence.

Li: Education in China is a mess. I hear that even your graduate students want to quit.

Fang: It is a mess. Of course my students want to keep studying with me in hopes of eventually going overseas. But they can barely feed themselves. Their wages and fellowships together come to less than 100 yuan a month. I have six graduate students now. Some students quit school because regulations require that they withdraw before they can go abroad, and one of mine is in that boat; he's been accepted by Princeton. There are also students who quit in order to go into business, but so far none of mine have done that.

Li: The middle-school situation is even worse.

Fang: Because wages are so low for primary and middle-school teachers, the quality of education is very inferior.

Li: Do you feel there's a sense of impending crisis in China, with nobody knowing quite what to do?

Fang: Yes. It's like a swarm of headless flies, buzzing around in every direction. The Central Committee is like that, too. When you have that much power, you're not reckless, because you want to hold on to it. But these people don't have any faith, either. Look how many of their children are in the United States, a disproportionate number of them with green cards [denoting permanent-resident status in the United States]. People are saying that if the government fell, most of them [the Central Committee] would flee the country.

The leadership is really getting down to earth now, and they're not talking Marxism-Leninism, either. What outsiders see is all this stuff about building socialism, the reforms, the Four Modernizations. But inside, it's every man for himself. This is a *fin de siècle* mindset, just waiting for things to collapse. The ship is sinking, and the rats are jumping off. First grab some money and stick it into a Swiss bank account. If you can't get to Hong Kong, go to Shenzhen—it's not that far from Hong Kong.

Li: Looking at it this way, it's no wonder that Hong Kong people don't have any confidence, either. Many Hong Kong business people who have dealings with the mainland know that you'd better be "nice" to your mainland counterparts or you don't have a chance of succeeding.

Fang: Not a chance. This isn't just routine corruption, it's a mindset that says grab all the money you can right now and don't even think about the long term. Give me money, help me get out of the country, now. Many joint ventures have failed for this very reason. The people you're dealing with are unreliable; they might just disappear on you tomorrow.

Li: Why are you always criticizing the leaders by name?

Fang: To goad them. Besides, look at it the other way: Why shouldn't I?

Li: On the outside it wouldn't matter, but in China it's dangerous. You've violated a taboo. On this trip you've repeatedly criticized Deng Xiaoping. Don't you think that this is going to haunt you when you go back?

Fang: Not really.

Li: They might not let you travel again. It's said that your trip last May was authorized by [Premier] Zhao Ziyang. Who authorized it this time?

Fang: Probably Hu Qili. It was definitely approved by the Central Committee, not CAS. Whether I'll be able to get out again depends on the situation in China.

Li: I understand your interview with Tiziano Terzani during last year's trip to Italy made people at the top furious.

Fang: Many people are saying now what I said to Tiziano last year. Every time they get infuriated it does some good, it moves things along a little. Lots of people now say that Marxism-Leninism is obsolete; no one considers it a big taboo.

Li: Given the kinds of things you said in that interview, from the perspective of the leadership you are getting further and further out of bounds. But in truth what you're doing is getting closer and closer to the way people act in a modern society where people are considered equal [and no one is on a pedestal]. Until the value of every individual is affirmed, there is no modernization.

Fang: People *are* equal, including Deng Xiaoping and me. If my criticism is off the mark, he can criticize me back. The students were saying such things on their big-character posters a long time ago.

Li: You say a multiparty system is a long-range goal for China. Do you think human rights can be gained in the short term?

Fang: We have no choice but to work on it. It is very difficult to do even the simplest investigation of human rights abuses, but we must try anyway. There are many, many cases involving prisoners of conscience. There are also such things as women being paid inhuman wages. There are certainly no fewer abuses in China than in the Soviet Union, but the Soviet Union at least has lists of prisoners' names. Except for a few celebrated cases such as Wei Jingsheng's, there are no such lists in China. In the villages, if you open your mouth too often, you'll just disappear, and no one will ever know what became of you.

Li: You're leaving tonight. Can you say what you think about your brief visit to Hong Kong, the questions you've been asked, your impressions of the people you've met?

Fang: Things look about the same as during my previous visit in 1982. But I can sense how dependent Hong Kong is on outside forces: Britain on the one hand, China on the other. People seem very anxious. They are intensely concerned about the 1997 political situation. I've seen a lot of reporters, and they've all asked me about 1997. I really have no business answering them; I don't have any special knowledge, I don't have any roots in Hong Kong, I don't know how the people here feel. But I'm aware that they are anxious, and that they want to know what to do. It's as if an earthquake were about to happen. I'm no seismologist, but people are asking me when the earthquake is going to come, anyway. I can't tell them, but they're just grabbing whomever they can and asking.

Li: Do you think Hong Kong's reverting to China will help or harm Hong Kong?

Fang: It will undoubtedly have an economic impact. In Australia I spoke with some "spacemen" who told me flat out that they don't trust China. These are people with money.

Li: Do you think the "one country, two systems" approach will work, whereby the Central Committee promises to preserve the capitalist system in Hong Kong?

Fang: It might work if there is international support, but it will be a kind of Finlandization. Finland is capitalist, but it has been politically controlled by the Soviet Union.

Li: The Central Committee has made it clear that it expects to have the last word on Hong Kong's legislative, judicial, and executive powers. Could these policies be subject to sudden changes in personnel, as in the case of Deng Xiaoping's health [taking a turn for the worse]?

Fang: It depends on the circumstances. As long as your ideas conform to theirs, it might be fine. In the same sense that we might be allowed to form new political parties in China as long as we accept the Communist Party's leadership. That's one way of doing things.

Li: What effect will the return of Hong Kong have on China itself?

Fang: If it fails, and Hong Kong's prosperity and status as a financial center are ruined, it will have very negative consequences for China.

Li: For several decades, Hong Kong has played the role of supervising China by means of public scrutiny and criticism. Consider the Tiananmen Incident,* which was widely covered in newspapers here. Who will perform this function after 1997 is hard to say. Some people on the mainland even say they're grateful for the Opium War:† It's allowed the outside world to know a little

---

*A demonstration in Tiananmen Square on April 5, 1976, which expressed massive public dissatisfaction with Mao Zedong and the Cultural Revolution. Harshly suppressed by security forces at the time, this demonstration was later officially credited with leading to the overthrow of the "Gang of Four."
†Hong Kong became a British territory as a consequence of the Opium War of 1839–42.

of what goes on in China. This has inhibited those in power a little—they can't just shut the door and beat the dog.

Last year's Campaign Against Bourgeois Liberalization is an example of this. There was very little coverage overseas, but it was headline news in Hong Kong. So our fears regarding what will happen to Hong Kong are not just about Hong Kong itself, but about China as well. Do you think China will permit press freedom in Hong Kong?

Fang: It depends on what level of freedom you're talking about. As long as you remember to acknowledge the Party's "guidance" when you're supposed to, things might be OK. Pay homage and submit your tribute, and otherwise you can do what you like. But at the level of things like the Tiananmen Incident or last year's campaign, I doubt they'd let you publish that. It's too embarrassing to the leaders. After 1997, Hong Kong's ability to oversee the top leadership in the Central Committee will be very much weakened.

Li: Thank you very much for consenting to this interview. Please take care of yourself.

LETTER TO DENG XIAOPING

The following is Fang Lizhi's now-famous letter of January 6, 1989, requesting that the Chinese government release Democracy Wall leader Wei Jingsheng and other political prisoners.

Central Military Commission
Chairman Deng Xiaoping:
This year is the fortieth anniversary of the founding of the People's Republic of China, and the seventieth anniversary of the May Fourth Movement. Surrounding these events there will no doubt be many commemorative activities. But beyond just remembering the past, the many of us even more concerned with the present and the future look to these commemorations to bring with them new hope.

In view of this, I would like to offer my sincere suggestion that on the occasion of these two anniversaries, a nationwide amnesty be declared, especially including the release of political prisoners such as Wei Jingsheng.

I believe that regardless of how Wei Jingsheng is judged, his release after serving ten years of his sentence would be a humanitarian act that would improve the atmosphere of our society.

This year also happens to be the two-hundredth anniversary of the French Revolution. From any perspective, the ideas of liberty, equality, fraternity, and human rights that the French Revolution symbolizes have won the respect of people all over the world. In this light, let me again express my earnest hope that you will consider this suggestion, and thus demonstrate even more concern for our future.

Sincerely, and with best wishes,

Fang Lizhi

January 6, 1989

PATRIOTISM AND GLOBAL
CITIZENSHIP

*The following talk was videotaped in Beijing on February 25, 1989,
by Orville Schell.*

Yesterday I attended a meeting of the History of Science Society
regarding commemorative ceremonies for the seventieth anniversary of the May Fourth Movement. Current plans for commemorating May Fourth do not include the theme of science and
democracy. Of course the student groups would like to talk about
science and democracy, but it seems that they will be forced to
use "patriotism" as a substitute. "Patriotism" is a slogan one hears
quite often right now. My name most likely will not appear on
the list of official speakers, but I do have a few things to say about
patriotism.

Patriotism is a big problem in this country. Criticize someone
for being unpatriotic, and it will shut him right up. But in my
opinion, and I want to say this very clearly, patriotism should not
be our guiding principle. Let me be a little more specific. "Patriotism" can mean many things, ranging from the purest of emotions to the dirtiest of politics, so the word itself is not too clearly
defined. In part, certainly, it refers to a deep love for your
homeland, your kith and kin. In this sense patriotism is a fine
thing, worthy of respect. But the way "patriotism" is being used
right now by no means carries such a simple meaning. Especially

when you emphasize the "-ism" part, it means that what you love is the nation-state.

In my younger days I would join in the criticism of our poor old teachers, who always defended themselves by saying, "At least I'm patriotic; at least I love my country." Our standard reply to that was "But what country do you love? A Communist country? Or a Guomindang country?" Of course what we were implying was that they really weren't patriotic at all.

In this context patriotism didn't mean loving your native place, its lands and rivers and people; it meant loving the state. Such a sentiment clearly has no business as our guiding principle. Because after all, what is the state? According to standard Marxist-Leninist teachings, the state is the instrument of repression! The most important tools of the state are the police, the courts, the prisons, and the army. Does that mean if we love our country we must love the police, the courts, the prisons, and the army? Obviously, such a patriotism is no lofty principle at all, but only a feeling that some would exploit for political purposes.

The first opposition to this kind of nationalistic patriotism that I know of came about during the First World War. (No doubt there were earlier examples, but this one concerns physics, and I'm a physicist, after all.) Though Germany and England were at war, the German and British physics communities continued to cooperate. Many felt that nationalism was wrong. At that time Einstein was setting out General Relativity, and his theoretical predictions were confirmed by the experimental observations of British scientists [led by Sir Arthur Eddington]. This was an outstanding act of cooperation. Why shouldn't we in China revere the same sentiments? At any rate, there is no way that patriotism, in the sense of "loving the machinery of the state," deserves to be exalted as the guiding principle of the May Fourth commemoration.

A second point I would like to make is that even very pure feelings of love for one's homeland have their limits. They can be quite parochial and do not constitute absolute criteria on which to base our judgments. Of course you should love your mother and the land of your origins. But when you encounter something new, should you automatically assume that it's good because it originates from your homeland or that it's bad because it does not? Such an attitude is the source of serious problems in China, and we need to rethink it very carefully. Einstein was a good model here, as well. Although he was a Jew, he did not feel compelled under every circumstance to speak as a Jew, but only as a human being.

In science, we approach a situation by asking if a statement is correct or incorrect, if a new theory is an improvement over an old one. These are our criteria. We do not ask if a thing originates with our race or nationality. This is extraordinarily clear in natural science: There is no Jewish physics or German physics. There is only physics that gives good answers and physics that doesn't. Where it comes from is irrelevant. There are no national boundaries in scientific thought, and science is not the exclusive property of any one race or nation.

I think that many scientists have a perspective that transcends their own particular culture. Local cultures should of course be respected, but not as an immutable principle that must be defended to the bitter end. In China, as well as in the West, there has long been a saying to the effect that "I love my teacher, but I love the truth more." You should love and respect your teachers, but their ideas shouldn't displace your own judgment and convictions. You have to love the truth more—you simply have to. Whether something is or isn't Chinese is not the issue. You can't go tiptoeing around for fear of challenging anything that is labeled "Chinese." That is not the nature of true knowledge.

The issue is whether a thing is true or false, not whether or not it's Chinese.

Things are trickier in the social realm than in natural science, but I think humanity has been slowly evolving in this area as well. As time goes on we arrive at principles that are more and more general in their application. Certainly science was the first such domain. The laws of natural science apply under all circumstances. But in the domain of the social sciences, in society itself, I believe we are also arriving at some increasingly universal precepts. As in science, these truths are not a function of skin color, religion, or nationality. They transcend such boundaries.

Human rights are such a precept. Human rights are not the property of a particular race or nationality. Every human being is born with the right to live, to find a mate, to speak and think freely. These are fundamental freedoms, and everyone on the face of the earth should have them, regardless of what country he or she lives in. I think humanity is slowly coming to recognize this. Such ideas are fairly recent in human history; in Lincoln's time, only a century past, it was just being acknowledged in the United States that blacks and whites should enjoy the same rights. In China we are only now confronting such an issue. The validity of human rights does not depend on the particular culture involved. Cultural biases are fine if you are not asking questions of right and wrong. You can like whatever kind of food you desire; what you eat is a question of preference, not of truth. Taste can be altogether a function of a particular place. But truth cannot. Truth doesn't distinguish between localities.

Of course, when you start asking detailed questions about democracy, such as whether to have a multiparty system, these are things that can differ from place to place. The specific framework of democracy in Britain is a constitutional monarchy, in France a republic, and so forth. These can differ. But they all start with the acknowledgment of human rights, and are built on this foundation. In this sense every place is equal, and China is no exception.

One reason I oppose patriotism is that it seems to become more narrow-minded as time goes on, while even the purest of patriotic sentiments is already too parochial for the world we now live in. Humanity is faced with a very new kind of reality. A century or two ago, a country could be quite isolated from the rest of the world. Relationships based on common interests between nations were rare. But from a scientific perspective today, the interests of all nations have become inseparably linked. We increasingly face common problems, such as energy and the environment. There are many environmental issues which now have to be considered on a global scale, including those of the oceans, the atmosphere, and outer space. Population is another global issue. These are collective problems, and no one nation alone can solve them. It simply can't be done. Desertification in Asia will cause the United States to suffer, and you can't run away from it, not even all the way across the Pacific Ocean. These are global issues, and they demand to be looked at from a global perspective.

In this regard, I would have to say that I personally have been guilty of something common to many scientists, which is believing that science inevitably leads to progress. In fact, one has to acknowledge that science has played a major role in creating many of these massive problems. With the advance of medical science came overpopulation, with the growth of technology came energy problems, and so on. Nonetheless, how do you deal with such problems? I believe that they require a holistic approach, looking at every aspect including the scientific and technological. And above all, they demand the creation of a truly global civilization.

Patriotism has little to contribute to solving problems of this nature. It is a throwback to an earlier stage of history. To restrict your love and concern to your own country at this point in time is completely misguided. We must face up to this. Our activities are now intimately linked with developments in the rest of the world.

You know, the earth is really very, very small. To those of us who work in astronomy, it is clear how small it is. People think that the atmosphere and the oceans are so vast that polluting them is of no consequence, but in fact if humanity continues on this course the earth will not be able to withstand it. Under such circumstances, it is very dangerous not to have balanced, co-operative management of the world's affairs. We need to develop a world culture. National boundaries must be weakened, not strengthened.

So one might speak of what China achieved on its own a millennium or two ago, but in the next century this won't be possible. Progress in China depends on progress in the rest of the world. There are those who speak hopefully of the twenty-first century as being the "Chinese Century," but I find this prospect unlikely. China can't overcome all its problems by itself precisely because the problems we face today don't involve only China.

Einstein's concept of world citizenship was profound. Of course, many of his ideas were poorly received while he was alive. Many critics called his work on a unified field theory, on which he spent the last thirty years of his life, a dead end. Marxist-Leninists blasted his work as philosophical "idealism." He had surprisingly few students. But time has shown the true profundity of Einstein's scientific thought. His ideas about world citizenship were also severely criticized at the time; they were labeled "cosmopolitanism." But in the years ahead, the human race will have to come to grips with this idea as well. It is in this vein that I say that patriotism is not a primary value. I would even call it narrow-minded.

CHINA'S DESPAIR AND CHINA'S HOPE

This essay appeared in The New York Review of Books *on February 2, 1989.*

Nineteen eighty-nine is the Year of the Snake in China. It is not clear whether this snake will bring with it any great temptations. But this much is predictable: The year will stimulate the Chinese into deeper reflection upon the past and a more incisive look at the present. The year will mark both the seventieth anniversary of the May Fourth Movement [a major intellectual and political movement marked by nationalism and Western cultural influence] and the fortieth year since the founding of socialist China in 1949. These two anniversaries may serve as telling symbols of China's hope and China's despair.

Forty years of socialism have left people despondent. In the 1950s, the catch phrases "only socialism can change China" and "without the Communist Party there could be no new China" seemed as widely accepted as physical laws. Today, a look at the "new" China makes one feel that the naive sincerity of those years has been trifled with, the people's enthusiasm betrayed.

True, the past forty years have not been wholly devoid of change or progress. But the standard of comparison for measuring the success or failure of a society should be this: Has the distance between it and the most advanced societies of the world increased or decreased? To measure our forty socialist years by this standard, not only was the Maoist period a failure; even the last ten years of "reform" provide insufficient grounds for the singing of praises.

The failure of the past forty years cannot be blamed—at least not entirely—on the Chinese cultural tradition. The facts clearly show that, of the other nations or territories sharing our cultural background and starting with conditions comparable to China's, nearly all have now joined or are about to join the ranks of the developed world.

Nor can these forty years of failure be blithely attributed to overpopulation. First, we must recognize that China's overpopulation is itself one of the political achievements of the Maoist years. It was Mao's policy in the 1950s to oppose birth control as a "bourgeois Malthusian doctrine" and encourage rapid population growth. Moreover, as everyone knows, one of the greatest factors obstructing China's economic development has been, for years, the parade of massive "class struggle" campaigns and large-scale political persecutions. Are we to believe that any over-populated society must by necessity generate such turmoil and repression? Such a view is plainly illogical.

Logic permits only one conclusion, that the disappointments of the past forty years must be attributed to the socialist system itself. That is why, in China today, pursuit of modernization has replaced faith in any ideology. Socialism of the Lenin-Stalin-Mao variety has been quite thoroughly discredited. At the same time, the May Fourth slogan "science and democracy" is once again circulating and becoming a new source of hope among Chinese intellectuals.

The reforms of recent years, which were begun against the background of this transition in thought, have indeed changed China considerably from what it was in the Maoist period. We should regard these changes as positive. The new emphasis on economics in domestic policy and the cessation of "exporting revolution" in foreign policy are both important examples of progress. On the other hand, the suppression of Democracy Wall nine years ago created the foreboding sense that, when it came to political reform, the authorities were not planning to do much. This fear has been confirmed by the experience of the ensuing years. Consider these examples:

—Even while admitting that the class struggle of the Maoist years was a mistake, the authorities have announced their Four Basic Political Principles, *i.e.,* maintenance of (1) the Communist Party's leading role; (2) the dictatorship of the proletariat; (3) the socialist system; (4) Marxism–Leninism–Mao Zedong Thought. These four principles, in actual content, are hardly distinguishable from Mao's own "Six Political Standards," which were the basic ideas underlying thirty years of class struggle.

—Although the Chinese Constitution provides for freedom of speech and other human rights, the Chinese government has, so far, failed to make its own endorsement of the United Nations Covenants on Human Rights. And in actual practice, even a basic right like freedom of scholarship, which has little political relevance, is commonly infringed. There have been instances, even very recently, in which lectures in the natural sciences have been banned on political grounds.

—Chinese education, which for years suffered the ravages of Mao Zedong's anti-intellectual, anticultural political principles, has left China with a population in which the proportion of illiterates remains about what it was forty years ago. Yet today's expenditures on education, as a proportion of China's GNP, are exactly what they were under Mao, or about 30 to 50 percent below the norm in countries whose economic levels are similar to China's. Ignorance serves dictatorship well. The true reason for the destruction of education is apparent enough.

—In recent years the authorities have repeatedly issued calls for "stability and unity," especially when any signs of political unrest have appeared. Stability and unity seem to have been raised to the status of supreme principles. But when it comes to one of the major causes of instability in Chinese society today—the continuing state of civil war with Taiwan—this supreme principle somehow ceases to apply. In its attempt to end the forty-two-year-old state of war, the Chinese leadership has so far refused, at least in theory, to accept the principle of no military force in relation to Taiwan.

These various problems have spawned continual conflict beneath the surface in Chinese society. The student demonstrations of 1986, which openly called for freedom and democracy in Chinese society, only brought these conflicts into the open. The authorities, in their efforts to curb the influence of the demonstrations, were obliged to fall back on the following two arguments:

1. Chinese culture lacks a tradition of democracy, and thus cannot accommodate a democratic system. The common people are not interested in democracy; they would not know how to use it if they were given it; they lack the ability to support it; etc.
2. Economic development does not necessarily require a democratic system. A dictatorial system may actually be more efficient in this regard. What best suits China is political dictatorship plus a free economy.

To present these arguments amounts, first of all, to public acknowledgment that what we now have is not democracy but dictatorship, and that slogans like "socialism is mankind's most democratic system" are simply a fraud. But if this is the case, how can Marxism still claim a place as the orthodox ideology of China?

The first of the two arguments above might be called "The Law of Conservation of Democracy." It holds that a society's

total capacity for democracy is fixed. If there was no democracy
to start with, then there will also be none later. Nobody, of
course, has set out to prove this law, because the counterexamples
are too numerous. The argument cannot save dictatorship in
China; it can only provide us with some comic diversion.

The second argument does seem to have a certain basis in fact.
There do seem to be some societies that have achieved success by
combining political dictatorship with a free economy. But there
are examples of failure among this group of societies as well. It
follows that the question cannot be decided by enumerating
precedents, but must be answered for China by asking this: Can
a free economy be made compatible with China's own form of
dictatorial government? A look at China in 1988 demonstrated
that, on the whole, the answer to this question must be no.

First, in comparison with other societies that have tried the
"political-dictatorship-plus-free-economy" formula, China dif-
fers in that its system of dictatorship is unable to fully accept a
free economy. This is because socialist dictatorship is closely
bound to a system of "public ownership" (in fact, official ownership), and its ideology is fundamentally antithetical to the kind
of private property rights that a free economy requires. Although
the severe inflation of 1988 has demonstrated quite clearly that
price reform is unworkable unless it is accompanied by reform
in property rights, the Chinese leadership's response to the inflation has been a resort to "the superior strength of politics." This
is but a retreat into the old Mao-era rut of "politics in command."

Second, it has already been shown, repeatedly, that China's
dictatorial system is ineffective in running the country. One need
only look at the corruption within the Communist Party itself
to appreciate this point. Ten years [since 1978] of "rectifying the
Party work-style" has in fact produced nothing but yearly increases in "unhealthy tendencies"—i.e., corruption. What began
merely as "unhealthy" misallocation of large living quarters to

Party leaders now has grown into extensive profiteering called "official turnaround." [The term refers to use of official power and connections to procure commodities or other resources at low prices in the state-run sector of the economy, then "turning around" to sell them at huge markups within the private sector.] Our minimum conclusion must be this: There is no rational basis for a belief that this kind of dictatorship can overcome the corruption that it itself has bred. Based on this problem alone, we need more effective means of public supervision and a more independent judiciary. This means, in effect, more democracy.

China's hope, at present, lies in the fact that more and more people have broken free from blind faith in the leadership. They have come to realize that the only avenue to progress for the society is through adoption of an oversight role for the public, which should have the right to express open criticisms of the leadership. The deputy editor of a newspaper in Guangzhou recently stated quite clearly that the function of his newspaper is to speak not for the Communist Party, but for the emergent middle class of Guangzhou. Not long ago, in an effort to stifle rising popular criticism of their performance, the authorities sternly announced their intention to "trace the rumor that top leaders and their children hold foreign bank accounts." The actual consequence of this effort, however, was only to cause the further spread of two basic ideas: first, that citizens have the right to evaluate the actions of their leaders; and second, that no holder of high office, even Deng Xiaoping himself, has the right to reject this supervision. The old idea that "superiors must not be opposed" is on the way out; democratic consciousness is moving in.

As democratic consciousness spreads, it is bound to lead to the formation of organizations with increasing power to weigh against the authority of the leadership. In fact such groups have already begun to appear in embryo. Right now, in many trades and professions, and at all levels of Chinese society, we are seeing the growth of unofficial clubs, associations, discussion groups, and other informal gatherings that have begun, in various degrees, to wield influence as pressure groups. Democracy is no longer just a slogan; it has come to exert a pressure of its own. The purpose of this pressure is to oblige the authorities, gradually and through nonviolent means, to accept changes that further political democracy and a free economy. Currently, the following are among the items most commonly discussed:

1. Guarantees of human rights. Most important, freedom of speech, freedom of the press, and freedom of assembly. Also, release of Wei Jingsheng and all other political prisoners.
2. Establishment of a free economic system. Gradual implementation of economic reforms that will include reforms in property rights.
3. Support for education. Abandonment of the "ignorant masses" policy; provision of the urgently needed and entirely feasible education commensurate with China's economic level.
4. Accountability for holders of public office. Use of open, *glasnost*-style means to root out corruption.
5. An end to China's state of civil war; promotion of peace in the Taiwan straits. The mainland side to call for mutual renunciation of force as a means of settling differences. A transition from mutual hostility toward peaceful competition.
6. Establishment of rule by law. Opposition to rule by individuals, whether directly or in disguised form, as when Party documents or policies override the laws of the nation.
7. Revision of the Constitution. Deletion of all language that relies on the principle of "class struggle" to support

dictatorship. Drafting of a Chinese constitution that provides for political democracy and economic freedom.

The road to Chinese democracy has already been long and difficult, and is likely to remain so for many years to come. It may take a decade, a generation, or even longer. But whatever the case, there can be no denying that a trend toward democracy has been set that will be very hard to turn completely around. Chinese history since the May Fourth period, including the forty years since 1949, makes it clear that democracy is not bestowed from on high, but must be fought for and won. We must not expect this fact to change in the decades to come. Yet it is precisely because democracy is generated from below that— despite the many frustrations and disappointments in our present situation—I still view our future with hope.

—Translated by Perry Link

PEACE PRIZE SPEECH

The following is Fang's letter accepting the Peace Prize jointly spon-
sored by the newspapers Politiken *of Denmark and* Dagens Nyheter
of Sweden. Fang received the award in absentia *in September 1989.*

I am delighted to be the recipient of this year's Peace Prize
awarded by *Politiken* of Denmark and *Dagens Nyheter* of Sweden.
This is a great honor for me. I regret that I cannot travel to
Copenhagen to participate in this distinguished gathering, nor
receive this prize in person. I can only express my heartfelt
appreciation from afar.

Perhaps my being forced to accept the prize in this manner is
a good illustration of what the cause of peace really means. It
symbolizes the difficulties that obstruct peace, and how much the
concern, the support, and the participation of people everywhere
are needed. It also symbolizes a cause that transcends national
boundaries, territorial boundaries, color, and race. As you con-
vene this gathering in Scandinavia, you can feel a resonance with
those of us on the opposite side of the earth. Indeed, the earth
is an inseparable whole. Humanity itself is also a whole, and our
consciousness is interlinked. No matter North, South, East, or
West, in ancient times or present, human beings know intuitively
to pursue peace, to pursue happiness, to pursue freedom, to pursue
a better world. In the expectant face of the mermaid of Copenhagen, and in the outstretched arm of the goddess of Beijing in June,
we see almost the same bright ideals.

Today's world is still far from ideal, yet it is not altogether without bright spots. The world is becoming more rational, more civilized. In more and more regions we see war being replaced with peace; between great-power blocs we see hostility being replaced with reconciliation; among more and more people we see hatred being replaced with respect. The spirit of science and reason and realism are bridging the gulf between faiths, dissolving the barriers between systems, tearing down the barbed-wire fences along borders. There is a tide in today's world, a rising tide of peace, democracy, reason, and tolerance.

Our world is changing with each new wave this rising tide brings in. The changes are evident in Europe and in Asia daily, in some cases almost *hourly*. And they are taking place in China as well.

These changes are not devoid of suffering. China has again shed fresh blood, blood which testifies to an oft-proved truth:

—Without respect for human rights, there will be resorting to violence;

—Without tolerance and pluralism, there will be resorting to prison;

—Without democratic checks and balances, there will be resorting to armed coercion.

China's history has long since proven, and continues to prove, that using violence and imprisonment and armed coercion to enforce upon a nation a single belief, a single point of view, a single superstition, will only lead to instability, poverty, and backwardness.

Freedom, democracy, human rights, and the rule of law are the indispensable guarantees of peace and prosperity.

Autocracy, dictatorship, force, and repression provide the breeding ground for turmoil and war: internal war, external war, cold war, hot war.

The philosophy of class struggle prevailed in China during the

Cultural Revolution. Under this orthodoxy, society was rampant with suspicion, bullying, oppression, hostility, and endless cruelty. From our vantage point today, it appears that this philosophy is not so much barbaric and evil as it is ignorant, a kind of primitive religion.

Faced with the current situation in China, one wants to cry out: If we once again incite suspicion, hostility, and cruelty, then we will reap the same results as the Cultural Revolution. China will sink into isolation, poverty, ignorance, and barbarism.

What China needs is progress, prosperity, and development.

What China needs is progress, prosperity, and development in an environment of peace, conciliation, and harmony.

What China needs is peace, conciliation, and harmony guaranteed by democracy, human rights, and the rule of law.

I firmly believe that China, along with the world as a whole, will eventually move toward peace, conciliation, and harmony, because peace, conciliation, and harmony are the true essence of nature and of humankind.

The great Danish physicist Niels Bohr discovered the Principle of Complementarity, which illustrates the natural tendency in the world for ideas to complement one another.

The famous Swedish mathematician Sophus Lie created the beautiful Lie Group. We have seen that when there is coordination and cooperation between the world's parts, they can form just such a harmonious and beautiful grouping.

Many of the ancient Chinese philosophers believed that harmony is the essential nature of the universe, and that peace is the true province of human beings.

I am optimistic. I believe that the spirit of peace, conciliation, and harmony will thrive in China; and that an ideal of freedom, democracy, prosperity, and development will materialize in China. My optimism is based on my faith in the truths spoken by many ancient sages. And it is also based on my faith in today's reality.

Although China has a vast territory and large population, it is still a member of the community of nations. China cannot stand apart from all worldwide currents and trends. The world is heading toward peace, democracy, and prosperity. China cannot but also head toward peace, democracy, and prosperity.

Individuals can stand apart from such trends, and China as a whole may, for a while, also stand apart. But China as a whole cannot permanently stand apart.

I hope everyone will remain as optimistic toward the future as I.

Thank you all.

KEEPING THE FAITH

The following is the text of Fang Lizhi's acceptance speech at the Robert F. Kennedy Memorial Human Rights Awards in Washington, D.C., on November 15, 1989. At the time, Fang and his wife, Li Shuxian, were in refuge within the U.S. Embassy in Beijing.

I am proud and deeply moved to have this opportunity to address you here today; at the same time, I am filled with sadness and remorse. I am moved because you have chosen to honor me with the 1989 Robert F. Kennedy Human Rights Award, which attests to the fact that I have not been, and am not now, alone. But I am full of sorrow that in the land of my birth, human dignity has once again been trampled upon. Indeed, having had my own basic rights stripped away, I am more acutely aware than ever how far we still have to go in promoting respect for the dignity of all human beings.

The values that underlie human dignity are common to all peoples. They are the universal standards of human rights that apply without regard to race, nationality, language, or creed. Symbolized by the United Nations' Universal Declaration of Human Rights, these principles are increasingly accepted and respected throughout the world. When a commemorative gathering was held last November in Beijing to honor the fortieth anniversary of the Declaration, many of us were delighted, because it seemed that the principles of human rights were finally starting to take root in our ancient land as well.

However, time after time such fond dreams have been shattered by a harsh reality. In the face of the bloody tragedy of last June, we now must admit to having been far too optimistic. Some of those responsible for this repression have attempted to defend their behavior by declaring that "China has its own standard of human rights," rejecting the world's censure by refusing to acknowledge the universal nature of human rights. They appear to think that by labeling something an "internal affair" they are free to ignore principles upheld throughout the world and do as they please.

This is the logic of feudalism. During ancient China's long isolation from the rest of the world, purporting to be the "master of all under heaven" may have been an effective means of controlling the country. But in the latter part of the twentieth century, declarations about "internal affairs" only serve to expose those who make them as the feudal dictators they are. Such statements have lost their capacity to intimidate or deceive.

To bring China into the modern world, we must incorporate into our society precisely those aspects of advanced civilization—science and democracy, especially—that have proven to apply everywhere. From the science and democracy movement of 1919 to the rising cry for intellectual freedom of 1957; from the protest marches of 1926, which were met by swords and rifles, to the demonstrations of 1989, which were confronted by tanks and machine guns—we can see how passionately the Chinese people have wanted a just, rational, and prosperous society. Although China has deep-seated problems that have caused it to lag behind the developed countries, our history shows clearly that the Chinese have long sought the same kind of progress as people around the globe, regardless of their race or nationality. When it comes to such aspirations, the Chinese are no different from anyone else. Like all other members of the human race, Chinese are born with bodies, brains, feelings, and souls. They ought to enjoy the same inalienable rights, dignity, and liberty as any other human beings.

Allow me to draw a parallel from Chinese history. Recent propaganda to the effect that "China has its own standard of human rights" bears an uncanny resemblance to pronouncements made by our eighteenth-century rulers when they declared that "China has its own astronomy." The feudal elite of two hundred years ago opposed the notion of an astronomy based on science and refused to acknowledge the universal applicability of modern astronomy, even that it might be of some use in formulating the Chinese calendar. They opposed it because the laws of astronomy made it apparent that their claim of a "heaven-conferred" mandate to rule was a fiction. By the same token, universal principles of human rights make it equally clear that the "natural" right to rule claimed by today's leaders is just as baseless. This is why rulers buoyed up by special privilege in every era have opposed the equality inherent in universal precepts.

The great advances of civilization have often followed on the heels of the discovery and development of general concepts and laws. Those who rejected the idea that science applied in China as well were, in fact, demonstrating their fear of modernity. The feudal aristocrats of two centuries past saw astronomy as the bearer of modern culture, and, as a result, ruthlessly persecuted those involved in its study and practice. Indeed, in one instance of oppression during the early Qing Dynasty, five astronomers from the Beijing Observatory were even put to death. But, far from demonstrating might, such brutality really only demonstrated fear. Equally fearful of the implications of universal human rights, modern-day dictators also resort to murder. But no more than in the case of their predecessors should we construe their actions as a sign of strength.

Some people say that the terror that has filled Beijing since June cannot help but make one pessimistic. And I must admit to such feelings myself. But I would also like to offer up a small bit of encouragement. Remember that in the current climate of terror, it may well be that those responsible for killing their fellow human beings are the most terrified. We may be forced to live in terror today, but we have no fear of tomorrow. The murderers, on the other hand, are not only fearful of the present; they are even more terrified of tomorrow. Thus we have no reason to lose our faith in the future. Ignorance, and the violence that serves it so well, may dominate in the short run, but in the long term it will be unable to resist the advance of universal truths. [As Galileo said while the Inquisition passed judgment on him,] "But the earth *does* move."

Of course, it takes time for the earth to move, and for China the movement may be slow, indeed. With this in mind, I would like to direct a few remarks to the young Chinese in the audience. I know that many of you have dedicated your lives to rebuilding our country. Since the road to rebirth will be a long one, I fervently hope that you will not abandon your education, but rather work harder than ever to broaden and deepen your knowledge.

We are all disciples of nonviolence. What power can nonviolence summon to resist the armed violence of the world? There are many ways that nonviolence can manifest itself, but I believe that at the root of them all lies the force of knowledge. Without knowledge to back it up, nonviolence can degenerate into pleading, and history is unmoved by pleading. [To paraphrase Einstein,] It is only when we stand on the shoulders of the giant that is knowledge that we can change the course of history. Only with knowledge will we be able to overcome ignorance and violence at their roots. Only with knowledge will we muster the compassion to deliver from their folly those who superstitiously worship the power of violence. As Ibsen said, "If you want to be of value to society, there is no better way than to forge yourself into a vessel for its use." I hope that all of us will strive to forge ourselves into just such vessels.

Many friends have expressed concern about our current situation, and I want to take this opportunity to thank both those of you whom we already know, and those of you whom we have not yet met, from the bottom of my heart. Because of the extraordinary circumstances under which we now live, I am unable to discuss the details of our daily lives. But there is one bit of news that may lighten your hearts somewhat. I am doing my best to exercise to the fullest extent possible two of my remaining human rights, namely the right to think and the right to inquire. I am continuing my research in astrophysics. In fact, since June of this year, I have written two research papers and am now in the middle of a third.

In my field of modern cosmology, the first principle is called the "cosmological principle." It says that the universe has no center, that it has the same properties throughout. Every place in the universe has, in this sense, equal rights. How can a human race that has evolved in a universe of such fundamental equality fail to strive for a society without violence and terror? And how can we not seek to build a just world in which the rights due every human being from birth are respected?

May the blessings of the universe be upon us. My thanks to you all.

Beijing
November 1989

THE END OF FORGETTING
HISTORY

The following was written while Fang was still in refuge inside the U.S. Embassy in Beijing, before his release in June 1990. It was published in The New York Review of Books *on September 27, 1990, under the title "The Chinese Amnesia."*

In November 1989, during the fifth month of my refuge inside the American Embassy in Beijing, I received two letters from New York, one from the president of a group called Human Rights in China, and one from a friend. Both letters asked me to contribute my calligraphy to the title page of a book called *Children of the Dragon** that the two were currently editing. At first I was inclined not to do it. For one thing, I couldn't find a writing brush or Chinese ink slab in the embassy. All I had was a Chinese typewriter, hardly appropriate for the kind of calligraphy that was needed. But second, I wasn't very fond of the four words "Children of the Dragon." To symbolize the Chinese people by a dragon, a creature that does not exist, may seem to imply that the Chinese people are unique in kind. This runs counter to my fundamental belief that human nature is universal and admits no distinctions of race.

Still, because I was entirely in agreement with the spirit and content of the book that the editors were planning, I eventually

*Human Rights in China, *Children of the Dragon* (New York: Collier, 1990).

found a way to do the calligraphy. Sometimes book titles are only convenient tags, I thought; there was no need to get overly scrupulous about it. Now that the book is published, I am delighted that it carries my four-word contribution.

• • •

As a four-word contributor I am technically one of the authors of *Children of the Dragon*. Authors of course wish that their books will circulate widely. But I wish to show, in the remainder of this essay, why I will be even happier if the circulation is only modest.

There seems to be no accurate count of all the books that have appeared about the Tiananmen events of the spring of 1989. But certainly there have been many. A friend at Columbia University recently wrote me that she and one of her Chinese colleagues, both of whom were eyewitnesses at Tiananmen, had originally planned to write a book about it. But publishers told them that so many Tiananmen books were already available that the market had become "saturated." The two reluctantly dropped their plan. It seems that a new Tiananmen book, for now, can have only a modest circulation.

In my view, a large but "saturated" market is itself one of the most important consequences to emerge from the events at Tiananmen. It signals the failure of the "Technique of Forgetting History," which has been an important device of rule by the Chinese Communists. I have lived under the Chinese Communist regime for four decades, and have had many opportunities to observe this technique at work. Its aim is to force the whole of society to forget its history, and especially the true history of the Chinese Communist Party itself.

In 1957 Mao Zedong launched an "Anti-Rightist Movement" to purge intellectuals, and 500,000 people were persecuted. Some were killed, some killed themselves, and some were imprisoned or sent for "labor reform." The lightest punishment was to be labeled a "Rightist." This was called "wearing a cap" and meant that one had to bear a powerful stigma. I had just graduated from college that year, and also in that year was purged for the first time.

After the 1957 Anti-Rightist purge, what worried me most was not that I had been punished, or that free thought had been curtailed. At that time I was still a believer, or semibeliever, in Marxism, and felt that the criticism of free thought, including my own free thought, was not entirely unreasonable. But what worried me, what I just couldn't figure out, was why the Communist Party of China would want to use such cruel methods against intellectuals who showed just a tiny bit (and some not even that) of independent thought. I had always assumed that the relationship between the Communist Party and intellectuals, including intellectuals who had some independent views, was one of friendship—or at least not one of enmity.

Later I discovered that this worry of mine seemed ridiculous to teachers and friends who were ten or twenty years older than I. They laughed at my ignorance of history. They told me how, as early as 1942, before the Party had wrested control of the whole country, the same cruel methods against intellectuals were already being used at the Communist base in Yenan. In college I had taken courses in Communist Party history, and of course knew that in 1942 at Yenan there had been a "rectification" movement aimed at "liberalism," "individualism," and other non-Marxist thought. But it was indeed true that I had had no idea that the methods of that "rectification" included "criticism and struggle"—which meant in practice forcing people to commit suicide, and even execution by beheading. People who had experienced the Yenan "rectification" paled at the very mention of it. But fifteen years later my generation was completely ignorant of it. We deserved the ridicule we received.

. . .

After another thirteen years, in 1970, it became our turn to laugh at a younger generation. This was in the middle stage of the Cultural Revolution that took place between 1966 and 1976. In the early stage of the Cultural Revolution, Mao Zedong had used university students, many of whom supported him fanatically, to bring down his political opponents. But in the early 1970s these same students became the targets of attack. In 1970 all the students and teachers in the physics department of the University of Science and Technology of China were sent to a coal mine in Huainan, Anhui Province, for "reeducation." I was a lecturer in physics at the time. The movement to "criticize and struggle" against the students' "counterrevolutionary words and deeds" reached its most intense point during the summer. Some students were "struggled"; others were locked up "for investigation"; a good number could not endure the torment of the vile political atmosphere and fell ill. One of my assignments was to pull a plank-cart (like a horse cart, but pulled by a human being) to transport the ill students. Of the group of forty-some students working in the same mine as I did, two were driven to suicide— one by jumping off a building, the other by lying in front of a train.

Most of these students, as innocent as I had been in 1957, never imagined that the Communist government could be so cruel in its treatment of students who had followed them so loyally. Later one of the students, who became my coworker in astrophysical research (and who is now in the United States), confided to me that he had had no knowledge whatever of the true history of the Anti-Rightist Movement. It was not until he was himself detained and interrogated that he slowly began to appreciate why some of the older people he knew lived in such fear of the phrase Anti-Rightist. The whole story of the main actors and issues of the Anti-Rightist Movement had, for this generation, become a huge blank.

This was all repeated again in 1989. According to one incomplete survey of students who participated in the Tiananmen democracy movement, more than half of them had no precise knowledge of what happened in the spring of 1979 when young activists posted independent views on the Democracy Wall in Beijing and were soon arrested for doing so. They did not know about Deng Xiaoping's persecution of the participants in the Democracy Wall Movement, or about "the Fifth Modernization,"or that Wei Jingsheng,* one of the most outspoken of the activists, was still serving time for what he did. Events of a mere ten years earlier, for this new generation, were already unknown history.

. . .

In this manner, about once each decade, the true face of history is thoroughly erased from the memory of Chinese society. This is the objective of the Chinese Communist policy of "Forgetting History." In an effort to coerce all of society into a continuing forgetfulness, the policy requires that any detail of history that is not in the interests of the Chinese Communists cannot be expressed in any speech, book, document, or other medium.

The year 1987 was the thirtieth anniversary of the Anti-Rightist Movement. In November 1986 Xu Liangying, Liu Binyan,* and I made plans for a scholarly conference that looked back on the Anti-Rightist Movement from a perspective of thirty years. Our primary aim was to establish a record of the true history of this period. Even though the movement had brought suffering to half a million people (the number persecuted to death was far greater than the number killed in the June 4 massacre), still we

*See Glossary.

looked in vain for any openly published materials on the history of the movement. The only records of the movement were inside the memories of those fortunate enough to have survived it. With the passage of time, those fortunate survivors were themselves becoming fewer and fewer, and for the younger generation, the impression of the Anti-Rightist Movement was growing fainter and fainter. We wished to create a record of the movement before those who could supply oral accounts disappeared.

Our plan was promptly suppressed by the authorities. In mid-December 1986, we sent out the first of our announcements of a "Scholarly Conference on the Thirtieth Anniversary of the Anti-Rightist Rectification." The response was quick. Within days some people sent us papers, while others expressed their support by sending money. But the authorities acted just as quickly. Xu Liangying and Liu Binyan were subjected to tremendous pressure (I was spared, since I was not in Beijing at the time). After two weeks there was no alternative except to announce that the conference could not be held. This showed that, even for events that had taken place thirty years earlier, the Communist authorities remained unwilling to allow the slightest opening for free discussion, and would permit only a thorough forgetfulness. Thus it remains the case today that there is no publication dealing in depth with the Anti-Rightist Movement of 1957 to be found on the open book market in China.

Regrettably, Western literature on China, so far as I know, also seems to lack such a book. Much of the history of Chinese Communism is unknown to the world, or has been forgotten. If, inside China, the whole of society has been coerced into forgetfulness by the authorities, in the West the act of forgetting can be observed in the work of a number of influential writers who have consciously ignored history and have willingly complied with the "standardized public opinion" of the Communists' censorial system.

The work of the late Edgar Snow provides one of the most telling examples of this tendency. Snow lived many years in China; we must assume that he understood its society. And yet, in his reports on China after the Communists took power, he strictly observed the regime's propaganda requirements—including the forgetting of history. In *Red China Today* he had this to say about China in the early 1960s:

> I diligently searched, without success, for starving people or beggars to photograph. Nor did anyone else succeed. . . . I must assert that I saw no starving people in China, nothing that looked like old-time famine, [and] that I do not believe that there is famine in China at this writing.*

The facts, which even the Chinese Communists do not dare to deny publicly, are that the early 1960s saw one of the greatest famines in more than two thousand years of recorded Chinese history. In the three years between 1960 and 1962 approximately twenty-five million people in China died of hunger. As for beggars, not only did they exist, they even had a kind of "culture," with Communist characteristics. In 1973 in Anhui I listened to a report by the "advanced" Party secretary of a peasant village. One of his main "advanced" experiences was to organize his villagers into a beggars' brigade to go begging through the neighboring countryside.

Snow's tomb is located on a quiet and secluded little hillock on the campus of Beijing University. He was respected in China during his lifetime; no one doubted the sincerity of his love for China and the Chinese people. But his writings have not received similar respect. His books have adopted too much of the view-

---

*Edgar Snow, *The Other Side of the River: Red China Today* (Random House, 1961), p. 619.

point of his old friend Mao Zedong, which is to say the view-point of official Communist propaganda. The works of China experts such as Snow have served, in fact, as a "Special Propaganda Department" for the Communists. They have helped the Communists' "Technique of Forgetting History" to become a completed circle, continuous both inside and outside China.

This foreign aid has helped the Chinese Communists, over a long period of time, to carry on their activities beyond the reach of world opinion and exempt from effective scrutiny. The Communists' nefarious record of human rights violations is not only banned from memory and discussion inside China, but has also been largely overlooked by the rest of the world, which never condemned its repression with the urgency and rigor that would have been appropriate.

The events in Tiananmen Square were the first exception to this pattern—the first time that Chinese Communist brutality was thoroughly recorded and reported, and the first time that virtually the whole world was willing to censure it.

• • •

Even though, inside China, the Communists are still doing all they possibly can to press ahead with their "Technique of Forgetting," their "Special Propaganda Department" no longer exists. The position of the world's opinion makers, and especially of the various reporters and observers inside China, has changed as well. In the early 1960s Edgar Snow was invited to stand next to Mao Zedong on top of the wall at Tiananmen and take part in the grand pomp and ceremony. By 1990, the lot of reporters had come to include beatings by troops at the base of that same wall. This has been one of the extremely significant changes occasioned by the Tiananmen events.

Hence, the "saturation of the market" by books about Tiananmen represents an important fact: While international concern about the regime's repression may have to some extent faded, no longer will the Chinese Communists be able to hide beyond the reach of world opinion. Facts will no longer be so easy to cover up, and the real history of last year's events cannot possibly be forgotten. This is an indispensable step in China's joining the world and moving toward progress.

—Translated by Perry Link

FREE TO SPEAK:
SECOND INTERVIEW
WITH TIZIANO TERZANI

The following interview with Der Spiegel *correspondent Tiziano Terzani took place in July 1990, shortly after the release of Fang Lizhi and Li Shuxian from their sanctuary within the American Embassy in Beijing. It took place at Cambridge University, where Fang accepted a temporary position as visiting researcher. Parts of this interview appeared in the* Far Eastern Economic Review *on August 2, 1990.*

Question: Professor Fang, over a year ago, immediately after the Tiananmen massacre, you and your wife took refuge in the American Embassy in Beijing. For that year you were locked up there, all the time uncertain about what would happen to you. Now you are in peaceful Cambridge. Do you consider your being here a victory or a defeat?

Fang: Both. The fact that the Chinese authorities were forced to let me go is a victory. The fact that I had to leave my own country, my friends, my colleagues is my failure.

Question: What do you think forced the Beijing government to let you go?

Fang: International pressure—this is in itself an important change. It is the first time that the Chinese authorities have allowed a dissident to go abroad, and this is because China has become responsive to the rest of the world.

276

Question: Don't you think that they allowed you to go also because, as a prisoner inside the American Embassy, you were becoming a martyr, while now, a free man outside of China, you may soon become politically irrelevant?

Fang: Yes, this is true. Away from China I shall be less effective.

Question: You have been called many times the Sakharov of China, but Sakharov was exiled within his country, while you are now far from yours.

Fang: That is why I regard my departure also as a defeat. Yet there is an important difference between China and the Soviet Union: There are large overseas Chinese communities present in most countries of the world. It is in these communities that some of the major political causes of China, like that of Sun Yatsen, were born and got their support.

Question: Let's go back to the events of last year and to Tiananmen. Let's try to reconstruct how you went through that experience. First of all let's clear the air on a major issue. You know that outside China there has been a great debate about what really happened on June 4, and even among some Western journalists there are doubts about the extent of the massacre that took place. The Chinese government on its part has played very shrewdly with this issue of the "Tiananmen massacre" by saying that not a single person was killed on the square, that there was no "Tiananmen massacre," and therefore no massacre at all. What is your assessment?

Fang: There is no point in discussing whether at a certain moment at a certain spot there was killing or not. The Chinese government itself admits that there were more than 300 dead people. This figure alone is higher than that of all the people killed in all the student movements of the last 100 years. Can we call it a massacre? The conclusion is obvious to anybody.

Question: Do you have any idea how many people were really killed?

Fang: It is very difficult to say because much evidence was immediately destroyed by the military. There is a lot that is still unknown about the suppression of the pro-democracy movement.

Question: During the whole period that led to the massacre, you kept a very low profile. You did not speak frequently in public, and you did not even show up on Tiananmen to address the mass rallies there. Why?

Fang: From the very beginning the authorities hinted that the movement was started and controlled by a handful of bad eggs, and that the top bad egg was Fang Lizhi. Of course I wholeheartedly supported the movement, but I wanted to make clear that it could not have been controlled by any one person and that it was a spontaneous, mass movement of intellectuals and students.

Question: The Chinese government has accused you of being the major conspirator of the "counterrevolutionary rebellion" of last year, and that is why, after the massacre, your name was put at the top of the "most wanted" list in China. You might not like to be called a "conspirator," but would you accept the appellation "inspirator"?

Fang: Yes. This is a label I have to accept. Before the previous student movement of 1986, I expressed my political views in many speeches. Those views were embraced by students and intellectuals, therefore I indeed had a role in what happened last year.

Question: To observers like myself, the movement, especially toward the end, looked ideologically rather confused. On one side there were people who seemed to be influenced by a sort of

Maoist nostalgia, on the other there were people who mistook Western affluence for Western democracy. Do you think that the movement had a clear idea of what it was and what it wanted?

Fang: No. I agree with your observation. The movement was made up of different people with very different backgrounds and with very different demands. Because of this it had no unified leadership and no clear objective. But it was still a very important movement.

Question: Why?

Fang: Because notwithstanding their different points of view, all the participants shared one thing in common: a profound disillusionment with the Communist Party. This was the common ground of everybody.

Question: Did you ever think in those days that the movement could succeed in toppling the government, as later happened in Eastern Europe?

Fang: Never! My expectations at the time were rather limited. At most I thought we could gain more freedom. For instance, not total freedom of the press, but less restrictions than before. I thought we could achieve the recognition of the independent student organizations, not in society as a whole, but on campus. What happened later in Eastern Europe was beyond even my dreams.

Question: What went wrong with the movement? Do you think that at the end it was manipulated? Did the factions fighting for power within the Party use the movement to their advantage?

Fang: There must have been some people within the Party who attempted to control the movement, but on the whole they did not have the strength to do it. The people's demand for democracy was certainly stronger than ever before, but as you all saw, at the last stages of the demonstrations all sorts of people joined in without unified leadership, and that made it easier for the government to launch the repression. . . .

Question: How widespread do you think the movement was in China? We know that there were demonstrations in many cities besides Beijing and Shanghai, but even if one adds up all the people who marched for democracy throughout China, one can say that ten million people did so. But that simply means that 1.2 billion Chinese did not move. What do you think?

Fang: I think the scale of the movement was unprecedented. Of course even ten million people in a Chinese context is a very, very small number, but compared with previous movements in China, none was so big, not even the demonstrations organized by the Communist Party.

Question: Tell us what happened to you in the last few hours of the demonstration, and how you reached the decision to take refuge in the U.S. Embassy.

Fang: The idea was suggested by some friends. The massacre convinced many people that the government had lost its mind and that it would go after all those who had been involved in the movement. On June 4, as soon as the shooting started at Tiananmen, I received various telephone calls from friends telling me that I was now in great danger. Some friends came to our house to persuade us to leave. Some had come with their cars to take us away. So on the afternoon of June 4 we left the house. We went into a hotel and spent the night there. On June 5 we left the hotel for the embassy.

Question: Why the American Embassy?

Fang: Well, I am a proponent of modern ideas, but I am still influenced by the Chinese tradition . . .

Question: Which tradition?

Fang: The tradition of putting oneself under foreign protection when in danger.

Question: When you got to the embassy, did you ask for political asylum?

Fang: Not at all. Our plan was to stay there for just a couple of days until the government could regain control of itself and start behaving rationally again.

Question: On June 5 you went into the embassy, but soon after you came out, only to go back again a few hours later. Why? What happened?

Fang: The embassy staff said that our presence there could not be kept secret, and I thought that the publicity would only further complicate the situation, so we left. Around five o'clock on June 5 we went to the Jianguo Hotel and stayed there. At eleven o'clock the same night, two American diplomats came to the hotel to tell me that I ought to go back to the embassy as a "guest of President Bush" and that we could stay there as long as we wanted. We got in their car and went to the embassy again.

Question: Looking back, was it a mistake to go into the American Embassy? Don't you think that putting yourself under the protection of a big foreign power has hurt your image? Would you do it again?

Fang: On the whole that decision has had some positive effects on the events that followed, but I do not know whether I would do it again. Even then I found it difficult to decide the way I did.

In any case I have a number of historical predecessors in this. In 1898 leaders of the reform movement took refuge by the arrangement of the British and Japanese embassies when the Beijing government went after them. Sun Yatsen managed to escape with his life thanks to British protection in Canton. Various Chinese Communist leaders were saved by foreign protection, like Li Dazhao, who in the twenties hid himself in the Soviet Embassy. . . . I am just the first to do so in forty years.

Question: Is it true that two days later you tried to leave the embassy again?

Fang: Yes, that was on June 8. But at that point the American diplomats were worried about letting me go and postponed the arrival of the car I had asked to take me out.

Question: Of course at that point the Americans had already boasted that they had you at the embassy and that President Bush was finally doing something to help the democracy movement.

Fang: I must say that my wife, Li Shuxian, also played an important role. She asked me not to leave. She was afraid that I would be killed. So I decided to stay.

Question: How have you spent the year in the embassy? How did you feel, locked up in the middle of Beijing? What were the greatest difficulties? What did you miss most?

Fang: After the first week my feelings stabilized. As I mentioned, I felt most uncomfortable during the first few days, then life took on its own routine. I spent most of the time pursuing my studies of cosmology and writing notes for an autobiography. Most of all I missed my friends.

Question: Did you ever think that you could spend that long a time in the embassy?

Fang: Yes. We had expected to from the very beginning. We knew of similar cases. In Hungary Cardinal Mindszenty was in for fifteen years; in the Soviet Union some dissidents were in for five years. So we thought that our stay in the embassy would not be too short. On the other hand, we did not expect it to be as long as fifteen years, either. At most it would last until all the old men in the leadership died! It could not have been any longer than that.

Question: Why do you think that the Chinese government tried to blame you as having been single-handedly responsible for all the events of those days?

Fang: The highest leader of China hates me.

Question: Deng Xiaoping. Why?

Fang: He has taken my criticism of the regime as a personal attack on himself.

Question: Let's come to your release and to the mechanism that brought it about. The Chinese authorities made a condition for your release: that you sign a document that they could call your "confession." Did you feel uncomfortable negotiating for your freedom?

Fang: No, because I did not accept any condition imposed by the Chinese authorities. I neither confess nor repent. The document I signed consists of three points. The first is the statement of my political views. I say there exactly what I told you in Florence in our interview for *Der Spiegel* three years ago. That is: I do not recognize the Four Basic Principles in the Constitution. The second point is the normal request for a travel permit that any Chinese citizen has to submit when going abroad. The third point is my commitment not to oppose China. This point is crucial, and it means exactly what it says: I will never oppose China.

Question: How about opposing the government?

Fang: The statement does not say anything about that.

Question: Did you negotiate directly with the Chinese authorities?

Fang: No. I never met anybody. All was done through American Ambassador James Lilley, who acted as the mailman.

Question: Still, though indirectly, you negotiated with the people responsible for the killing of hundreds of unarmed people and for this some of the most radical dissidents have criticized you. What do you think?

Fang: It is very simple. The Communist Party is still in power in China, and if we want anything done in China, we have to negotiate with that Party. I see nothing wrong with it. . . .

Question: If China is as sensitive to foreign pressure as you say, what do you think the West should do in order to help the democratization of your country? Should the West maintain its sanctions, should the West discourage investing in China?

Fang: The important thing now is not to isolate China. We cannot afford to break the connection between China and the outside world. One principle should be the strengthening of all kinds of links: economic, cultural, scientific, educational. The other principle should be to relate these links to the progressive forces in China. The West, for instance, should insist on the respect of human rights in China. Only in this way can we maximize the effectiveness of outside pressure.

Question: So you are not calling for the West to stop credits and loans, reduce contacts to China?

Fang: Not at all. That would be a mistake. On the contrary, I think it is important for everybody to deal with the Chinese authorities, to maintain contact with your adversary so that you have a chance to push him to the ground.

Question: You then take a completely different attitude from Nelson Mandela, who, since his release, has gone around the Western world to ask various governments to maintain their sanctions against South Africa.

Fang: I cannot comment on Mandela, because South Africa has its own history. But in the Chinese context we have to look at the history of the last 100 years: Every attempt by China to open itself to the rest of the world has been in response to outside pressure. That is when the country has made some progress. No contacts now would only mean no chances of development in China. Nobody wants that.

Question: Could China close herself again?

Fang: We cannot rule out this possibility. China is still a very big country, and it can survive in isolation. Mao did just that. He understood that if he opened the door that would mean his end, so he kept it closed. Now the situation is different from that of Mao's time, but a return to isolation is not out of the question. That is why a policy of complete sanctions against China will not work.

Question: What will work, then?

Fang: Strength, determination. The present Chinese government does not operate according to internationally recognized rules. It behaves like a bandit who does not use reason, but guns. Yet just as a bandit gives in when he meets a stronger force, so this government makes concessions when faced with strength.

Question: Do you think Deng is very strong?

Fang: He looks strong, but he is no Superman. He respects only power, that is why he was so afraid of Mao.

Question: You once said that Mao was better than Deng because at least the old Helmsman had a vision, while Deng has none. Was Mao really better?

Fang: No. He was not better. He was different. Mao was a philosopher, Deng is not. Deng's intellectual abilities are much less than those of Mao.

Question: Yet he is still in charge. Do you think that he and the other leaders of the old generation are the major obstacle to change in today's China?

Fang: The big obstacle is that the Chinese Communist Party still thinks it is possible to pursue a policy of reforms and openness while maintaining the Four Basic Principles. Now it is clear to everybody that these principles were the ultimate cause of the massacre and that we cannot continue with them.

Question: So how is this change going to take place? Do you see it happening slowly within the framework of the Chinese Communist Party, or dramatically with a big upheaval?

Fang: I don't wish any chaos or violence in China. This is my desire, but the development of history will not necessarily conform to my wishes. No matter whether the changes come from outside or inside, they will have to come. Whether this time they come slowly or suddenly also depends on the international climate.

Question: In our interview three years ago, you said that if there was a Communist country that really had a chance of reforming itself, that country was China. Your argument was that Communism in China had no major achievements to claim, and therefore China was in an even better position than the Soviet Union under Gorbachev. Well, the events of the last three years have proven you wrong. Not only is the Soviet Union undergoing major reforms, but the whole of Eastern Europe is changing, and one country after the other has renounced Communism.

Fang: I was too optimistic then, but I still think that China has a chance. Democracy as a social system is the trend of the modern world, and I believe that China will also progress in this direction. It is almost like a natural law. The popular demand for such progress is strong and has not subsided because of the Tiananmen massacre. The only difference is that now people do not express it as openly as last year.

Question: Do you think the present leadership is seriously worried about what happened in Eastern Europe?

Fang: Of course. What happens in Eastern Europe has a great impact on China. For forty years China and Eastern Europe belonged to the same ideological community.

Question: Do you think that China will experience something similar to Romania, or something similar to Poland, Hungary, and East Germany?

Fang: It is difficult to answer. That there will be change is certain; less certain is the way change will take place. I consider the Romanian experience one of the ways of changing, and although I wish a peaceful evolution, I do not rule out that it could happen that way in China as well.

Question: Ceauçescu was taken prisoner and shot as a criminal. Can you imagine that a man like Deng Xiaoping could be treated the same way for the Tiananmen massacre?

Fang: Those who gave the order to kill should bear the legal responsibility.

Question: In the case of the USSR and Eastern Europe, there is no question that the changes were brought about by popular demand, but above all by the presence on the political stage of a man like Gorbachev. Is there a Chinese Gorbachev?

Fang: Up to now I have seen no traces of him.

Question: Did you think that Zhao Ziyang could have been China's Gorbachev?

Fang: Not very likely.

Question: How about Li Ruihuan, the former mayor of Tianjin?

Fang: I have seen no traces in him, either. It is very difficult to see these things now. Under the Chinese system there is only one man who matters, Deng. For the time being the others do not express their own ideas.

Question: Are you saying that we will have to wait until the death of Deng Xiaoping to see whether China has a Gorbachev?

Fang: Yes.

Question: What will happen when Deng dies?

Fang: The direct result of Deng's death will be a power struggle among today's leaders. How intense a struggle we cannot predict.

Question: Do you see yourself joining a future government?

Fang: I am not thinking about this now. I am a scientist, not a professional politician.

Question: Havel was a writer, but now he is the president of Czechoslovakia.

Fang: I do not think we can compare the present situation in China with Czechoslovakia, or me with Havel. . . .

Question: In one way or another the present leadership of China seems to have been discredited by the events of last year. On the other hand what we see in Eastern Europe indicates how difficult it is to have continuity from the past Communist regimes to the present non-Communist ones. So where will the future leaders of China come from?

Fang: This is a problem we have to face, but there is a Chinese saying that goes, "The situation creates the hero."

Question: You now are the hero. The situation has already created you.

Fang: It is true that I have become well known due to the circumstances. But when the right situation develops again, there will be other people who will become more well known than I.

Question: When we met last time, you formulated the situation in China in a way that has now become famous. You said: "Marxism-Leninism is like an old dress that must be put aside." Are you not worried about that moment when China will be left naked?

Fang: China is already that way, because most people have already thrown away that dress. Only the authorities are still wearing it. So we should say that China is already naked.

Question: So how to cover her?

Fang: I cover her with my religion, which is science.

Question: What do you mean by that?

Fang: I mean that there are certain basic laws in this world. The world can be known, can be understood. Each religion has something to pursue. Well, my pursuit is that we can know and understand more. Even in judging policies this should be our starting point. . . .

Question: Did Marxism-Leninism have any positive effect on China? Did it not impose some kind of public morality?

Fang: Not at all. I disagree with this idea that Marxism brought morality to China. Especially during the last forty years the moral standards in China have been declining rather than ascending. Rather than the so-called morality of Marxist-Leninism, we will have the morality of humanism, we will have mutual respect among people, and not class struggle. I think that any principle of morality has to conform with those of human rights, because the principles of human rights are universal. Those of Marxism-Leninism are not.

Question: You give great importance to the role of intellectuals in the future of China. Yet the past record of intellectuals in your country is not one to be very proud of. Over the last half century most Chinese intellectuals have let themselves be either co-opted, lured, silenced, or repressed by power. Why is it going to be different from now on?

Fang: The situation has changed. In my generation, for instance, it was quite difficult to become completely independent, because we were young during Liberation. For the intellectuals of the new generation it is quite another matter. They will have a much more independent relationship with the authorities. This is a turning point. Take for instance the situation of the intellectuals during the Anti-Rightist Campaign of the fifties and the situation last year. In the fifties people who tried to advocate independent thinking were easily eradicated. This time the authorities had to resort to harsher methods. I think that now the Chinese people in general have seen the meaning of freedom.

Question: You have been the first to stand up and play the role of the independent intellectual. You have said it was enough that one voice arise to set the tone. Now that voice is gone. Do you think that the tone will now be set by others?

Fang: Since we met last time in Florence, more and more people have stood up to speak out. There are now many independent intellectuals besides me. The reason is that Chinese intellectuals are becoming more and more part of the international community, and from those contacts they gain strength themselves. If we increase the contacts, their strength will increase.

Question: What happened to the group that you had at the University of Science and Technology?

Fang: Unfortunately, many have been pushed out. Many of them are now in the United States.

Question: Throughout the history of Communist China every new generation has had its expression of intellectual dissent, yet every generation has been methodically decapitated in one way or another of its best elements, from the Anti-Rightist Campaign, to the Cultural Revolution, to the Tiananmen massacre. Do you think that this time a generation has again been lost, and that China has to wait another generation for change?

Fang: Yes, every generation of Chinese intellectuals has met with the same fate, but it has become more difficult nowadays for the authorities to eradicate people with independent ideas. There are too many of them. I have seen a recent survey in which the majority of people expressed their conviction that the demonstrations of last year were right. The restoration of brainwashing during the past year has not achieved what the authorities expected. It has been completely useless. Very few people have admitted they were wrong. While I was in the American Embassy I heard this story: An American academic delegation had come to China. During their visits to various universities they met government officials who told them that the situation was stable, that the students and the authorities were united, etc. At the end of the translation the young Chinese government interpreters assigned to the group would whisper to the American visitors, "Do not believe a word." This would have been impossible years ago.

Question: How unstable is the situation in China, in your view?

Fang: On the surface all looks normal, but in China instability is hidden. If you go to the students and listen to them, you will hear and see some obvious symptoms of a general dissatisfaction within the society.

Question: But students are a minority. Is there dissatisfaction among the peasants?

Fang: I do not dare to comment on this, since for a long time I have had no contacts with the peasants. But I think that the entrepreneurs among the peasants have relatively independent ideas about the society.

Question: Do you think the fact that some of the students managed to escape means that they had the support of the people and maybe the support of some section of the army and the security forces?

Fang: I am sure that the students who participated in the demonstration had massive support. I am also sure that they had support even within the security forces and the military. What I do not know is the extent of that backing. . . .

Question: What do you think of the Front for Democracy in China [FDC], which was founded with great publicity last summer in Paris soon after the massacre and is now headed by Wu'er Kaixi, Yan Jiaqi, and Wan Runnan?

Fang: I don't think we should single out this particular organization from all the other overseas Chinese organizations. Over the last 100 years many people have left China because of repression by the authorities; and FDC is not the first and not the only one. The very first movement of this kind was a century ago, that of the Taiping rebels. We cannot say that they were the best, but under the pressure of the Qing Dynasty many of these people managed to escape. Later on the leaders of the 1898 Reform movement escaped, and they were followed by others in turn. They all became part of the overseas Chinese political movement. I think that the FDC is only the latest group in this tradition. If we regard this overseas Chinese political movement as a whole, its main purpose remains the same, which is to push the cause of progress in China.

Question: What role do you see yourself playing among all these organizations?

Fang: So far I have no definite idea. I have just arrived. Up to this day I have had little contact with them.

Question: Do you plan to join any of them?

Fang: No, it is too early. For the time being I prefer to be self-employed, to belong to the independent brigade. The important thing is to realize that for the first time, China has a dissident movement operating abroad against the Communist Party. This is a very positive development.

Question: Do you think the FDC should organize itself as a party?

Fang: I do not think so. The key point is to exert influence in China. Whether you call it a party or not does not make any difference.

Question: Should the dissident movement organize an underground in China, aimed, for instance, at spreading pro-democracy information?

Fang: This exists already. Even when I was inside the American Embassy I received leaflets that were sent to me by the movement. . . .

Question: Are you really free? Or are you bound by a gentleman's agreement with the Chinese authorities, who have let you and your family go, to refrain from politics and not to rock the Chinese boat too much?

Fang: There is no gentleman's agreement, but a year inside the embassy certainly has had an effect on me. Everybody is influenced by his immediate history. Nobody can escape from this, yet I feel completely free talking to you.

Question: There are over 100,000 Chinese students now studying abroad. Most of them support the democracy movement, and they want you to talk to them. What is your message to them?

Fang: Study, study hard. The changes we all wish for China are not only political; they are above all cultural ones.

Question: What do you mean?

Fang: If we look at the problems of China from an historical and a detached point of view, we realize that China is a huge isolated country that has begun to blend into the ocean of the world. The process of blending is not only a matter of politics. It requires changes in many aspects. A nation is like a person. Only when a person has acquired a background of modern civilization, including science and other aspects of culture, will that person have his or her own political perspective, be able to think independently. China, as a nation, has to be infused with modern culture, and then it can assimilate into the modern community. That is why the priority for every Chinese who studies abroad is to take advantage of the situation and absorb these modern ideas. I came to my own views about democracy through my conception of science.

Question: Don't you think that many of your young supporters will be disappointed by this call of yours to study and wait passively?

Fang: Well, do we want to be democratic? Then we have to learn that democracy requires a confrontation of ideas and not a leader who says one thing and everybody follows. And besides, to fill oneself with knowledge does not mean to wait passively.

Question: Don't you feel that many Chinese today expect you to play a more active role now that you are free?

Fang: I think that if the Chinese people are expecting the appearance of a hero, it had better not be me. This expectation in itself is very unhealthy.

Question: China has always needed an emperor; maybe now she expects one who can bring democracy.

Fang: That is exactly what I call dangerous. The Chinese people tend to put all their hopes on the next leader, but, as is often the case, their hopes are not realized, and disillusionment immediately follows. Three years ago I told you that some people called me the "teacher of youth." I dislike this term immensely. Of course I do not mean to avoid my responsibility. Especially because of the experiences of the last few years, I am aware of that responsibility, and I shall definitely try to fulfill it, but this does not mean that I want to be a leader.

Question: Isn't it strange? Here you are, the most famous Chinese dissident. Thousands of people have been waiting for you as a sort

of Messiah of dissent who would give them the ten command-
ments of democracy, who would lead the way, who would tell
people what to do—and you just plan to avoid doing this?

Fang: If you ask me what to do next in China, I find it very
difficult to answer. I am not one who knows everything, who can
do everything. I am not God. I know that all the young people
abroad are thinking of what to do next. I also am puzzled by this
question. I don't have ideas that are much wiser or otherwise
superior to those of others. I want very much to do something
to influence things in China, but I think that different people have
different ways of doing things, and we should not have a situation
in which one person says, "We have to do this," and everybody
else must follow. If that is the case, I disagree.

One of the urgent issues in the pro-democracy movement is
to demand of Chinese authorities that they release all people who
are accused of participating in the Tiananmen events last year.

Question: The recent history of China is one of ambitious leaders
struggling for power. You seem to be reluctant in the face of
power and not to have much ambition.

Fang: My personal ambitions are in the scientific world, and even
there they are not too big.

Question: What are they?

Fang: I want to pursue truth, and as Einstein said, I consider that
pursuit much more important than the possession of truth itself.

Question: No other ambition?

Fang: On the general level my greatest ambition is to contribute
to the development of China and to her catching up with the rest
of the world.

Question: Do you believe that China can still make it?

Fang: Yes, but it will not be decided by China alone. If we look to the long run, I think the whole world will become more unified. Modern science and technology make anything else impossible. The greenhouse effect, the population explosion, are issues that cannot be solved without a global solution. If China cannot catch up with the rest of the world, the world will make China catch up with it.

Question: And with all this in front of you, you insist on refusing the political role that people thrust upon you?

Fang: I feel that I have been thrust into the middle of politics by circumstances, but the fact is that each time I could have avoided a commitment, I have had to say what my heart was telling me. That got me involved ever more deeply. Three years ago you asked me about the Four Basic Principles. I could not say that I supported them. That brought me some trouble and got me even more deeply involved in politics. You are one of the people who pushed me into this.

Question: Please, then, describe the role you want to have in the future.

Fang: I just want to plant some seeds in the spirit of China. Let's say four seeds to replace the Four Principles. My seeds are: science, democracy, creativity, and independence. I want to be an activist for human rights. I feel that I have a moral responsibility in this, now that I am free. We have to campaign for the release of all the political prisoners.

Question: Do you consider yourself expelled from China? Do you consider yourself in exile?

Fang: In a formal sense I am not expelled, because I have been given a travel permit, and I am not in exile, because I have a Chinese passport and I have not asked for political asylum.

Question: So theoretically you could go back anytime.

Fang: Yes, and I have to tell you that the idea of going back has been in my mind since the moment I left Beijing on board that military plane the Americans had sent to fetch me and my wife.

Question: In order to speak freely three years ago we met in Florence; now we meet in Cambridge. When do you think we will be able to meet in China and talk in the same way, without fearing the consequences?

Fang: For sure within the next ten years.

APPENDIX

The following appeared in The New York Review of Books, *July 20, 1989. It contains letters of support that Fang received from sympathetic Chinese citizens following his expulsion from the Communist Party in 1987.*

After the 1986 Chinese student movement, a fair number of foreign friends and journalists asked me, "Why is there only one Fang Lizhi in China?" and, "Being one lone person, don't you feel isolated?"

I hope that the following letters will serve as a kind of reply to these questions by providing proof that China has many people whose thoughts are similar to my own, and thus that I am not really alone. Moreover, the dozens of letters I have selected for publication are not even one percent of the number I actually received.

In the Chinese scheme of things, letters are not seen as an inviolable means by which people can communicate. Although Chinese law stipulates that freedom of correspondence is protected, during the last few decades there have been an enormous number of cases in which people have been persecuted because of what they wrote in personal letters. The best-known case was that of the so-called counterrevolutionary clique of Hu Feng.* In 1955, Mao Zedong personally made public certain "counterrevolutionary materials" ascribed to Hu Feng, almost

---

*One of the first well-known dissident intellectuals to be purged after "Liberation." See Glossary.

all of which where lifted from private letters. In actuality the so-called counterrevolutionary parts were nothing more than a few phrases of complaint about the situation at that time.

At the end of 1986, just as the student demonstrations were reaching a crescendo, the mail that normally came in and out of the University of Science and Technology of China where I was vice president, not only suddenly started to turn up more slowly, so that letters which had normally taken no more than two days to arrive began to take a week, but also the number of "lost" letters increased sharply. The reason was self-evident.

Ironically, one cannot make a blanket statement that China has had no openness, or *glasnost.* In fact, so far as the people in authority in the dictatorship of the proletariat are concerned, the letters of select people have long been subject to an official form of *glasnost* treatment. Because of this, just to write a personal letter in China has often required tremendous courage, a courage that is not necessarily any less than what it requires to give a public speech.

Some really courageous people have simply taken to using this type of "openness" for their own good purposes. For instance, a portion of the correspondence that I received in 1987 was written openly, right on the back of postcards. The intention of the writers, who usually signed their names, was clear. Since they knew that this kind of mail was going to be examined anyway, they reasoned, why not just send it openly for all to inspect in the first place? Not only could the censoring authorities easily read the correspondence, but everyone else could see what had been written. These postcards were a means of more broadly disseminating ideas. Indeed, by the fall of 1987, when authorities were most strenuously suppressing democracy and freedom, people eagerly came each day to wait at the mailroom of the Beijing Astronomical Observatory, where I had subsequently been assigned to work, just so that they could read the freshly arrived crop of postcards. Some of these cards protested the actions of the authorities, some supported the views of the students, some derided the so-called Anti-Bourgeois Liberalization Campaign. In a country that has neither freedom of speech nor freedom of the press, one values any kind of freedom all the more, even if it can be exercised only on the back of a tiny postcard.

Precisely because of this, I believe that publishing these letters will not violate their authors' original intentions. Needless to say, I could not get everyone's approval for publication, simply because I had no way of doing so. But I feel that one way I can express my deep gratitude to all those who have encouraged and supported me is by openly circulating their letters. What I regret is that these Chinese letters cannot first be published in China itself. What is worse is that even long after they may appear abroad, their authors will probably still not know it, much less be able actually to see them in print. However, come what may, their voices will finally have been recorded as part of the historical record. And here, at least, they will serve as evidence that even when Deng Xiaoping admonished the police "not to be afraid of letting a little blood flow," China still gave rise to voices which, in crying out for freedom and democracy, refused to be suppressed.

Beijing, December 20, 1988

January 20, 1987
Dear and Most Respected Teacher Fang:
Greetings and how are you? We are a group of high school students who live in Qiqihar, way up on the northern frontier where our motherland borders on the Soviet Union. Last night, after we finished listening to a radio program criticizing you, we found ourselves feeling angry, but also happy at the same time. What made us feel angry was the utter irrationality of those who are politically dominating us and the way in which they confuse black and white. For the life of us, we were unable to find anything wrong in what you had said in your speeches. In fact, quite to the contrary, the more we heard of them, the more we felt the truthfulness of those thoughts advanced by you. What made us feel happy was the notion that our country still has a person such as you. You are our hope.

You have said that if one wants democracy, one must struggle for it. And now, among students, this has already become a familiar quotation which has circulated widely. You have said that the yearning for democracy and the rejection of autocratic control is a developing and unstoppable trend in the world. But now our newspapers, radios, and television stations talk nonstop about the "state of the nation" and how we should strive not to fall prey to "wholesale Westernization." But we feel that such talk is just a pretext used by those who dominate us to protect their domination.

Only by actually changing the circumstances of the "state of the nation" will our country ever have hope. And, without being too extreme, one could say that what most characterizes our "state of the nation" is the growing polarization between the rich and the poor. What is more, it is government officials, gangs of hooligans, and pickpockets in the street that are the segments of society to "get rich first." Even our parents say that the police these days are more fearful than the police of the Guomindang era.

Of course, our opinions may not quite be correct, and it is possible that you might even find them laughable. But all that we really want to tell you is this: The more they criticize you, the higher your reputation will rise, just as happened when Chairman Mao began to criticize Deng Xiaoping and ended up criticizing him right into office. And when Deng Xiaoping first became the leader, we believed that our situation would improve. Never in the farthest reaches of our imagination did we expect that it would become as bad as it is now.

Please forgive us for not signing our names.

A group of high school students in Qiqihar

P.S. We are on your side (even though it may be useless)!

P.P.S. As one individual in the group, allow me to add a few additional words. My father works in the Qiqihar municipal government, and I have never seen him do even one good deed to really help the people. All that I have seen him and his cronies do is intrigue against each other, using any tactic in their rivalry to become mayor. As a result, right now in Qiqihar eight out of ten people view the mayor as nothing more than a skunk.

But, alas, the mayor is still our mayor. So from this we can see the importance of democracy.

Dear Teacher Fang:

Although Beijing and Hefei are a thousand *li* apart, it is not hard for us to imagine your plight. Please accept this as an expression of high tribute to you.

All of us writing have lived through the great calamity of the so-called Cultural Revolution and are now Chinese Communist Party members, and most of us are now in some kind of leadership positions either in the central government or in other state organizations. As for the students who have been demonstrating in the street, we don't believe that this is necessarily a particularly good way to strive toward democracy. But as for those who view these demonstrations as an enormous outrage, and those who have opened up a battlefield of vengeful criticism, we abhor them even more.

Recently the tactics of our propaganda organs seem hardly different from those used during the Anti-Rightist Campaign in 1957 and the movement to criticize President Liu Shaoqi in 1966. Still we have the tyranny of a single voice, and still we are confronted with the same kind of criticism, which will not tolerate people defending themselves. Reality has shown us once again that in China what we actually confront is not the threat of a capitalist restoration, but havoc wreaked by a still-volatile core of feudalism wrapped up in Marxism. China's process of democratization is going to be a long and painful one.

It may make you feel somewhat relieved to know that a great majority of people our age, and even a fairly large number of older comrades in central state organizations as well, have all expressed disgust at the way things are now being handled. Of course, at official meetings everyone must put on a mask, and contrary to their real convictions, mouth official jargon. But privately they not only express real outrage about phony Marxists, but evince great admiration and respect for you.

There are some older intellectuals who, having been themselves duped by others for decades, now in turn help dupe other people. Standing before such members of their own generation as Lu Xun, Wen Yiduo, and Li Gongpu,* one wonders if they do not now feel ashamed. But perhaps not. Once these sorts of people become officials, even though their positions are actually worth no more than a rubber stamp, they no longer heed such things as shame.

In thirty or forty years, when we look back on the farce that is now being enacted, we will doubtless feel its complete ludicrousness, not to say its utter tragedy. Does China have hope? We think so, but such hope lies with the country's youth.

When we compare ourselves to you, we feel unworthy because we have not had the courage to stand up without regard for our own safety and forcefully make appeals for democracy and freedom. But please believe us when we say that we will never ride roughshod over democracy just to preserve our official positions. We will wait until we have the ability to speak out, until the advance of time is able to push us forward into more important positions, and then we will make our great effort to strive for democracy, a legal system, and freedom.

Please forgive us for not revealing our positions. We know all too well what kind of "democracy" and "freedom" is around us. We have even had to have this letter copied in the hand of younger siblings.

Once again, accept our tribute.

                              Several older youths from the Capital

---

*See Glossary entries for each.

OPEN LETTER OF THIRTY-THREE INTELLECTUALS

On February 16, 1989, thirty-three prominent Chinese writers and artists signed the following open letter in support of Fang Lizhi's request for an amnesty for political prisoners.

To the Standing Committee of the National People's Congress, and the Central Committee of the Chinese Communist Party:

Having heard of Mr. Fang Lizhi's open letter [to Deng Xiaoping] of January 6, 1989, we would like to express our deep concern. We believe that on the occasion of the fortieth anniversary of the founding of our country, and the seventieth anniversary of the May Fourth Movement, a general amnesty, especially including the release of political prisoners such as Wei Jingsheng, would create an atmosphere of harmony beneficial to the reforms. At the same time it would be in accord with the current worldwide trend of increasing respect for human rights.

[signed by] Bei Dao, Shao Yanxiang, Niu Han, Lao Mu, Wu Zuguang, Li Tuo, Bing Xin, Zong Pu, Zhang Jie, Wu Zuxiang, Tang Yijie, Yue Daiyun, Zhang Dainian, Huang Ziping, Chen Pingyuan, Yan Wenjing, Liu Dong, Feng Yidai, Xiao Qian, Su Xiaokang, Jin Guantao, Liu Qingfeng, Li Zehou, Pang Pu, Zhu Wei, Wang Yan, Bao Zunxin, Tian Zhuangzhuang, Mang Ke, Gao Gao, Su Shaozhi, Wang Ruoshui, Chen Jun

OPEN LETTER OF FORTY-TWO SCIENTISTS

The following open letter of February 26, 1989, also triggered by Fang's plea for the release of political prisoners, was signed by forty-two prominent academicians, including twenty-seven natural scientists. It was organized by historian of science Xu Liangying.

To General Secretary Zhao Ziyang, Chairman Wan Li, Chairman Li Xiannian, Premier Li Peng, the Central Committee of the Chinese Communist Party, the Standing Committee of the National People's Congress, the People's Consultative Congress, and the State Council:

Since the Third Plenum of the Eleventh Party Congress, which took as its guiding principle emancipation of the mind and as its basic policy openness and reform, our country's achievements in the undertaking of modernization have caught the world's attention. Although there have been some mistakes and setbacks, the general direction of developments has been in accord with the will of the people and the currents of world history. These ten years have unquestionably been the best period since the founding of the People's Republic. Today, however, the progress of our reform is impeded by serious obstacles: widespread corruption, rampant official profiteering, skyrocketing prices, and a general lack of enthusiasm among the people. Our science, education, art, and literature face severe crises. Chinese intellectuals, heir to a tradition that holds "All the people share responsibility for the fate of the country," cannot help but feel deeply troubled about this situation. In order to prevent our modernization efforts from coming to a tragic and premature end, we older and middle-aged intellectuals, who have long been battling on the scientific, educational, and cultural fronts, with a sense of our social responsibility to the nation and to our people, and with true patriotic hearts beating in our breasts, earnestly offer to you the following suggestions:

1. Maintaining the basic premise of openness and reform, vigorously carry out simultaneous reform of political

institutions—that is, political democratization—and of the economy. World history and the present reality of China both tell us that democratization (including the rule of law) is the indispensable guarantee of economic reform and the whole modernization endeavor. Only in realizing democratization will the people's initiative and active participation be brought into play. Only through democratization can the whole people gladly shoulder their burdens when inevitable difficulties arise in the reform process, and pooling our efforts and our wisdom, find that there is no obstacle that cannot be overcome. Furthermore, under the conditions of a commodity economy, only the realization of democracy with expanded accountability to the people and effective public supervision will allow clean government to exist. Without supervisory power in the hands of the people, there will be no way to put an end to corruption. This is an inescapable law of history that has long been recognized by all.

2. The first condition for political democratization is to thoroughly guarantee all the basic rights of citizens stipulated in the Constitution, especially the rights of citizens to freedom of speech and freedom of the press. As long as the people can speak out freely, and differing opinions can be openly expressed, and leaders can be criticized without fear of attack or revenge, then the atmosphere in our country will be lively, uninhibited, and harmonious, and the citizens will fully exercise their democratic consciousness. This is the only reliable guarantee of unity and stability. From this starting point the reforms can proceed smoothly.

3. In order to stop further occurrences of the historical tragedy of making political criminals out of those who express, in speaking or writing, dissenting political views, please instruct the various departments concerned to release all young people who have been sentenced to prison or labor reform for ideological reasons. In putting an end to the prosecution of political crimes, our country will be entering a new political era.

4. Provide the necessary support for science and education, which, even if it does not benefit the economy directly, nonetheless will determine our country's future fate. Increase as much as possible the proportion of GNP earmarked for funding education and scientific research (especially basic research). Increase the wages for intellectuals (young, old, middle-aged, and retired), so that they will not be living under hardship conditions forever. Right now there are former first-rank professors of the 1950s who are reduced to applying for hardship assistance. There was very recently also a seventy-eight-year-old engineer of the second rank who jumped off a building because his living conditions were intolerable. Such tragic occurrences are of no benefit to the modernization effort and tarnish the nation's image.

5. If these suggestions are adopted, it will bring great fortune to the Chinese people. Science and democracy, as advocated by the pioneers of the May Fourth Movement seventy years ago, will truly flourish in our great land, and the atmosphere surrounding the fortieth anniversary of our country's founding will be one of joy and celebration.

Respectfully,

Qian Linzhao, Wang Ganchang, Shi Yafeng, Xu Liangying, Guo Xingxian, Xue Yugu, Ye Duzheng, Huang Zongzhen, Hu Shihua, Zhu Yaoxiang, Zhou Mingzhen, Xu Guozhi, Jiang Lijin, Sun Keding, Wang Rong, Liu Yuanzhang, Mao Yushi, Hu Jimin, Yan Rengeng, Zhang Xuansan, Du Ruji, Yu Haocheng, Zhang Xianyang, Li Honglin, Bao Zunxin, Liu Shengji, Shao Yanxiang, Wu Zuguang, Wang Laidi, Gu Zhiwei, Ge Ge, Liu Liao, Zhang Zhaoqing, Liang Xiaoguang, Zhang Zonghua, Hou Meiying, Wu Guozhen, Cai Shidong, Cao Junxi, Su Shuxi, Zhou Liquan, Liang Zhixue

February 26, 1989

THE IDEALISTIC DOCTRINE OF A "FINITE UNIVERSE" MUST BE CRITICIZED

The following criticism of the Big Bang model and its Chinese proponents—namely, Fang Lizhi and his colleagues at the University of Science and Technology—appeared in Acta Physica Sinica No. 4, *1976. The author is Liu Bowen.*

On the question of whether the universe should be infinite or finite, there has been throughout the history of physics a struggle between materialism and idealism, between dialectics and metaphysics. Materialism asserts that the universe is infinite, while idealism advocates finitude. At every stage in the history of physics, these two philosophical lines have engaged in fierce struggle. Although developments in physics always demonstrate the failure of the finite-universe doctrine, with every new advance in science the idealists distort and take advantage of the latest results of physics to "prove" with varying sleights of hand that the universe is finite, serving the reactionary rule of the moribund exploiting classes.

In the early part of this century, after the rise of quantum theory and relativity theory, physics arrived at a new stage of development. After General Relativity was announced in 1916, a lot of people used it and similar theories of gravity to produce all sorts of models of the universe. The "finite-universe" point of view became even more fashionable. Lenin pointed out: "That certain schools of the new physics have various dealings with Machism and other variants of modern idealism, is a fact not to be doubted for a moment." It is clear from reading all sorts of foreign literature that the schools of physics promoting a finite universe are linked up with all sorts of idealist philosophy, including theology.

We wish to emphasize that this idealist concept is finding expression right here in our own country as well. In the last year or two, an article has appeared in some publications calculating "cosmological solutions" and constructing "models of the universe."* They hold that the discovery of the 3 K black-body radiation supports an evolutionary theory of the universe, whose early state was a fireball, raising the need to discuss models of the universe with mass and black-body radiation. The article states right at the outset that the early universe was a fireball of finite extent. It makes a few assumptions about the whole universe, such as that it is homogeneous and isotropic, and after making further assumptions about the relevant pressure and the energy-flux density, proceeds to insert these "data" into the corresponding gravitational-field equations, and obtains a so-called rigorous cosmological solution. (The article is mainly concerned with closed models, namely the finite-fireball models of the universe.) From these solutions the authors obtain the relationships among the radius of the universe, the age of the universe, and the radiational energy of matter. The format and conclusion of the article are not very different from a foreign article of the same variety, except that it does not literally use the words "finite-universe model." It changes the terminology a little, the radius of the universe being written as "radius," and the age of the universe as "time scale of cosmic evolution." But the premises and conclusions of the paper are clear enough; they all go to advocating that the universe is finite in both time and space, and moreover to making actual calculations that the universe was born only about ten billion years ago.

Consequently the idealistic philosophical tendency of the article is perfectly apparent. In actuality, when thinking about a finite universe, the radius of the universe aside, you can't avoid answering such questions as these: What was there before the universe was created and what will there be after it is destroyed? How was it created? Does it or does it not have an objective existence? There can be no answer other than some God or absolute being. The article went on to cite certain important observational facts of astrophysics, such as the 3 K microwave radiation, and the redshift, and so forth, and lump them together as supporting evidence for the Big Bang Theory.

*This refers to Fang Lizhi *et al.,* "A Solution of the Cosmological Equations in Scalar-Tensor Theory, with Mass and Black-Body Radiation," *Physica,* 1 (1972). This was the first article in the People's Republic to introduce the Big Bang model.

In our opinion, controversies over whether the universe is infinite or finite, over whether experiments and observational data support Big Bang cosmology, are not so-called purely scientific-academic debates. Rather they reflect a basic difference between philosophical lines. "Among physicists there are already many different sects, and on this basis definite schools are formed. Therefore, our duty is limited to exposing clearly the following: What is the essence of the difference between the schools, and what is their relation to the basic philosophical lines?" The school that argues for a finite universe is just a school founded on the idealistic philosophical line. As to their so-called "scientific" basis and explanation of empirical findings, these are nothing but tools serving this philosophical foundation.

The dialectical-materialist conception of the universe tells us that the natural world is infinite, and it exists indefinitely. The world is infinite. Both space and time are boundless and infinite. The universe in both its macroscopic and microscopic aspects is infinite. Matter is infinitely divisible. The judgment of dialectical materialism on the infinitude of the physical world is the result of a profound philosophical synthesis of the fruits of thousands of years of science. The fundamental mistake of the school of physics that advocates a finite universe is that it runs counter to the basic position of dialectical materialism on the infinite nature of the universe. On the theoretical side, they exploit finite closed-form solutions of General Relativity or similar field equations of gravitation. On the empirical side, they take advantage of facts like the redshift or 3 K microwave radiation. We must point out that relying on the finite closed-form gravitational-field equations to address "cosmological solutions" is a fundamental mistake. The universe can be understood, but the process of understanding the universe by human beings is infinite. "Systems claiming comprehensive, final, and complete understanding of nature and history stand in basic contradiction to the laws of dialectical thought." That which humans have probed of the material world is only the minutest fraction of the universe. In terms of levels we go up only as far as the metagalaxy, and down as far as fundamental particles, which are but a few of the infinitely many tiers of the structure of matter. On this basis, fundamentally one cannot have, and there cannot be, a unified description of the whole universe by mathematical physics. As far as the redshift and 3 K microwave radiation and so forth go, they are data obtained from observations made in a certain region of space-time, descriptions of a partial state of the universe. Employing these theories and experimental results to discuss the entire universe is incorrect. The so-called age of the universe, radius of the universe, and other results derived in this way are just so many absurdities.

Many a critical essay has been written against the sheer folly of the physical and philosophical theories of a "finite universe." Here I wish merely to communicate a few private thoughts.

Chairman Mao has recently remarked, "Why did Lenin insist that the question of dictatorship over the bourgeoisie must be made clear? Because as long as this question is not made clear, we can fall into revisionism. Let the whole country know." In the socialist stage of history, the struggle between proletariat and bourgeoisie, between the socialist and capitalist lines, is prolonged, tortuous, and at times extremely intense. This demands that we insist upon the Party's basic line, and support complete dictatorship over the bourgeoisie in every sphere, including politics, economics, ideology, and culture.

In the field of physics the struggle between the proletarian worldview and the bourgeois worldview is extremely acute. In the theoretical foundations of modern physics, the philosophical viewpoints of the main originators of quantum theory and relativity theory are permeated with metaphysics and idealism. An idealistic and metaphysical orthodoxy in physics not only inhibits the development of physics itself, but also influences other disciplines of the natural sciences and other domains. In our country, the presence of idealism and metaphysics also has deep class origins, not to speak of epistemological origins. Thus all sorts of worldwide idealist trends find expression in our country's physics community. Hence it is not difficult to understand why the viewpoints of the finite-universe school have been accepted by many scientific workers, and moreover turned into research topics.

We must "read and study conscientiously, and get a good grasp of Marxism," deepen our understanding of the theory of proletarian dictatorship, and raise our proficiency in criticism and analysis, the better to mark out clearly the boundary between dialectical materialism and idealistic metaphysics. We must ferret out and combat every kind of reactionary philosophical viewpoint in the domain of scientific research, using Marxism to establish our position in the natural sciences.

DECISION REGARDING THE EXPULSION OF FANG
LIZHI FROM THE CHINESE COMMUNIST PARTY

*The following document specifying the grounds for Fang Lizhi's
expulsion from the Chinese Communist Party was issued on January
17, 1987, by the CCP Discipline Inspection Committee of Anhui
Province.*

Fang Lizhi, male, born 1936. Entered the Party in 1955, entered the
workforce in 1956. Former vice president of the University of Science
and Technology of China, removed from this post on January 12, 1987.

Over the last few years, Fang Lizhi has on all manner of occasions
openly propagated bourgeois liberalization, opposed the Four Basic
Principles, repudiated the leadership of the Communist Party, repudiated the socialist system, attempted to sow discord between intellectuals and the Party, and incited students to create disturbances, leading
to serious consequences. Despite the Party's many attempts to criticize
and educate him with regard to these errors, he has adopted a two-faced
attitude, refused to reform, seriously jeopardized the Party, and damaged our political unity and stability. The facts clearly show that Fang
Lizhi is no longer qualified for membership in the Chinese Communist
Party.

The facts regarding his main errors are as follows:

1. He has proclaimed that Marxism is obsolete and repudiated the
   guiding role of Marxism. In his attacks, Fang Lizhi has said: "As
   far as being a science is concerned, Marxism has already completed
   its historical mission. What we need now is to search for new
   truths." "[Marxism's] so-called guidance can only lead to
   erroneous results. It has never been successful." "In our country,
   so-called Marxist guidance really refers to the guidance of the
   leaders, the government, those in power, the Party. We need this
   even less."
2. He has repudiated the socialist system and propagated "wholesale

Westernization," and advocated the capitalist road. His slanders include the following: "I think that what we have been doing these last thirty years, in terms of the socialist system, has been a failure." "The results of orthodox socialism from Marx and Lenin to Stalin and Mao Zedong have been a failure." "Now we have nothing but bitter regret over these things of the last thirty years." "Very few good things have been done in these thirty years." He has advocated "complete openness, or to put it another way, complete Westernization." "Complete Westernization includes studying everything about Western science, technology, culture, politics, economics, ideology, and ethics." "Including our political system, and our system of ownership." He has attacked our country's socialist system as "modern-day feudalism" and "feudalism under the banner of nationalism, in essence just dictatorship, the concentration of power."

3. He has publicly proclaimed his desire to "change the Party" and repudiated the leadership of the Party. He has made such attacks as: "One of the distinguishing characteristics of Chinese feudal rule was that the center of power and the center of ethical authority were combined into one. The Communist Party is just like that today." "The Party is now Black." "I approve of people joining the Party. After they join it, they can change its color. I formally suggest changing the Party." He was "very dissatisfied" with the contents of the resolution of the Sixth Plenum of the Twelfth Party Congress opposing bourgeois liberalization, and he publicly stated: "This [resolution] is very wrong. What it means is very unclear, and it will just be used to bludgeon people."

4. He has advocated that universities eliminate Party leadership, called for universities to be "completely independent," and driven a wedge between intellectuals and the Party and government. He claims that "the relationship between government and universities should be purely one of providing funding." "The government should give the money to the university presidents, and other than that shouldn't interfere

with them." "Universities are independent." "They should be independent of the government, independent centers of thought." "There can't be some external control directing universities from above." He incited people, saying: "Chinese intellectuals have still not awakened to the fact that they should be an independent force, a leading force. They are still dependent, feudal." "If intellectuals don't become an independent force, China's reforms have no chance of succeeding."

5. He has called for bourgeois "democracy" and "freedom," incited the students to create disturbances, and damaged political unity and stability. At several universities he incited the students, saying: "The Keda students aren't lively enough. Why don't you show a little 'troublemaking' spirit?" "Students are a force for the progress of democratization." He called on students "to confront the society," saying that "There are many things that appear strong but are actually weak. Once you challenge them you find there isn't anything so awesome about them." "Just a little prodding will have a big impact." "Very small actions can make things tense all over the country." His provocations also included the statement that democracy "can be fought for in many ways . . . and of course this includes confrontational methods." On the evening of December 4, 1986, when most of the students at USTC were planning to create disturbances, he further incited them by saying, "Democracy is not a gift bestowed by our superiors. It depends on us to fight for it." The next day, students from USTC and other Hefei schools went on a protest march.

In summary, Fang Lizhi's errors of openly calling for bourgeois liberalization and opposing the Four Cardinal Principles are very serious. He has turned his back on the Party rules and the "Regulations Concerning Political Life Within the Party."

According to the Party rules, Fang Lizhi is hereby expelled from Party membership.

BEIJING MUNICIPAL PUBLIC SECURITY BUREAU
ARREST WARRANT

The arrest warrant below was published in the People's Daily *on June 13, 1989, after Fang Lizhi and Li Shuxian had taken refuge inside the U.S. Embassy in Beijing.*

Fang Lizhi and Li Shuxian have committed the crimes of disseminating counterrevolutionary propaganda and inciting counterrevolutionary activities, in violation of the Penal Code of the People's Republic of China, Article 102. An arrest warrant has been applied for and granted by the Beijing Municipal Branch of the People's Office of Prosecution. The arrest of Li is further authorized by the Standing Committee of the People's Congress, Haidian District.

Fang Lizhi, male, born December 12, 1936. A native of the city of Hangzhou, Zhejiang Province. Researcher at the Beijing Astronomical Observatory of the Chinese Academy of Sciences. Approximately 1.72 meters tall, slightly chubby, hair worn longer on one side, square face with rounded features, wears corrective glasses for nearsightedness, walks with erect gait and head uplifted.

Li Shuxian, female, born January 28, 1935. A native of Jiashan County, Anhui Province. Assistant professor of physics at Beijing University. Approximately 1.60 meters tall, slightly thin, short permanented hair, elongated face, visible freckles; walks at a fast gait.

The criminals Fang and Li have fled in order to avoid punishment, and are to be arrested on sight. All district and county security organs are hereby notified to deploy personnel to investigate and apprehend the guilty parties immediately following receipt of this notice. All provincial, autonomous-region, and directly administered municipality security organs are requested to cooperate with this search. Fang and Li are to be detained upon apprehension, and the Beijing Municipal Public Security Bureau notified immediately.

Beijing Municipal Public Security Bureau
June 11, 1989

GLOSSARY

Ah Q: The main character in Lu Xun's biting 1920 short story "The True Story of Ah Q," the story of a gullible and badly victimized peasant who lacks the moral strength to honestly confront his situation. For Lu Xun, Ah Q symbolized China's cultural backwardness. (See Lu Xun, below.)

Alienation *(yi hua)***:** A theory advanced by Marxist reformers in the early 1980s, which held that state socialism had "alienated" its populace from control over their lives, just as capitalism had alienated the working classes from their labor. This concept was an integral part of the program of humanism attacked during the Anti-Spiritual Pollution Campaign of 1983–84.

Anti-Bourgeois Liberalization Campaign: A political campaign that came on the heels of nationwide student demonstrations in late 1986, and focused on opposing Western influences, especially ideas of liberal democracy. The campaign began in January 1987 and resulted in the removal of Hu Yaobang as General Secretary of the CCP, and in the expulsion from CCP membership of three prominent intellectuals: Wang Ruowang, Liu Binyan, and Fang Lizhi.

Anti-Rightist Campaign: A 1957 political campaign directed against intellectuals who had criticized the Communist Party. During this campaign, one-half million or more people were labeled "rightists," resulting in jail terms or lengthy periods of manual labor in the countryside. The "rightist" label made its bearers unemployable, effectively ending their careers.

Anti-Spiritual Pollution Campaign: A political campaign in 1983–84 against Western influences in politics and culture. The campaign focused criticism on reformist thinkers who proposed a "humanism" that transcended class interests.

April Fifth Incident: See Tiananmen Incident, below.

Beijing University (Beida): China's oldest and most prestigious university, founded in 1898 by imperial edict. Beida and its students have played a key role in numerous pivotal events in twentieth-century China, including the May Fourth Movement, the founding of the Chinese Communist Party, anti-Japanese activism prior to World War II, the Hundred Flowers Movement, the Cultural Revolution, and the spring 1989 democracy movement.

Big Bang Theory: The theory that the universe began in a primordial fireball some 10 to 20 billion years ago, subsequently expanding and coalescing into the universe we observe today.

Bo Le system: Bo Le was the "celestial master of horses" in Chinese legend, able to select potential "thousand-league horses" and develop their talents accordingly. The "Bo Le system" is an informal term for the selection of officials by Party leaders based on personal recommendations.

Bo Yang (b. 1920): The pseudonym of Guo Yidong, a Taiwanese writer who spent ten years in Nationalist prisons for political crimes, and author of *The Ugly Chinaman,* a critique of flaws in the Chinese national psyche.

Bruno, Giordano (1548–1600): Italian philosopher burned at the stake in 1600 by the Catholic Church for advocating, among other things, that the earth revolves around the sun.

Cai Yuanpei (1868–1948): President of Beijing University from 1916 to 1926, who turned the floundering former imperial academy into China's most prestigious university. Cai was an important figure of the

May Fourth period, known for his advocacy of intellectual freedom and diversity on the university campus.

Calendar debates in the Ming and Qing dynasties: In traditional Confucian China, unforeseen celestial events such as comets and solar eclipses were taken as omens that the reigning dynasty had begun to lose its cosmic mandate to rule. Calendar-making and accurate predictions of events in the heavens were therefore matters of great political sensitivity, and emperors maintained sizable bureaucracies to do the necessary observation and record keeping. The Jesuits became active in sixteenth- and seventeenth-century politics at the imperial court, as they sought to convert China to Catholicism by first converting the Chinese emperor. They gained access to the court because of their command of emerging European science and technologies. Their expertise in astronomy in particular allowed them to predict eclipses more accurately than could Chinese astronomers, an ability that made them valuable to the emperors but also the object of political intrigues at court.

Campaign Against Bourgeois Liberalization: See Anti-Bourgeois Liberalization Campaign, above.

Campaign Against Spiritual Pollution: See Anti-Spiritual Pollution Campaign, above.

Chinese Academy of Sciences (CAS): China's highest scientific research body, with over 100 research centers and institutes and 100,000 employees. Unlike the National Academy of Sciences in the United States (and like the Soviet Academy), CAS administers and coordinates basic research nationwide on a day-to-day basis.

Chinese Academy of Social Science (CASS): China's highest social sciences research body, with thirty-four affiliated research centers and institutes. Formed in 1977 from the former Department of Philosophy and Social Sciences of CAS.

Cosmology: The branch of astrophysics concerned with the origins, overall structure, and evolution of the universe, and consequently with such related issues as the fundamental nature of matter, space, and time.

"Decision on Reform of the Science and Technology Management System": A landmark document issued on March 13, 1985, by the Communist Party Central Committee, which mandated sweeping changes in the organization and funding of research and the diffusion of technology into the general economy.

Democracy Wall: A public wall near Tiananmen Square in Beijing on which for a period in late 1978 and early 1979 democracy activists placed posters calling for democratic reforms. These activities were suppressed by Deng Xiaoping beginning in March 1979, leading to the imprisonment of a number of the movement's leading figures.

Deng Liqun: Ideologically conservative former Politburo member and director of the Party Propaganda Department.

Deng Xiaoping (b. 1904): Born to a peasant family in Sichuan Province, Deng joined the Chinese Communist Party while a student in France during the 1920s. A Long March veteran and a capable administrator, Deng rose to high positions during the fifties and sixties. Driven out of office during the Cultural Revolution, Deng returned to power to become China's paramount leader in the late 1970s. He overturned Maoist policies of class struggle in favor of a pragmatic program of economic growth and modernization under Communist Party rule.

Dialectics of Nature (natural dialectics): The Marxist natural philosophy that originated with Friedrich Engels's book of the same name in the 1880s, and that was codified under Lenin and Stalin as the official Soviet philosophy of science. Natural dialectics and historical materialism together compose the integral Marxist-Leninist philosophy called dialectical materialism, which aims to provide a unified set of principles and categories by which to understand all phenomena in the natural and social worlds.

Feudalism: According to Marxist-Leninist historiography, a stage of socioeconomic development characterized by agrarian production, autocratic politics, and patriarchal social relations. While in this view China's feudal stage formally ended with the overthrow of the Qing Dynasty in 1911, the Communist leadership of the Deng era has explained the excesses of the Cultural Revolution as a consequence of lingering "feudal" traditions. Liberal intellectuals of the 1980s appropriated the term to criticize the Deng regime itself, claiming that Communist Party rule generally is characterized by "feudal" patriarchy and dependency. (Western historians use the term in a different sense, to describe certain technical features of the medieval social order in Europe.)

Four Big Freedoms: The freedoms of "speaking out freely, airing views fully, holding great debates, and writing big-character posters" invoked by Mao Zedong in encouraging Red Guards and others to attack factions in the Party leadership to which he was opposed. These freedoms were incorporated into the 1978 Constitution of the People's Republic, but deleted in 1980.

Four Cardinal Principles: The basic political and ideological guidelines set down by Deng Xiaoping in 1979, which call for upholding (1) the socialist road, (2) the dictatorship of the proletariat, (3) leadership by the Communist Party, and (4) the leading role of Marxism–Leninism–Mao Zedong Thought. Also known as the Four Upholds, the Four Basic Principles, or simply the Four Principles.

Four Modernizations: The policy (originally announced in the 1960s by Zhou Enlai, revived in the mid-1970s by Deng Xiaoping) of promoting modernization in the areas of industry, agriculture, science and technology, and national defense.

Galileo Galilei (1564–1642): Great Italian pioneer of physics and astronomy. Galileo's *Dialogue on the Two Chief World Systems* supported the Copernican view that the earth moves around the sun, leading to Galileo's trial before the Inquisition in 1633 and subsequent house arrest until his death. Tradition has it that after being forced to recant the Copernican doctrine, Galileo was heard to mutter, "But it *does* move."

Gang of Four: A group of Party leaders, consisting of former factory official Wang Hongwen, radical theorists Yao Wenyuan and Zhang Chunqiao, and Mao Zedong's wife, Jiang Qing, who were officially blamed for starting and directing the Cultural Revolution. They were arrested shortly after Mao's death in 1976 and convicted in a highly publicized trial in 1980–81. They remain in prison.

Great Leap Forward: Mao Zedong's effort, launched in May 1958, to create a self-reliant path for China's development, emphasizing collectivization and rapid industrial development. The failure of these policies led to serious economic dislocations and widespread famine in the period the Chinese call the "three bitter years" [1959–61].

Guiding role of philosophy over science: The doctrine that scientific research requires the guidance of Marxist philosophy in the selection of research topics and the interpretation of results.

Guomindang (Kuomintang, or KMT): The Nationalist Party, founded by Sun Yat-sen and long led by Chiang Kai-shek.

Hat: A political label. During the Cultural Revolution, Red Guards often required those whom they were criticizing to literally wear hats—dunce caps on which were written such labels as "capitalist roader."

Hu Feng: A well-known author and Communist Party member who in the early 1950s complained of Party domination over intellectual life. In 1955, a nationwide campaign was launched to "criticize Hu Feng," and in the process to ferret out other intellectuals who had overtly opposed Party policies. Hu remained in prison until 1979.

Hundred Flowers Movement: A very brief period of liberalization in May 1957, when Mao invited intellectuals—using the classical expression "let one hundred flowers bloom, let one hundred schools of thought contend"—to criticize the Chinese Communist Party. The movement ended abruptly when Mao reversed himself in June 1957 and ordered the Anti-Rightist Campaign, which led to severe consequences for those who had spoken out.

Hu Qiaomu (b. 1911): Conservative former Politburo member and first president of the Chinese Academy of Social Sciences. As a leading expert on ideology and Party history, Hu has provided the formal rationale for many key aspects of Deng's policies, as well as defenses of the basic tenets of Marxist-Leninist philosophy.

Hu Qili (b. 1929): Politburo Standing Committee member, considered a leading reformer but removed from office along with Zhao Ziyang in the wake of the Tiananmen protests and massacre of 1989.

Hu Shi (Hu Shih, 1891–1962): Professor of philosophy at Beijing University and leading exponent of liberal ideas during the May Fourth period. A student of John Dewey's at Columbia during the 1910s, Hu served as Chinese ambassador to the United States during World War II.

Hu Yaobang (1915–1989): Long March veteran and protégé of Deng Xiaoping, who rose through the ranks of the Communist Youth League to become General Secretary of the Communist Party in 1980. Considered a leading reformist and patron of intellectuals, Hu was dismissed from his post in 1987 for supporting liberalization. Hu's death on April 15, 1989, triggered the first of that spring's mass demonstrations for democracy in Tiananmen Square.

Idealism: A general description of philosophies holding that the mind itself is the source of knowledge, or that underlying reality is nonmaterial in nature. Marxist philosophy, known as dialectical materialism, holds idealism to be an incorrect viewpoint. In Marxist-Leninist theory, materialism is identified with revolutionary and proletarian values, and idealism with bourgeois and reactionary values, making "idealism" a damning political label.

International Center for Theoretical Physics (ICTP): Located in Trieste, Italy, this institution was founded by Abdus Salaam, the Pakistani physicist and Nobel Prize winner. (During the period in which China was isolated from contact with the West and the Soviet Union, Pakistani scientists were a major conduit of scientific information to China.) Following Deng Xiaoping's inauguration of an "openness" policy in the late 1970s, ICTP arranged research trips for numerous Chinese scientists.

Kaifang: "Opening," referring to the policy of *dui wai kaifang*— "opening to the outside world"—that Deng Xiaoping declared in order to end the isolation of the Mao period and promote rapid modernization with foreign ideas and technologies.

Key institutions: In 1978, to improve educational standards following the Cultural Revolution, eighty-eight universities throughout China were designated "key institutions" at which academically rigorous admissions and instructional standards would be maintained.

Lei Feng: A young soldier in the People's Liberation Army who was elevated after his accidental death to become a national role model, exemplifying selflessness and devotion to the Communist Party. The first "learn from Lei Feng" campaign was launched in 1963.

Li Dazhao: One of the founders of the Chinese Communist Party, in April 1927 Li was arrested while hiding in the Soviet Embassy in Beijing by troops of the warlord Zhang Zuolin, and hanged.

Li Gongpu: Leader of the China Democratic League, assassinated by the Guomindang in 1946.

Liu Binyan: A well-known investigative journalist, whose exposés of official malfeasance brought him both popular acclaim and political recriminations. He was a widely respected intellectual leader in China during the 1980s.

Li Zhengdao (T. D. Lee, b. 1926): Chinese-born winner of the 1957 Nobel Prize in physics, shared with Yang Zhenning (Frank Yang). Li's international stature has allowed him access to the top echelons of Chinese leaders, even during periods of national isolation such as the Cultural Revolution. Li has been an important booster of China's scientific relations with the rest of the world.

Lu Xun (Lu Hsün, 1881–1936): One of China's most famous modern writers and a leading figure of the May Fourth Movement. His short stories and essays employed dark humor and compassionate ridicule in criticizing China's backwardness. (See Ah Q.)

Mach, Ernst (1830–1916): An Austrian physicist and philosopher whose arguments against the existence of absolute space and time stimulated Einstein to ponder the connection between matter and the geometry of space-time (a line of investigation which culminated in the general theory of relativity). Lenin believed that Mach's ideas were philosophically idealist because they called into question the objective existence of matter. He attacked Mach's views in his 1908 tract *Materialism and Empirio-Criticism,* a polemic that became the *locus classicus* for discussions of relativity and quantum theory from the perspective of Marxism in the USSR and China.

Materialism: A general term for philosophies that emphasize the existence of matter as the ultimate source of reality, and of human knowledge about reality. Marxist philosophy holds materialism to be a correct viewpoint, and idealism to be incorrect.

May Fourth Movement: Beijing students held massive demonstrations in Tiananmen Square on May 4, 1919, to protest the acquiescence of the Chinese government to the Treaty of Versailles, which ceded large amounts of Chinese territory to Japan. The protests galvanized public concern about national survival. The "May Fourth Movement" and the "New Culture Movement" are used somewhat interchangeably to describe the period of intellectual ferment immediately prior to and following the May Fourth protests, which produced vigorous explorations of Western cultural and political models, and major innovations in art, literature, and language.

Neo-authoritarianism *(xin quanwei zhuyi)*: A doctrine of the late 1980s holding that China would be best served by concentrating power in an authoritarian leader, for the sake of economic development.

New Culture Movement: A movement among Chinese intellectuals between approximately 1915 and 1927, broadly focused on investigating and transforming the socially and intellectually repressive features of the traditional culture.

Official turnaround *(guan dao)*: A prevalent form of economic crime in China, in which officials obtain products at subsidized prices in the state-run sector of the economy, and then "turn around" to sell them at vastly higher prices on the open market.

"Practice is the sole criterion of truth": A slogan put forward by Deng Xiaoping in 1978 to promote pragmatism over strict adherence to Maoist ideology.

Qian Xuesen (H. S. Tsien): Physicist and father of China's ballistic missile program, educated at MIT in the 1940s. Now a politically conservative elder statesman in China's scientific establishment.

"Resolution on Guiding Principles for Building Socialist Spiritual Civilization": An ambiguous document produced by the Sixth Plenary Session of the Twelfth Communist Party Congress in September 1986, which called for both ideological purity and a conducive atmosphere for professional work. The plenum itself is now seen as having marked a decisive setback for reform forces, especially for Hu Yaobang, who is said to have lost Deng Xiaoping's support at this time.

"Science and democracy" (*kexue yu minzhu*): A main slogan of the May Fourth era, encapsulating the idea that the key to the wealth, power, and stability of modern countries lay in these two institutions. The slogan was revived in the 1989 Tiananmen demonstrations.

Song Jian: Current director of the State Science and Technology Commission, China's highest policy-making body in the science and technology arena.

Synchrotron accelerator: A device that accelerates charged particles, producing high-energy X rays (used in physics experiments).

Third Plenary Session of the Eleventh Party Congress: The pivotal Communist Party plenum of December 1978, at which Deng Xiaoping consolidated his position as China's paramount leader and announced a new policy direction emphasizing modernization and economic growth.

Three Great Discoveries (*san da faxian*): The nineteenth-century scientific discoveries held by Engels and subsequent Marxist philosophers to epitomize the dialectical laws of nature: the conservation laws of physics, the existence of cells as the fundamental constituents of organisms, and biological evolution.

Tiananmen Incident (April Fifth Incident): A demonstration in Tiananmen Square on April 5, 1976, occurring during the traditional "tomb-sweeping" (Qingming) festival and marking the death of Zhou Enlai earlier in the year, which expressed massive public dissatisfaction with Mao Zedong and the Cultural Revolution. Harshly suppressed by security forces at the time and condemned by the government. The verdict on the Tiananmen Incident was officially reversed in 1978, and the event given credit for leading to the overthrow of the "Gang of Four."

Ti-yong: A term with a long history in Chinese metaphysics, adapted by nineteenth-century officials in the expression *Zhong xue wei ti, Xi xue wei yong*—"taking Chinese learning for the essential things, taking Western learning for the practical application." When this prescription was first voiced in the 1860s, it represented a fairly radical rationalization for an expanded view of the world. By the end of the century, however, *ti-yong* had become the slogan of conservative officials who advocated the acquisition of Western technology while screening out Western cultural influences such as religion and political ideas.

University of Science and Technology of China (USTC, also known as Keda): China's premier technical university, located in Hefei, Anhui, in central China. Originally established in 1959 in Beijing, it was moved to Hefei in 1970 to escape the Cultural Revolution activities in Beijing, which had brought higher education to a standstill.

Wei Jingsheng: A young worker and leading figure of the 1978–79 Democracy Wall movement in Beijing. Wei was the author of a tract arguing that Deng Xiaoping's Four Modernizations program would fail unless democracy, "The Fifth Modernization," was also instituted. He was arrested in March 1979, and a few months later tried and convicted of publishing counterrevolutionary documents and of selling classified information to foreigners. Wei is still in prison.

Wen Yiduo: A respected Chinese poet assassinated in 1946 by the Guomindang for his criticism of the regime.

Xuan Zang: A Tang Dynasty monk who traveled to India in the latter half of the seventh century to obtain Buddhist scriptures. A highly fictionalized and allegorical account of his adventures was set down in the sixteenth-century epic *Journey to the West.*

Xu Liangying: Director of the Institute for the History of Natural Science at the Chinese Academy of Social Sciences, translator of Einstein's works into Chinese, and participant in the debates over natural dialectics. Xu organized the letter of forty-two prominent academicians in February 1989 calling for release of political prisoners and other liberalizations.

Zhang Baifa: The vice mayor of Beijing who joined a party of twenty-five Chinese scientists and officials on a 1985 scientific mission to the United States organized by Chinese-American physicist T. D. Lee. In a speech at Beijing University in November 1985, Fang Lizhi questioned Zhang's value to the mission, implying that he had taken a junket at public expense. This led to subsequent recriminations as the Beijing Party Committee demanded a public apology from Fang, which never came.

Zhao Ziyang (b. 1919): Onetime protégé of Deng Xiaoping, considered a leading reformist. Named premier in 1980, Zhao was the main overseer of Deng's economic reforms. Zhao became General Secretary of the Party following Hu Yaobang's ouster in 1987, and was himself ousted and arrested for "attempting to split the Party" in the wake of the spring 1989 demonstrations in Tiananmen Square.

BIBLIOGRAPHY

The bibliographical entries below appear in the same order as the thirty-two texts by Fang Lizhi contained in this book. The following abbreviations are used:

Zanmei = Fang Lizhi, *Zanmei wozhu zhi hou: Fang Lizhi zi xuan ji zhi yi* [After Praising the Lord: Selected Speeches and Writings by Fang Lizhi], vol. 1 (Singapore: World Scientific, 1988).

Weiji = Fang Lizhi, *Weiji gan xia de zeren: Fang Lizhi zi xuan ji zhi er* [Responsibility Under Crisis: Selected Speeches and Writings by Fang Lizhi], vol. 2 (Singapore: World Scientific, 1989).

Zhexue = Fang Lizhi, *Zhexue shi wulixue de gongju* [Philosophy Is a Tool of Physics] (Changsha: Hunan kexue jishu chubanshe, 1988).

"Expanding Universe" = James H. Williams, ed. and trans., "The Expanding Universe of Fang Lizhi: Astrophysics and Ideology in Peoples's China," *Chinese Studies in Philosophy,* vol. 19, no. 4 [1988].

TEXTS

1. PREFACE

"Yingwen ban qian yan" [Foreword to the English Edition], unpublished, 1990.

2. PREFACE TO THE CHINESE EDITION

"Xu" [Preface], *Zanmei.*

3. FROM NEWTON TO EINSTEIN

"Qian yan" [Foreword], Fang Lizhi and Chu Yaoquan, *Cong Niudun dinglü dao Aiensitan xiangduilun* [From Newton's Laws to Einstein's Theory of Relativity] (Beijing: Kexue chubanshe, 1981), pp. iii–v. Translated in "Expanding Universe," pp. 27–28.

4. FROM ''WATER IS THE ORIGIN OF ALL THINGS''
TO ''SPACE-TIME IS THE FORM OF THE EXISTENCE
OF MATTER''

"Cong 'wanwu yuan yu shui' dao 'shikong shi wuzhi cunzai de xingshi'," *Zhexue yanjiu* [Philosophical Research], no. 6 (1982), pp. 18–20. Reprinted in *Zhexue,* pp. 91–94. Translated in "Expanding Universe," pp. 40–42.

5. PHILOSOPHY IS A TOOL OF PHYSICS

"Zhexue shi wuli de gongju," preface to Zhou Lin, Yin Dengxiang, and Zhang Yongqian, eds., *Kexuejia lun fangfa* [Scientists on Method], vol. 2 (Inner Mongolia: Nei Menggu renmin chubanshe, 1983). Reprinted in *Zhexue,* pp. 143–145. Translated by David A. Kelly in "Expanding Universe," pp. 43–45.

6. PHILOSOPHY AND PHYSICS

"Zhexue he wuli," *Zhexue shi wulixue de gongju* [Philosophy Is a Tool of Physics] (Changsha: Hunan kexue jishu chubanshe, 1988), pp. 1–6.

7. A NOTE ON THE INTERFACE BETWEEN
SCIENCE AND RELIGION

A Note on The Interface Between Science and Religion, Robert J. Russell, ed., *John Paul II on Science and Religion: Twenty Reflections on the New View from Rome* (Geneva: Vatican Press, forthcoming 1991).

8. CHINESE DEMOCRACY: THE VIEW FROM
THE BEIJING OBSERVATORY

"Cong Beijing tianwentai kan Zhongguo minzhu jincheng—jinian wusi qishi nian" [Chinese Democracy: The View from Beijing Observatory—(On the Seventieth Anniversary of the May Fourth Movement)]," unpublished, 1989. Translated by Geremie Barmé.

9. WRITTEN AT MIDNIGHT, AFTER PRAISING THE LORD

"Xie zai 'zanmei wozhu' zhi hou de wuye li," *Shenghuo* [Life], 1980. Reprinted in *Zhexue,* pp. 1–5.

10. A HAT, A FORBIDDEN ZONE, A QUESTION

"Yi ding maozi, yi kuai jindi, yi ge wenti," *Beijing keji bao* [Beijing Science and Technology News], October 19, 1979. Reprinted in *Zhexue,* pp. 59–61. Translated in "Expanding Universe," pp. 29–31.

11. A LETTER FROM JAPAN

"Fang ri tong xin yi ze," *Zanmei,* pp. 31–33.

12. ARASHIYAMA MEMOIR

"You Lanshan hou ji," *Zanmei,* pp. 35–42. Translated in "Expanding Universe," pp. 34–39.

13. GALILEO AND MILTON: PHYSICS AND POETRY

"Jialilüe, Mierdun, wuli he shi," *Zhongguo Keda* [University of Science and Technology of China], 1985. Reprinted in *Zanmei,* pp. 29–30.

14. MY FEELINGS ABOUT ART

"Wo dui meishu de ganshou," *Zhongguo meishu bao* [China Art News], no. 8 [1988]. Reprinted in *Zanmei,* pp. 95–97.

15. RETURN TO CAPRI

"Chong fang Kapuli," *Zanmei,* pp. 89–93.

16. THE END OF OLD THINKING

"Tuo diao jiu sixiang cai neng jinru weilai" [Only When We Discard Old Thinking Can We Enter the Future], speech at 2nd National Conference on the Science of Science, Hefei, Anhui, December 1980. Transcript in *Weiji*, pp. 5–7. Translated in "Expanding Universe," pp. 32–33.

17. THOUGHTS ON REFORM

"Gaige de sikao," speech at Zhejiang University, March 24, 1985. Transcript in *Weiji*, pp. 9–51.

18. REFLECTIONS ON TEACHERS' DAY

"You gan yu jiaoshi jie," *Zhongguo Keda* [University of Science and Technology of China], September 12, 1985. Reprinted in *Zanmei*, pp. 65–67.

19. A NATURAL SCIENTIST VIEWS THE REFORMS

"Yi wei ziran kexue jia kan gaige—Fang Lizhi jiaoshou dawen lu" [A Natural Scientist Views the Reforms—An Exchange with Professor Fang Lizhi], *Shehui bao* (Society), October 28, 1986. Reprinted in *Weiji*, pp. 105–110. Translated in "Expanding Universe," pp. 75–79.

20. ON POLITICAL REFORM

"Tan zhengzhi tizhi gaige" [Discussing Reform of the Political Structure], speech to Conference on Political Reform, sponsored by the Research Center for Economics and Culture, Anhui Provincial People's Government. Transcript in *Weiji*, pp. 111–130.

21. DEMOCRACY, REFORM, AND MODERNIZATION

"Minzhu, gaige, xiandaihua," speech at Tongji University, November 18, 1986. Transcript in *Weiji*, pp. 195–240. Translated by James H. Williams as "Peering Over the Great Wall," *Journal of Democracy*, vol. 1, no. 1 [1990], pp. 32–40.

22. MY LIFE ON MAY 21ST, 1987

"Wode yi jiu ba qi nian, wu yue, ershi yi ri," *Zanmei*, pp. 83–88.

23. INTERVIEW WITH TIZIANO TERZANI

"Farewell Marx and Mao; Your Party Is Over," interview with Fang Lizhi by Tiziano Terzani, *Far Eastern Economic Review*, October 22, 1987, pp. 52–55.

24. LEARNING ABOUT DEMOCRACY

"Gei Huang Yuchuan xiansheng de yi feng xin" [A Letter to Mr. Huang Yuchuan], *Zanmei,* pp. 107–109.

25. WILL CHINA DISINTEGRATE?

"Zhongguo yao jiesan? Zhuanfang Fang Lizhi" [Will China Disintegrate? An Interview with Fang Lizhi], *Jiushi niandai* [The Nineties], October 1988, pp. 70–77.

26. LETTER TO DENG XIAOPING

"Fang Lizhi zhi Deng Xiaoping han," *Jiushi niandai* [The Nineties], March 1989, p. 18.

27. PATRIOTISM AND GLOBAL CITIZENSHIP

Videotaped in Beijing on February 25, 1989, by Orville Schell. Translated directly from tape by James H. Williams as "Patriotism and Global Citizenship," in George Hicks, ed., *The Broken Mirror: China After Tiananmen* [London: Longman, 1990].

28. CHINA'S DESPAIR AND CHINA'S HOPE

"Zhongguo de shiwang he xiwang," unpublished, 1989. Translated by Perry Link as "China's Despair and China's Hope," *The New York Review of Books,* February 2, 1989.

29. PEACE PRIZE SPEECH

"Heping jiang di yanjiang ci," acceptance speech in absentia at Peace Award Ceremony of *Politiken* of Denmark and *Dagens Nyheter* of Sweden, September 1989. Unpublished.

30. KEEPING THE FAITH

"Robert F. Kennedy renquan jiang yanjiang ci" [Speech on the Occasion of Receiving the Robert F. Kennedy Human Rights Award], November 1989. Unpublished. Translated by James H. Williams and Orville Schell as "Keeping the Faith," *The New York Review of Books,* December 21, 1989.

31. THE END OF FORGETTING HISTORY

"Lishi jiang buzai bei yiwang" [History Will No Longer Be Forgotten], unpublished, 1990. Translated by Perry Link as "The Chinese Amnesia," *The New York Review of Books,* September 27, 1990, pp. 30–31.

32. FREE TO SPEAK: SECOND INTERVIEW WITH TIZIANO TERZANI

Interview with Fang Lizhi by Tiziano Terzani for *Der Spiegel.* Translated into English by Tiziano Terzani as "Free to Speak," *Far Eastern Economic Review,* August 2, 1990, pp. 21–22.

A Note About the Author

Fang Lizhi was born in Beijing in 1936 and trained in physics at Beijing University. For joining other young intellectuals in demanding greater freedom of thought and expression, Fang was expelled from the Communist Party in the Anti-Rightist Campaign of 1957, and later imprisoned during the Cultural Revolution.

Despite these setbacks, Fang emerged as one of China's leading experts in astrophysics and cosmology. Officially rehabilitated in 1979, Fang was appointed vice president of the prestigious University of Science and Technology of China. Student unrest in late 1986 resulted in Fang's removal from his post and a second expulsion from the Communist Party, which attacked his outspoken advocacy of democratic reform as "bourgeois liberalization." In the turmoil following the Tiananmen Square massacre of June 1989, Fang and his wife sought sanctuary within the U.S. Embassy in Beijing, where they remained for over a year.

Fang is currently a visiting scholar at the Institute for Advanced Study in Princeton, New Jersey.

A Note on the Type

The text of this book was set in a digitized version of Bembo, a well-known Monotype face. Named for Pietro Bembo, the celebrated Renaissance writer and humanist scholar who was made a cardinal and served as secretary to Pope Leo X, the original cutting of Bembo was made by Francesco Griffo of Bologna only a few years after Columbus discovered America.

Sturdy, well-balanced, and finely proportioned, Bembo is a face of rare beauty, extremely legible in all of its sizes.

Composed, printed, and bound by The Haddon Craftsmen Inc., Scranton, Pennsylvania

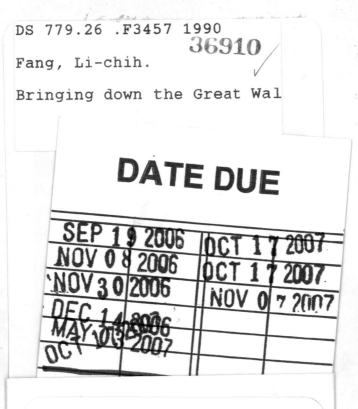